Saving Florida

UNIVERSITY PRESS OF FLORIDA

Florida A&M University, Tallahassee
Florida Atlantic University, Boca Raton
Florida Gulf Coast University, Ft. Myers
Florida International University, Miami
Florida State University, Tallahassee
New College of Florida, Sarasota
University of Central Florida, Orlando
University of Florida, Gainesville
University of North Florida, Jacksonville
University of South Florida, Tampa
University of West Florida, Pensacola

Saving Florida

Women's Fight for the Environment in the Twentieth Century

Leslie Kemp Poole

University Press of Florida

Gainesville / Tallahassee / Tampa / Boca Raton
Pensacola / Orlando / Miami / Jacksonville / Ft. Myers / Sarasota

Frontis: Four women with two students in 1913 display a seventy-foot petition to save Florida's robins. Courtesy of the Florida Audubon Society.

First cloth printing, 2015
First paperback printing, 2016

Library of Congress Cataloging-in-Publication Data
Poole, Leslie Kemp, author.
Saving Florida : women's fight for the environment in the twentieth century /
Leslie Kemp Poole.
pages cm
Includes bibliographical references and index.
ISBN 978-0-8130-6081-1 (cloth)
ISBN 978-0-8130-6232-7 (pbk.)
1. Women in conservation of natural resources—Florida. 2. Women conservationists—Florida.
3. Women in development—Florida. 4. Environmental management—Florida. I. Title.
QH76.5.F6P66 2015
363.70082'09759—dc23   2014043923

The University Press of Florida is the scholarly publishing agency for the State University
System of Florida, comprising Florida A&M University, Florida Atlantic University, Florida
Gulf Coast University, Florida International University, Florida State University, New
College of Florida, University of Central Florida, University of Florida, University
of North Florida, University of South Florida, and University of West Florida.

University Press of Florida
15 Northwest 15th Street
Gainesville, FL 32611-2079
http://www.upf.com

To my husband, Michael,
who joined me on this long journey
and kept me on the path.

Contents

Figures

Figures follow page 119.

Acknowledgments

Many thanks to the wonderful people who joined me on the journey that led to this book. Dr. Jack E. Davis, of the University of Florida, has been my guide and mentor since I took his fascinating environmental history class. Dr. Stephen Noll, Dr. Vassiliki "Betty" Smocovitis, Dr. Louise Newman, Dr. Paul Ortiz, and Alyson Craig Flournoy, all of the University of Florida, also offered needed encouragement and help. Likewise at UF, Florence Turcotte provided superb direction at the archives and Dr. Margaret "Peggy" Macdonald answered all my email inquiries and willingly shared her research about Marjorie Harris Carr, now included in her terrific recent book.

Dr. Bruce Stephenson of Rollins College, author Bill Belleville, and Dr. Jim Clark of the University of Central Florida guided me along the long path to book publishing, offering sage counsel, suggestions, and friendship. Rollins College colleagues Dr. Robert Smither, Dr. Joseph Siry, and Dr. Julian Chambliss always were willing to point me in the right direction. Dr. Patricia Lancaster, Dr. Barry Levis, and Joanne Hanley, all from Rollins, also supported my work.

James Murphy shared his unpublished biography of Doris Leeper, helping to paint a stronger portrait of her accomplishments. Clay Henderson offered his recollections of "Doc," shared his many contacts with the state's environmental movers and shakers, and suffered through many readings of different versions of this manuscript. Cynthia Barnett and Dr. Judith Poucher read early drafts, and their suggestions have made it stronger and livelier. Bruce Hunt has been a great friend, offering his vast expertise in photography. Kim den Beste and Deirdre Macnab provided valuable photographs and encouragement. Kay Davidson-Bond and Stacey Matrazzo have been wonderful readers, and Gerry Wolfson-Grande has been an insightful, good-natured copy editor, formatting genius, and manuscript advisor.

I could not have completed my research without the help of personnel and archivists at the Atlantic Center for the Arts, Florida Audubon Society, Florida Historical Society, HistoryMiami, Maitland Historical Society, Orange County Regional History Center, Rollins College, State Archives of Florida, Stranahan House and Museum, University of Central Florida, University of Florida, University of North Florida, University of Miami, and University of West Florida. Special thanks to the Florida Federation of Garden Clubs and the Florida Federation of Women's Clubs for repeatedly opening their doors, files, and email to help quench my academic thirst. Thanks also to Dr. Connie Lester and the *Florida Historical Quarterly,* which published an article that has been expanded into this book's first chapter. A portion of chapter 2 was previously published in volume 22 of *FCH Annals: Journal of the Florida Conference of Historians* and is used with FCH permission.

I have been blessed to work with Sian Hunter at the University Press of Florida. She has guided me astutely, answering my multitude of questions along the way. Marthe Walters and Sally Antrobus have been wonderful guides through the final publishing and copyediting processes. I send my warmest thanks to my many girlfriends who listened, encouraged, and happily celebrated each milestone through the years.

My family has been my rock. During the many years of this project my husband Michael has given unwavering support and my sons Blake and Preston—and now my new daughter-in-law, Mary Kathryn—have been by my side on this trek into unknown territory. Remember who loves you.

Finally, I thank the twenty-five women and men who participated in the formal oral interviews used in this book. They opened their homes, minds, and hearts to discuss their important activism on behalf of Florida's environment. Their love of Florida and optimism about its future are inspiring; they are models for us all, carrying on the tradition started more than a century ago in Clara Dommerich's living room.

Introduction

The scene is breathtaking and remarkably soothing. A long stretch of tan, sandy beach disappears into mist and glare. Surf that alternates between sapphire and aquamarine rhythmically pounds the shore. Sun worshipers lazily examine wave-tossed shells as wading birds hurry to catch silvery baitfish. Birds flit among vegetation-crested dunes, at the base of which thousands of sea turtles have nested, their young now hatched and swimming in ocean currents.

This is Canaveral National Seashore, the longest undeveloped public beach on Florida's east coast. It is a twenty-four-mile refuge in a state where critics joke that the official bird should be the construction crane. Once upon a time, however, this beautiful beach was in jeopardy, threatened by development projects and cars that plowed through its dunes.

Then Doris Leeper got involved.

The strong-minded, straight-speaking Leeper hassled the business community, gathered like-minded area citizens, and pressed federal officials for help, leading to the establishment of the national seashore in 1975. Four decades later her name is missing from the seashore's history and website, but those who witnessed the fight know that Leeper's footprints are permanently embedded in the park's very existence.

Farther south, near Florida's peninsular tip, the Royal Palm Visitor Center hosts visitors to Everglades National Park who come from around the world to see alligators, birds, and sawgrass wetlands. The site has few of the stately trees for which it is named—most disappeared after decades of hurricane damage. But if you concentrate on the few that continue to sway in the subtropical breeze, it is wonderful to imagine when 168 cars, many with clubwomen, traveled to this hammock, a rise in the vast wetlands, to celebrate the 1916 dedication of Royal Palm State Park, the first state park in Florida. Under a

November sky, these women, clad in long skirts and wide-brimmed hats, celebrated the culmination of years of efforts to save a piece of Florida they feared would disappear.[1]

Men who ran the state legislature had regularly ignored their efforts and refused to fund a park in what they viewed as "wastelands." But the women saw something different—a unique refuge of colorful birds and striking plants that they crusaded to save until legislators caved in to their demands. Three decades later Royal Palm became the core of Everglades National Park, biologically one of America's richest national parks. Women, before they could vote, had forced action to save the state's natural beauty.

Today these sites are the tangible remainders and reminders of a century of work by Florida's environmental women. Others are found in parks, jungle-lined rivers, nature preserves, and the continued presence of endangered species, their very existence due in part to these women's insistence that humans curb imperiling behavior. Their legacy also lives on in ways that most Floridians take for granted—bays made safe from untreated sewage, estuaries protected from dredge-and-fill development projects, and air safeguarded from poisonous industrial discharge. And their work continues in efforts to stop pollution of the Fenholloway River, to get medical attention and treatment for pesticide-exposed farmworkers, and to eliminate a dam that for too long has blocked what was once one of the state's most scenic rivers.

This book offers a comprehensive study of Florida women's conservation and environmental activism across the twentieth century, synthesizing previous scholarship with the untold stories of women who were vital forces in these movements. I investigate what it meant to be a woman involved in these efforts, using their written, reported, and recorded words. The book charts how women navigated difficult and often biased social structures to be heard and to effect change. As the movement evolved—absorbing new understandings in ecological science and taking inspiration from the century's other social causes—so did the role of women, who had their own sensibilities and concerns. Along the way multiple surges in the women's equality movement eliminated a number of societal constraints and brought new opportunities to exercise power. Together, the women's rights and environmental movements forced a more open and aware society, advancing new visions for the state's natural systems, including the new idea of sustainability. The intersection of the two makes for a fascinating and significant history.[2]

To be clear, not all Florida women were involved in such efforts. And the ones who were often had complex relationships with the landscape. Many profited from development activities in which they or their families were engaged. Bertha Honoré Palmer, a wealthy widow, was a developer in her own right, at one point owning 140,000 acres in Sarasota and Hillsborough counties. Palmer developed some of the property and used other acreage for agriculture; her children donated nineteen hundred acres in her honor to become part of Myakka River State Park. Mary Kenan Flagler benefited greatly from her late husband Henry's vast railroad and hotel empire, but her donation of approximately 960 acres of land kick-started the Royal Palm State Park efforts. May Mann Jennings led the charge to create and preserve Royal Palm but was comfortable with her husband's encouragement of Everglades drainage elsewhere.[3]

This book encompasses a number of historical topics, primarily serving as a history that examines the changing relationship between humans and our natural surroundings during the twentieth century, and how each has indelibly influenced the other. My goal is to achieve what eminent scholar J. Donald Hughes prescribes—that environmental history "be a corrective to the prevalent tendency of humans to see themselves as separate from nature, above nature, and in charge of nature." The entire century is surveyed because it truly is America's "environmental century," a period of unprecedented change in attitudes and understanding of the nation's natural resources and systems.[4]

By the end of the 1800s, many women had expanded their interests and duties from the home into the community, a movement that historians labeled "municipal housekeeping." Florida's middle- and upper-class women—the movers and shakers behind early natural resource protection—in large part followed this model, working within women's clubs to address issues as diverse as education, prison reform, and protection of native flora and fauna. They also brought their interests and talents into garden clubs and Audubon societies, which worked in conjunction with women's clubs to seek statutory protections and wider public awareness. As women became more important within such groups, and as their social roles expanded, so did their power and prominence. At the beginning of the twentieth century, women had no vote. By the end of it they were creating and leading nonprofit ecological organizations and advising presidents. One Floridian, Carol Browner, ran the U.S. Environmental Protection Agency (EPA), arguably the most powerful bureaucracy of its kind in the world.[5]

The pivot of this changing female role was that much of the activism was a response to destruction of the state's flora and fauna by male-dominated business and government. For the entire century, men controlled these fields, often viewing harmful, polluting practices simply as the cost of doing business. Women, however, often had a different sensibility. Initially upset by the aesthetic damage rendered by clear-cut logging, roadside billboards, and dirty streets, Florida women, along with their sisters across the country, demanded cleaner cities and better forestry practices.

As knowledge increased by midcentury, bringing the science of ecology into the public consciousness and revealing public health risks of air, water, and land pollution, a number of Florida women became alarmed that their homes and families were imperiled. Armed with this information, women helped reframe the debate, elevating public health issues onto the agenda alongside saving trees, animals, and beautiful places. Often working from outside the system and with little care for political allegiances, women entered into public debates in which they demanded that industry and government clean up the crises of their own making. In doing so, women established themselves as important public advocates. They also found new and expanded identities that included holding public office—an accomplishment that was only dreamed of by women in the early part of the century.

It is important to recognize that as white, wealthy, and well-educated women, many female environmental figures led lives that included a certain level of independence. Several were widowed, some unmarried, others retired—a status that additionally shielded them from pressures from business and government. The poised and self-confident Jennings continued to be a conservation leader for decades after the death of her husband, a former governor with whom she shared great political savvy. Katherine Bell Tippetts managed her deceased husband's real estate holdings in St. Petersburg while also becoming a local, state, and national advocate for saving birds. Gloria Cann Rains retired with her husband to Florida; soon they were trying to save the beauty that had attracted them to the state. The unmarried Leeper, a nationally recognized artist, was free to criticize and publicize issues she felt were important.

Others found resolve to counter the status quo through their communal efforts in women's and garden clubs and by participating in organizations that sprang up to address local issues. Grassroots work tends to free activists from any outside authority, allowing them to draw from their own morals to create their own approaches to issues. Such was the case with many Florida women.[6]

The scope and geography of this book encompass material from numerous state and local resources, including historical societies, women's clubs, garden clubs, museum and college archives, newspapers, and four interviews plus twenty-one formal oral histories of people involved in Florida environmentalism. Taken together, these records provide the first century-long synthesis focused on the wide-ranging efforts and successes of state women.

It begins with early Audubon efforts in Florida, specifically a 1900 meeting in Clara Dommerich's winter home in Maitland. There the Florida Audubon Society was formed to confront the devastating overhunting of the state's wading birds and sale of feathers to the millinery industry—ironically, for women's hats. Women were vital to the organization's success, running the day-to-day operations, writing articles, lobbying the state legislature, and proving skilled organizers and leaders. The Audubon experience was an unusual one for women of this era, as it combined the efforts of both men and women. As the first four chapters of this book show, most women accomplished their conservation activism in female-only groups during the early half of the century.

Female efforts also were critical in saving and managing the state's forests. By the late nineteenth century it was clear that poor lumber practices were devastating timberlands. Florida's clubwomen, joining with those in other parts of the country, raised public awareness and pushed state leaders to protect these important natural and economic resources. Jennings, called the "Mother of Florida Forestry," was a powerful force in the politics of forestry and conservation in the state. As already noted, she led the effort for establishment of Royal Palm State Park, the first state park created by clubwomen in the United States. For much of the twentieth century women helped launch parks around the state, some by donating their own property to be preserved in perpetuity.

While parks added to Florida's attractiveness, women also drove campaigns and programs to make the state and communities more beautiful. During the first three decades of the century, women across the state worked to counter declining aesthetics brought on by rising development. They fought proliferating billboards, planted thousands of trees, helped create playgrounds, and urged local governments to enact city planning and to improve or remove slums.

No story of Florida environmentalism is complete without a discussion of the three Marjories whose impact on the state is indelible: Pulitzer Prize-winning author Marjorie Kinnan Rawlings, who taught the nation to appreciate the state's natural landscape and people; Marjorie Harris Carr, who embodied the grassroots fight to stop the Cross Florida Barge Canal; and Marjory Stoneman Douglas, an author and late-in-life activist for the Everglades. Their work reflected the nation's rising ecological consciousness, heightened by author Rachel Carson's groundbreaking book *Silent Spring*, which warned of the consequences of overuse of pesticides. Carr and Douglas were leaders in an era in which women and men began to work together regularly in organizations to address specific ills, whether on a local, state, or national level. Women's clubs were still important, but the dawning environmental movement and growing recognition of women's rights brought a new bi-gender activism to the forefront.

After World War II Americans began to realize that the country was being degraded in a variety of ways, often from postwar technology. Florida women rightly became worried about the consequences of air pollution arising from industrial smokestacks in urban and rural areas—a concern that first arose in the nineteenth century. For business leaders, smoke in the air might have been the smell of success; for women, it was an unacceptable health risk.

Threats to the state's water supplies as well as to its wetlands and coastal estuaries also arose in midcentury. Women challenged a number of damaging practices, including the dumping of untreated municipal sewage into water bodies—an unthinkable practice today. As a result numerous female activists found new roles as elected officials and as appointees to recently created water regulatory boards.

The story of Florida's environmentally minded women also includes their efforts to save endangered species and landscapes. As scientific knowledge about the natural world increased, and a number of crises struck, Floridians became aware of how the state's rapid development affected the natural world. A variety of women fought to protect endangered species such as manatees and sea turtles, while others tried to defend fragile coastal beaches and estuaries that were threatened by pollution and development schemes.

By the last two decades of the century Florida women were leading a suite of environmental efforts in the state. Many women focused on seeking justice for people whose lives were adversely impacted by the state's changing environment. Their work included securing land and livelihood for Seminole and Miccosukee people in the Everglades; a campaign to relocate African American residents living near a toxic dump in Pensacola; a crusade to stop industrial pollution of the Fenholloway River; and efforts to help agricultural workers. Each example involves women addressing the needs of low-income, marginalized people—often of minority races—who frequently become the first victims of pollution and ecological degradation.

I conclude with an examination of the rise of Florida women into environmental leadership roles in the latter decades of the century. These women used hard-won female rights and opportunities to gain stature in the workforce, often finding new professional opportunities in environmental quarters. In unprecedented numbers, they established and led organizations and ran bureaucracies in a state where business and government remained under male domination. Others elected to office on environmental mandates or appointed to political boards kept such issues on the public agenda.

This is not an exhaustive account of all the efforts by Florida women to save the environment. I have not examined the records of all women's groups in the state, but my experiences indicate that most would hold additional stories of female concern for and efforts to mend their surroundings. Women were not solely responsible for conservation and environmental victories—a host of men were involved in these causes too, leading groups, appointing women to boards and bureaucratic positions, and providing the needed governmental votes. However, the concentration here is on the role of women and how it demonstrates not only the changing gender order but also the grassroots organizing necessary to effect change through a group with little political or economic power.

Largely missing is the perspective of the state's minority women, who struggled within the social and economic constraints of Jim Crow and racism for much of the century. A few, such as Eartha M. M. White in Jacksonville and Alice Mickens in West Palm Beach, helped establish city playgrounds for their youth, but these efforts usually had the goal of improving the lives of families in the African American community, not of saving or protecting the environment. Across the country, the National Association of Colored Women, the umbrella organization for African American clubwomen, advocated a number of urban-centered ideals, including playgrounds and camps for children, clearly viewing nature as an antidote to city problems. At century's end African American women became involved in environmental justice issues after learning that pollution and hazardous chemicals disproportionately affected their communities and workplaces. Margaret Williams successfully fought to get Pensacola families relocated from contaminated land, and African American farm workers in the Apopka area spoke out about how chemicals and pesticides had damaged their health and that of their families. Views of the state's Seminole and Miccosukee women are even more difficult to determine. These areas deserve more academic scrutiny.[7]

For Florida's environmentally minded women it was a dramatic century. From founding Florida Audubon to running the EPA, they forged unprecedented changes in how residents understood and valued their natural resources. As their roles in society expanded, women found different ways to adapt their tactics and activism to be effective advocates. Their interests evolved from creating beauty and preventing ugliness to stopping toxic assaults on human health—focuses that changed as scientific knowledge and the visible results of Florida's booming growth became evident. They set the foundation for the next century's environmental agenda, which came to include the idea of sustainability: of meshing ecology and economy to enhance energy efficiency and the functioning of natural systems. The history of the state's twentieth-century environmental movement reflects a montage of individuals who, as a collective force, made a difference in the way others saw the natural world. Because of their advocacy, we can walk on the beach at Canaveral National Seashore or under the royal palms at Everglades National Park, marveling at the beauty of Florida that remains today.

Part I

Working through Women's Groups

For the Birds

It was March 2, the time of year when the intoxicating aroma of orange blossoms from nearby groves perfumed the airy thirty-room estate. Gathered congenially in the living room were fifteen prosperous, educated men and women—the "Who's Who" of Central Florida, including a college president, a wealthy grain merchant, and female community leaders. Clara Dommerich summoned them to her home to discuss their mutual concern about the alarming loss of birds in Florida and, more important, to do something about it.[1]

While they met, hunters in Florida's wetlands busily sought out raucous, crowded rookeries of wading birds. In a matter of minutes, a nesting colony could be wiped out by gunshots, leaving eggs that would never hatch and crying orphaned chicks sentenced to certain starvation. Hunters stripped showy nuptial feathers from the backs of adult egrets, herons, and roseate spoonbills and shipped their booty to faraway millinery markets in New York and Europe. There, far from the bloody reality of their origin, the plumes, often worth more than their weight in gold, were fashioned into ladies' hats to meet a booming demand. The preserved bodies of songbirds and hummingbirds often met the same fate.

This was a horrifying reality to Dommerich. She and her husband Louis brought their family every winter from New York City to Hiawatha Grove, a grand lakefront estate in Maitland, where they could enjoy mild weather, grow citrus, and observe wildlife. A prosperous silk importer and textile manufacturer, Louis would take a moment every morning to fill bird feeding stations and whistle to call his avian friends to breakfast. On the four-hundred-acre property, which included a bird sanctuary, the family enjoyed a variety of birds, among them cranes, owls, quail, doves, hummingbirds, and turkey. That any of these creatures might end up as hats was abhorrent to the Dommerichs and the nature-loving friends seated in their home that spring day. But in 1900 it was a real possibility.[2]

Although Dommerich's words, likely accented with her native German, were not recorded, her energy and insistence were. It was time to act to save Florida's birds. The first step was to establish an Audubon Society in the state. The Rt. Rev. Henry B. Whipple, Episcopal bishop of Minnesota, was another wintering Maitland resident—or "snowbird." He became the first president of the Florida Audubon Society (FAS), and he lauded Dommerich "for the interest which she has awakened for the protection of the birds of Florida. No state or territory in our country has been as richly endowed in plumage and song birds as this state." By the time of the meeting, Dommerich had researched Audubon organizations in other states and collected financial support for one in Florida. The group established a five-member committee to draw up a constitution, adopted it, and named Dommerich the secretary-treasurer.[3]

Unfortunately, just eight months later she died at forty-three of a lingering illness back in her urban home, never seeing the far-reaching effect of the organization she created. The new FAS secretary, Harriet Vanderpool, an FAS founder, wrote: "This society owes its existence to her loving interest in our feathered friends. . . . She had watched with righteous indignation the wanton destruction of the beautiful birds which . . . added so much to the charm and beauty of our Southland. It was this womanly love which led her to ask others to unite in the creation of a society whose object is the protection of birds in Florida. We cannot speak too highly of her wise thoughtfulness and earnestness in this blessed work."[4] Twenty-five years later, FAS President Hiram Byrd described the society's founders as "a little group of people who had a vision for the future." Dommerich, he noted, was "probably the leading spirit in the movement, but as so frequently happens in this world of affairs, the hand that presses the button is not seen."[5]

It made perfect sense to form an Audubon group in Florida, the ground zero for a rising movement that sought to protect colorful birds from death by rampant consumerism. A number of bird species were in trouble, particularly passenger pigeons and Carolina parakeets, both of which would be extinct within eighteen years. And the FAS founders were witnesses to the devastation. On one occasion, Whipple wrote in 1900, he had observed "not less than two thousand paroquets" (Carolina parakeets) at a Central Florida lake. "Many of these beautiful creatures are no longer to be found, unless in the Everglades," he lamented. "The murderous work of extermination has been carried on by vandals, incited by the cupidity of traders who minister to the pride of thoughtless people."[6] Those who had been drawn to Florida by the abundance of nature were witnessing its disappearance, all in the name of fashion and profits.

Men and women had long been adorning their headwear—military items for men and hats and everyday clothing for women—with feathers and bodies of birds. In the eighteenth century Marie Antoinette, nicknamed "Feather-head" by her brother, set the trend in court for women to wear feathers in their elaborate hairstyles. Her death briefly ended that fad, but it was revived in the late nineteenth century as fashion magazines and journals extolled the style often worn by popular actresses.[7]

In 1886 on two late afternoon excursions in New York City shopping areas, ornithologist Frank Chapman, a leading national Audubon force, noted that three-quarters of the seven hundred women's hats he counted displayed feathers that came from "40 different kinds of native birds, including sparrows, warblers and flycatchers." In Paris dresses were edged with wings, feathers, and skins. In London a woman wore a gown hemmed with finch heads.[8] By the late 1800s, a period dubbed the "so-called age of extermination," hundreds of thousands of birds were being killed. Feathers and bird parts gathered by hunters were shipped to northern markets for processing and big profits in the $17-million-a-year industry, which employed an estimated 83,000 people in 1900 and included trade with European countries.[9] One London firm reported that one and one-half tons of "aigrettes"—the term used for the flashy feathers—passed through its salesroom in a year, the equivalent of almost 200,000 birds, which excluded the number of lost chicks and eggs.[10]

The results were nothing short of tragic. In *Some Kind of Paradise: A Chronicle of Man and the Land in Florida*, Mark Derr recounts tales of rookeries being wiped out along Florida's west coast, from the Tampa area south to the Everglades: "White ibis, roseate spoonbills, pelicans, and herons and egrets of every hue and size were gone. Many hunters thought survivors had fled to rookeries inland or farther south: They couldn't conceive that the birds would not come back. A similar situation existed on the east coast above Lake Worth. So thorough was the destruction of plume birds that within several generations collective memory of the rookeries was as dead as the birds themselves."[11]

In 1883 a group of concerned professionals founded the American Ornithologists' Union (AOU) to try to stop the plume trade's devastation. An AOU committee that included George Bird Grinnell, a hunter and editor of *Forest and Stream* magazine, created a "Model Law" to press state legislatures to enact provisions protecting nongame birds and their eggs and nests. Three years later Grinnell founded the nation's first Audubon Society, named after John James

Audubon, the famed painter of America's birds. As a boy, Grinnell had known the artist's widow. Grinnell hoped public opinion could be swayed to stop the bird deaths without the need for legislation, and he found widespread support. He launched the *Audubon Magazine*, but it folded after its second issue in 1888 and with it the Audubon Society. Although the organization was short-lived, Grinnell continued to be an important player in conservation efforts. In 1887 he had helped found the Boone and Crockett Club, an organization of one hundred wealthy sportsmen including Theodore Roosevelt, who would later become U.S. president. They worked to preserve large game in the United States, particularly in the West, and to promote natural history research. This conservation idea would move from a male-dominated realm to capture the attention of women and would lead to reemergence of the Audubon Society in groups across the nation.[12]

The American conservation movement blossomed in the early 1900s during the reform-minded Progressive Era that developed in response to a rapidly industrializing nation. The toll that the nation's growth had taken on wildlife and natural resources was staggering, almost unimaginable to a citizenry who had embraced the myth that it would never disappear. Bison, estimated to have numbered up to 60 million in North America, had long symbolized the American West and had been a staple of native peoples, who prized them for their meat and hides. Commercial demand for hides and overhunting led to vast slaughter, placing bison on the brink of extinction by the end of the 1800s. Perhaps no creature defined the Audubon supporters' fears as much as the passenger pigeon, which once blackened the skies of North America for hours with enormous traveling flocks. Hunters had easy pickings; the birds were easily captured or shot and shipped to food markets. Once estimated at 5 billion birds, passenger pigeon populations were decimated in the late nineteenth century. The last of the species died in 1914—an extinction that alarmed bird lovers and conservationists alike.[13] Four years later the last brilliantly colored Carolina parakeet died in captivity.

These concerns led Americans to revive the Audubon crusade. Harriet Hemenway, a wealthy and well-connected Bostonian, was an early leader, gathering influential women and male ornithologists to found the Massachusetts Audubon Society in 1896. Its goals were to discourage buying and wearing of any goods adorned with wild bird feathers and to promote bird protection. Almost thirteen hundred adults and children were members by the end of the year, which also marked the beginning of a Pennsylvania society. The movement quickly spread to other states, mostly in the Northeast, and by 1900 five states had enacted laws based on the AOU Model Law. The Audubon effort was alive once again and growing, thanks in large part to its female membership.[14]

Another important player on the national scene was Mabel Osgood Wright, a founder of the Connecticut group and later a leader in the national group. Wright wrote extensively about nature to a receptive national audience. She also served as an associate editor of *Bird-Lore*, a national bird-lovers' magazine that later became *Audubon* magazine. Her articles and books, which included an 1895 bird guide, were widely read and were lauded by her literary peers, including heralded naturalist John Burroughs as well as women writers and readers. At the same time, women, who considered the home and garden their domain, used conservation and Audubon activities to engage in larger community issues and exert greater influence.[15] This expanding female role, dubbed "municipal housekeeping," was embraced enthusiastically by many middle- and upper-class women. "The idea that women as the center of home life were responsible for the moral tone of a community did not vanish, but increasingly it was said that such responsibility did not end with the four walls of a home, but extended to the neighborhood, the town, the city," notes historian Anne Firor Scott.[16] Although they were unable to vote until 1920, these women had the financial stability, aesthetic appreciation, leisure time, and desire to spread their wings in activities that ranged from creating parks to fighting for pure food and improving child welfare—efforts that were considered to be within the woman's realm. They were "indispensable in every environmental cause in the United States," agrees historian Adam Rome.[17]

Saving Florida's colorful birds from hunters was a top environmental issue, and like women elsewhere, the FAS women attacked the issue with zeal, carrying the organization into the state and national arena.[18] Their actions also reflected the shifting national consciousness, which would move during the early twentieth century from a focus on conservation—namely the largely science-based development, management, and use of natural resources—into the modern environmental movement, which was concerned with the quality of the human environment. The Audubon women wanted a world with beautiful, singing birds—an aesthetic value that would help spur the future environmental movement.[19] They shared the long-held human affinity for birds, with which people have much in common: both "build homes, raise young, and then head south to avoid cold weather," writes historian Kurkpatrick Dorsey. As renowned evolutionary biologist Edward O. Wilson notes, "birds have been the most pursued and best known of all animals" for centuries, perhaps owing to *biophilia*—a word he uses to describe a phenomenon in which humans bond emotionally with certain life forms.[20]

A love of birds drew the eight women and five men to the afternoon meeting in Clara Dommerich's living room. They were a cross section of the area's elite and included the Dommerichs; Dr. G. M. Ward, president of nearby Rollins College, and his wife Emma; Harriet Vanderpool, wife of a local citrus grower who was a Maitland founder; W. C. Comstock, a Winter Park businessman and civic leader; Lida Peck Bronson, wife of businessman and former Maitland mayor Sherman Bronson; and Laura Norcross Marrs and her husband Kingsmill, a wealthy Massachusetts couple who wintered in Maitland. The community was a small one at the time, and several of these FAS founders became involved in other civic activities, from founding a public library to establishing a church and serving in various leadership capacities at Rollins College.[21] Although the first FAS president was the eloquent Whipple, who was succeeded by men until 1920, the organization's successes were reliant on the work and community connections of its female members. With passion and diligence, these women, some of them snowbirds, worked with year-round residents to gain public support for the FAS mission, leading to bird protection laws, the creation and operation of bird preserves, and extensive school programs. Women held long-term leadership positions; kept track of the group's finances, records, and correspondence; led meetings; wrote articles and pamphlets; and worked with people in other organizations to further the cause.

Initial FAS memberships were $1 per year, $5 per year for sustaining members, 25 cents for children, and free for teachers. A $25 payment would make someone a patron. The organization also wisely attached itself to influential people. As an Episcopal bishop, Whipple had negotiated with eleven presidents as an advocate for reforms in U.S. relations with the native Indians of his midwestern region.[22] FAS honorary vice presidents included Governor William Bloxam of Florida, New York governor Theodore Roosevelt (who became U.S. president the next year), and Kirk Munroe, a nationally known author of children's books who lived in Coconut Grove, Florida. Of the twenty-eight vice presidents representing different regions of Florida, twenty-two were male, including journalists, clergy, the presidents of nearby Rollins College and Stetson University, and *Bird-Lore* editor Frank Chapman of the American Museum of Natural History. Six women were named vice presidents, among them Marrs; Evangeline Whipple, wife of the bishop; and Rose Cleveland, sister of former U.S. president Grover Cleveland and a close friend of Evangeline Whipple. However, the gender spread was more even on the executive committee, which would be the guiding force of the organization during the next two decades. Half its members were female—including Marrs, Bronson, and Vanderpool.[23]

In its second year FAS worked diligently to improve bird protection laws in Florida, which had little beyond an 1877 statute that protected mockingbirds during breeding season. That law also forbade the destruction of nests, eggs, and young of "sea birds of plume," but it had been repealed two years later. In 1891 the state gave protection to wading birds, but this had little effect on the plume trade. In May 1900 the federal government provided some hope when it adopted the Lacey Act, which prohibited interstate commerce in birds that had state protections. Florida needed to adopt the AOU Model Law to be under that umbrella, so the FAS went to work, calling in nationally recognized bird leaders for help. William Dutcher, then chair of the AOU's committee on bird protection, came to Florida in May 1901 to fight alongside Audubon leaders for the Model Law passage. Although the legislature approved a new statute, it excluded certain birds that FAS had hoped to protect: robins, shore birds, meadowlarks, and hawks. Nevertheless, the group was off to a strong start, having made a statewide impact in its first year.[24]

FAS women carried much of the organizational workload and became prominent leaders. Bronson was elected treasurer in 1901 and served in that role until 1915, gathering contributions and dues and disbursing funds for projects. After her death in 1926, she was remembered for her efficiency, devotion, and regular attendance. She "was one of a small group in Maitland whose constancy and faith kept the Audubon movement alive in Florida," according to an FAS resolution.[25] Vanderpool's contribution was invaluable. From 1901 to 1917 she served as the FAS secretary, which put her in charge of correspondence, record keeping, and hand-written minutes of annual and executive committee meetings. She communicated with local Audubon groups around the state, gathering reports from each, and read them at executive committee meetings. Vanderpool also tirelessly sent mailings to newspaper editors around the state, provided thousands of leaflets to school board heads to encourage school participation, gathered information about school programs, and shipped posters about bird regulations to all Florida post offices. Since a number of the early FAS members had northern residences, she handled much of the business during the summer months. It was a multifaceted job but perfectly suited for Vanderpool, a community activist born in England who came to Maitland in 1876 with her husband, Isaac, to live on property homesteaded on Lake Maitland and planted as an orange grove. Isaac, who had helped plan the city of Maitland, served as its mayor in 1887 and helped establish the nearby African

American city of Eatonville. Like her progressive sisters, Vanderpool was involved in various aspects of improving her community, helping Whipple with the founding of the Church of the Good Shepherd in Maitland and working with Dommerich to establish the Maitland Public Library.[26]

Vanderpool shared an ardent passion for saving her adopted home. "It may be of interest to some of your readers to know that Florida, the land of sunshine, flowers and balmy breezes, has at last awakened to the fact that these combined are not *all* that make their state so attractive and so different," Vanderpool wrote in 1901. "They find (even the most unconcerned) that their rivers, lakes and woods are strangely silent, and that some of the old-time charm and beauty has gone." FAS founders, "to whom these feathered songsters are real friends, and who grieved to see them so wantonly destroyed," had started work, distributing "literature and leaflets," she wrote, adding that member numbers were growing and "we trust in a few years our eyes and ears will be gladdened as of old. Sunshine, flowers and the happy song of our thousands of native birds, and Florida *is* Paradise indeed."[27]

As integral to FAS success as Bronson and Vanderpool were, perhaps no woman—or, arguably, man—was as influential as Marrs, whose efforts impacted the direction of FAS as well as other national bird groups. Marrs, daughter of Otis Norcross, who was elected mayor of Boston in 1867, was a member of Massachusetts Audubon when she became a founder of FAS and chair of its executive committee—a position she held until her death in 1926. She and her husband Kingsmill, a wealthy traveler and art collector, wintered at "Maitland Cottage," in the same town as Evangeline Whipple; the bishop's wife was Kingsmill's sister. With a background much like that of Harriet Hemenway at Massachusetts Audubon, Marrs was just as important to the Florida group, taking up an even stronger leadership role. A 1926 FAS resolution declared that she "gave continuously and unstintedly of her time, sympathy, council and money to its work as long as she lived," and at her death she left $25,000 to the National Association of Audubon Societies to promote bird study and protection. Marrs was involved in other local community issues, leading a women's club and supporting the Hungerford School in Eatonville.[28]

Unless she was traveling, Marrs led executive committee meetings, often at her home, where the operations and structure of FAS were discussed. Marrs wrote annual reports for *Bird-Lore* and traveled to national meetings to represent the group, participating in efforts leading to the 1905 creation of the National Association of Audubon Societies for the Protection of Wild Birds and

Animals, later named the National Audubon Society. Wright, the influential writer, also was part of the national group.[29]

Marrs was instrumental in hiring bird warden Guy Bradley to stop plume hunters in southern Florida. The state's new bird protection laws had failed in one important way—they did not fund law enforcement officers. In 1902 Kirk Munroe, an FAS vice president, wrote to Marrs about the continuing damage to bird populations in the Florida Keys and along the southern coastline. He suggested that Bradley, a former plume hunter, would be the right person to serve as a game warden in the area. Marrs sent the letter to New York to Dutcher, who had hired lighthouse keepers to protect rookeries since the state had failed to provide the personnel to do so. Dutcher put Bradley, at a salary of $35 per month, in charge of patrolling Florida Bay and the Everglades. It was a dense 140-mile frontier of wetland marshes, tiny islands, rookeries, and poachers who ignored state and federal laws for the opportunity to make money in the hardscrabble area. Bradley worked hard, sending Dutcher lists of New York companies he believed acted illegally in the plume trade. To help, FAS raised money to purchase Bradley a boat, named *Audubon*. Marrs worried about Bradley's dangerous work for good reason. As author Stuart B. McIver notes, "sooner or later the warden would have to confront, face to face, a plume hunter caught in the act at the scene of a crime. And that plume hunter would necessarily be holding a gun in his hands." On July 8, 1905, Bradley was shot and killed after responding to a possible poaching incident on an island near his home. A local man was arrested, but a Key West grand jury refused to indict him. Bradley had become America's first martyr in the plume wars, and FAS later erected a monument to him. "The murder of Warden Guy M. Bradley fills not only our Society in Florida, but the people of the United States, with horror," wrote Marrs. "A brave man shot at his post, defending the helpless against brutality, and all for what? A feather, to adorn the head of some woman!!"[30]

With Bradley's death and the subsequent failure to punish his murderer, the Audubon movement was temporarily disheartened and did not replace the warden. Marrs noted that few others would be "willing thus to jeopardize their lives, for, if the laws of the state cannot be enforced and criminals brought to justice, no man has a guarantee" of safety. Three years later, another Audubon warden was killed in Charlotte Harbor in southwest Florida; his boat was sunk in the bay, his body never found.[31]

Still, the movement picked up momentum. FAS reports from the early years showed growing membership and activities, much of the energy supplied by the female members. By 1901 the society had published seven leaflets for distribution throughout the state, of which women wrote five. Marrs wrote two: *John James Audubon* and *Katie's Pledge*, the latter for children. Her sister-in-law Evangeline Whipple wrote *A Letter to the Boys and Girls of the Audubon Society*, and her friend Rose Cleveland penned *The Rights of the Man Versus the Bird*. The group also worked with Orange County school representatives to bring weekly half-hour bird lectures to classes. In coming years the society sponsored essay contests for children in different areas of the state, offered prizes, and provided educational materials about birds—all part of a national push to influence the adults of the next generation. FAS also paid for traveling lecturers and sent articles to local newspapers and national publications. Educating the Florida public would take much time, Dutcher noted in a 1904 report: "Progress in this direction must be slow. Prejudices and instincts of generations must be overcome; all the signs, however, are encouraging."[32]

In 1903 FAS lauded another major event at its doorstep: the creation of the first national bird refuge in the United States. On March 14 President Theodore Roosevelt, at the urging of FAS members, established by executive order the Pelican Island National Wildlife Refuge to protect a prime bird roosting and nesting islet in the Indian River on Florida's central Atlantic coast. It was a momentous occasion—the first of fifty-three federal sanctuaries that Roosevelt created.[33] And a Florida woman played a large role in its creation.

Frances "Ma" Latham, along with her husband, Charles, ran Oak Lodge, a ten-bedroom wooden boarding house built in 1881 in Micco on the Indian River. It was a "magnet for scientists, naturalists, museum curators and artists wanting to observe and document the natural history conditions in Florida," according to a history of the refuge. Some would stay for months, gathering specimens from forays into local areas, and then gathering together at night to compare notes. Audubon's Chapman stayed at the inn during his 1898 honeymoon and described Latham as "a 'born naturalist' having 'great enthusiasm and energy' for the work of collecting and processing specimens." The "salty, no-nonsense and razor smart" Latham donned overalls to accompany visiting scientists on area walks. She was a capable naturalist, collecting loggerhead sea turtle eggs and embryos, enhancing her reputation among her distinguished visitors. She was an early observer of loggerhead nesting habits and voiced concerns that unrestricted fishing could wipe out important fish species. It was Latham who directed Chapman to the 5.5-acre Pelican Island, located nine miles away from her inn. There he studied the nesting brown pelican colony at a site once home to thousands of wading birds that had disappeared as a result of the plume trade. When he returned two years later, Chapman discovered the pelicans had declined by 14 percent to 2,364 birds, an alarming number. In 1902 Latham was hired by the AOU to oversee the island, and at her recommendation, the group hired Paul Kroegel as a warden for $1 per month. It was a difficult task, and by 1903 Dutcher concluded that the best way to protect the pelican colony was by purchasing the island—a daunting task given bureaucratic issues and dealing with the federal government, which owned the island. Dutcher began pressing his Washington D.C. connections to purchase the island, but resolution came instead with Roosevelt's groundbreaking designation of the refuge.[34]

Roosevelt's creation of the national wildlife refuge system was federal acknowledgement of the plight of birds but also of the growing American conservation movement. At the end of the nineteenth century it was clear to Americans that their much-loved natural resources were jeopardized in many ways. People were concerned about dwindling wildlife but also about the diminishing amount of timber and arable land caused by exploitative uses such as overgrazing, mining, and monoculture farming. In response Americans embraced the conservation movement, which advocated protection and "right use" of natural resources to benefit humans. Roosevelt was a prime figure in the conservation movement as well as in the concurrent Progressive Era of the early 1900s, during which citizens demanded government-led reforms in areas such as business and public health. The conservation movement melded well with the progressive reform agenda, advocating better use of resources and controls over the actions of business and exploitative individuals, such as plume hunters.[35]

Although they were unable to vote and participate in the political process until 1920, Progressive Era women activists exerted indirect influence through volunteer and charitable groups to pursue their civic interests, which extended from their domestic agenda and included providing safe, proper homes for their families. They pressed for public sanitation, orphanages, and hospitals. They also proved to be very effective in tackling conservation issues around the country.[36] So effective, in fact, that like-minded men often felt the need to preserve their masculinity by distancing themselves from protection arguments considered "feminine," observes Rome. "Though some men were comfortable arguing for environmental reform in the same terms as women, many were not." Rome writes that arguments for "beauty, health, [and] future generations" were seen as the "province of women." The movement to save birds, culminating in the 1900 Lacey Act, stands out because it was achieved through a "cross-gender alliance" that men often were reluctant to enter in other conservation realms. The Sierra Club welcomed female members, but women of that persuasion generally kept their activism within female-only clubs and organizations.[37]

The Audubon movement also galvanized women because it was female fashion that drove the avian destruction. Not only was it a question of conserving resources, but the issue also had become a moral one that called into question the vanity and responsibility of women. This gender-driven argument hit home with the female populace, although it ignored the fact that men were hunting the birds and running the millinery trade that profited from the bloody slaughter. Both sexes were responsible for the plume trade, but women were assigned and assumed greater guilt. Environmental scholar Jennifer Price notes: "At a time when many people were ready to embrace conservation as a moral issue, the glaring complicity of the distaff half, who were supposed to be the moral caretakers for all society, made this issue resonate at a higher moral volume than any other. . . . Throughout the rancorous debate that raged in newspapers and legislative halls and clubhouses and hat shops across the country, outraged Audubon activists proclaimed reasons to save not only birds but also the moral guardianship that women were supposed to ensure."[38]

In Florida the battle between females could be fierce. In her history *The Florida Audubon Society: 1900–1935*, Lucy Worthington Blackman, an ardent bird activist, described South Florida's Mary Barr Munroe, wife of author Kirk Munroe, as "probably our most militant power," commenting:

> Wheresoe'er Mrs. Munroe's keen eye saw an aigrette waving, there she followed, and cornering the wearer—be it on the street, in the crowded hotel lobby, on the beach, at church or entertainment or party—there compelled her to listen to the story of cruelty and murder of which her vanity was the contributing cause. And Mrs. Munroe was eloquent. It was not unusual for women to be reduced to tears, whether of anger or humiliation or repentance, and several were known to have taken off their hats and destroyed their aigrettes as a result of their encounter with Mrs. Monroe [*sic*].[39]

In a 1915 article "the dynamic, blue-eyed" Munroe, a founder of the Coconut Grove Audubon Society, disputed claims by women that the plumes on their hats came from long-dead birds, that the feathers were gathered from the ground, or that purchasing them helped "poor Indians" who sold them. "But it is not the Indian's sin: it is the women who demand the plumes, so that white men have hunted the birds in such numbers that after a few more years of such reckless slaughter during the breeding season the egret and snowy heron will be classed among the extinct birds of the country," she wrote, firmly placing the guilt on feminine consumerism. Besides scolding women, she also took practical steps to stop the slaughter, writing a leaflet for public education and starting Bird Defenders, a boys' club that encouraged youths to love rather than kill birds.[40]

Florida Audubon worked hard to gain female support. In 1908 FAS started a campaign against wearing plumage and distributed a pledge to women around the state, especially women's organizations, asking them to refuse to adorn themselves with bird products. Audubon members asked Miami authorities to enforce prohibitions on the plume trade during tourist season, particularly that of "Indians who brought their spoils by the boat load from the interior of the Everglades, and spread a veritable bargain counter before the women at the hotels and boarding houses," according to Blackman. Audubon women "preached their holy war," she wrote, until "after a time the tourist women became shy about wearing their aigrettes and plumage ornaments in Florida. But it did not prevent them from receiving Indian emissaries in their rooms, where they hid their bargain treasures until they went north."[41]

In an effort to garner grassroots support, FAS worked closely with the Florida Federation of Women's Clubs (FFWC). From its beginning in 1895 the FFWC led conservation efforts that included bird protection and tree planting, and later turned its attention to endangered species and wetlands preservation. At the 1905 FFWC annual meeting, during which delegates were entertained at Munroe's bayside home, the chair of the bird preservation committee "urged clubs to encourage their members to put out food and water for birds and boxes for martins, bluebirds and wrens." By its second decade FFWC members were attuned to the loss of birds, due not just to plume hunting but also to sportsmen who traveled along the state's waterways, particularly the St. Johns and Ocklawaha rivers. "They had killed not for good or even for the feathers of these birds but just to prove their marksmanship or for the fun of seeing live birds fall," wrote historian Jessie Hamm Meyer, adding that although "there were not a great many environmentally minded people working in organizations during those years," the FFWC had a strong, effective response that resulted in campaigns to preserve birds as well as efforts to conserve forests and plant trees in urban areas. "Their efforts intensified as they witnessed the further degradation of Florida's natural beauty and resources," she added. Other FFWC efforts mirrored Progressive Era initiatives: self-improvement, domestic science, drug education, libraries, health care, and food for the poor.[42] The addition of FFWC as a sustaining member of Florida Audubon was a strategic triumph, which increased the Audubon base around the state. The FFWC represented 1,600 women in 36 clubs by 1910 and grew to more than 9,000 women by 1917, making it one of Florida's largest and most influential groups.[43]

Florida Audubon also extended its appeals to the most influential of the Progressive Era women's groups—the General Federation of Women's Clubs (GFWC), whose members were 2 million strong by 1915. Created in 1890, this national umbrella group composed of clubs of diverse interests and actions galvanized America's women into a force with which to be reckoned. GFWC members formulated platforms that covered a wide range of issues—from conservation to public sewage, factory conditions, and women's rights and suffrage. At its 1910 biennial meeting, the GFWC adopted a resolution endorsing Audubon bird protection work.[44]

It was only natural that several FAS female leaders were active clubwomen. Munroe, who helped found the Coconut Grove and then the Miami Audubon societies, served on the FAS executive committee. She also spread her attention to other issues, helping to start the Housekeeper's Club, an early Dade County women's club, and was the first president of the Dade County Federation of Women's Clubs. Blackman wrote the early Audubon history and was active as an FAS vice president and member of the executive committee (where her husband was president). She was a charter member of the Woman's Club of Winter Park, founded in 1915, and she established the first domestic science program at Rollins College, with the goal of improving women's cooking and sewing as part of their college education. In 1940 Blackman also authored a two-volume work, *The Women of Florida*, to pay homage to other activist females and show "the part individual and organized women have played" in the state's history.[45]

As impassioned as these women were about Florida's birds and nature, none could surpass Katherine Bell Tippetts of St. Petersburg for sheer determination and influence. Endowed with writing talent and business savvy, Tippetts moved easily between the worlds of women's clubs, male-dominated politics, and community service, leaving a trail of accomplishments that would be noteworthy for man or woman. The well-educated widow of a foreign correspondent, Tippetts was a businesswoman who had the time and energy to be involved in various aspects of her community. In 1909, the same year her husband died, Tippetts took over his hotel and real estate interests, then followed one of her own, founding the St. Petersburg Audubon Society (SPAS). In a 1910 newspaper article she explained her passion, noting that she had been birdwatching long before her 1902 move to Florida. Tippetts described an incident that led to the founding of SPAS. One day she saw a boy shoot a cardinal; when she approached him, she found four additional birds that had been beheaded and skinned. "Five beautiful song-birds killed in one short afternoon and no means of redress," she recalled. "It was at this crises [sic] I resolved to organize the Audubon Society"—something she accomplished in 1909, serving as its president from its founding until 1940, the longest tenure of any SPAS president.[46]

In its first year SPAS worked in a variety of realms to save the area's birds. The group posted summaries of state bird laws and successfully urged the Chicago publisher of a boys' publication to remove air-gun advertisements. SPAS later fought for protection of the meadowlark and encouraged its members to build birdhouses. Tippetts foresaw that saving birds would create a confrontation with agricultural interests that wanted to rid their field of birds they considered a nuisance. Her response was to apply common sense and a business approach that men could appreciate: "The sooner the up-to-date farmer learns to leave a corner of his domain in the natural state to attract the birds, the sooner he will derive the benefit accruing from their invaluable aid, for 'the birds are the natural allies to agriculture, forestry and fruit growing as has been proved.'"[47] Tippetts wrote: "This is not an appeal to the aesthetically-minded, but a plain statement of facts, given to all in the hopes that it will be read with thought and will induce an awakening of public sentiment toward making St. Petersburg known for its myriad song birds. I long for the time to come when the passion for bird-protection will have become so commonplace for that state only can be reached when all humanity assists in the work."[48]

SPAS started Junior Audubon classes in local schools and offered annual prizes to children who participated in the programs. Tippetts, a novelist dubbed "The Florida Bird Woman," used her media acumen and connections to win local and state protections, including eleven bird sanctuaries, the passage of a 1913 law to establish the Florida Fish and Game Commission, and a city ordinance requiring licensing of cats, considered then and now to be a scourge to bird populations. Tippetts also made it a SPAS mission to save the robin, considered an agricultural pest, but which she argued instead was a friend to farmers as well as an aesthetic delight. A photograph in the SPAS scrapbook, hand-dated March 1913, shows Tippetts with three other women and two elementary school girls, all in long white dresses, holding a seventy-foot petition with signatures that asked the state legislature to save the robin—a measure that passed two months later.[49] They looked feminine and friendly in their appeal to the all-male legislature—and they got their way.

Despite the spotlight on pelicans provided by the 1903 Pelican Island National Wildlife Refuge designation, the ungainly birds remained unpopular in the St. Petersburg area, where local fishing interests claimed the pelicans competed with working folks for food. By 1918 some area residents wanted to exterminate the area's pelicans, claiming that the species ate more than 169 million pounds of fish per year that should instead go to hungry families. "Not only do we say stop the pelicans from breeding for five years, but kill the pelican altogether," the *Largo Sentinel* recommended. "When it comes to a question of the usefulness of the pelican, it can't be found. Of course, there are people—fanatics if you will—who put up a howl if you kill any living thing; but they should be treated as fanatics and ignored."[50]

Tippetts organized an Audubon response that was rapid and controlled—anything but fanatic—and relied upon support from clubwomen. May Mann Jennings, a powerful women's club leader and respected wife of a former governor, replied in a published statement that there was no way to verify the amount of fish pelicans ate, that fishermen wasted large amounts of fish in their practices, and finally, that the "pelican is one of Florida's most picturesque attractions, especially to our winter tourist, as inseparable of association with the state as the storks of Holland, Japan or Spain." T. Gilbert Pearson, as secretary of the National Association of Audubon Societies, raised objections at the national level and later assured Florida groups that the bird would be protected. In a letter to SPAS, Pearson thanked the "local society for its activity in the matter and assured the members that their alertness in passing resolutions and taking other steps in behalf of the pelican were appreciated by the national body." SPAS also worked to protect black and turkey vultures and helped fund a warden to protect local bird colonies.[51]

By contributing articles to local newspapers and women's club publications, Tippetts kept her message at the forefront. Her two-punch arguments always stressed the beauty of birds along with their usefulness—an appeal to aesthetics as well as practicality that engaged female and male sensibilities. "The love of nature is your heritage and there is no lovelier thing in nature than our birds," she told a local art club in 1924 in an effort to garner support for bird protection. "But if you will not listen to the aesthetic appeal, surely you will see the economic value of saving bird life. As tree protectors, health protectors and crop preservers, our birds have no equal, and once they are gone, even millions of dollars in chemicals and labor cannot replace what they do for us. Do you know that scientists declare we humans could not exist a score of years if we were entirely deprived of all the help the birds give us and could not have that help replaced?"[52]

In 1920 Tippetts became the first female FAS president—the same year American women won the right to vote. It signaled a new start for FAS and acknowledged the powerful role that women had come to hold in the organization. "Conservation was the watchword of her administration," wrote Blackman, adding that Tippetts "emphasized the municipal and private sanctuary movement in Florida, and her familiarity with legislative requirements and her close touch with National conservation groups made her a very valuable leader for the Audubon Society." Tippetts "brought to the new office enthusiasm, knowledge of bird life and experience not alone in Audubon work, but in the Woman's Club interests," Blackman wrote. By the third anniversary of her leadership, Florida had thirty new sanctuaries, and Volusia County was the first county in the country to be designated a sanctuary by a state legislature.[53]

In 1922 Tippetts and Myrtice McCaskill of Taylor County became the first women in Florida to run for seats in the state legislature. They were unsuccessful, but Tippetts's race was so close that it forced a recount—an indication of her political interests, accomplishments, and support base. Like numerous women of her era, Tippetts was involved in a host of other groups, including the National Park Association, Boy Scouts of America, Florida Chamber of Commerce, local and state women's clubs, and the General Federation of Women's Clubs, where she served as bird chair. She succeeded in getting the mockingbird named the official Florida state bird, encouraged similar bird campaigns in other states, and worked to have the wild rose named the national flower.[54] Despite her many activities and crippling arthritis resulting from a 1920s automobile accident, Tippetts held an attitude often shared by those of the same gender during her era, declaring that her priorities put her children first, business second, and "club work is my recreation."[55]

Munroe died in 1922, the same year as Tippetts's attempt at elected office. The passing of the woman who once scolded others about wearing plumed hats left the state's birds "without an 'especially kind friend,'" according to mourners. Munroe once wondered in a newspaper commentary what would happen if women's clubs disbanded. A century later historian Jack E. Davis had this reply: "Without the female protagonists, conservation in Florida would have languished at the level of resource conservation and game protection, so fatuously wedded were men to market values and sporting activities. As it happened, the insouciant plundering of nature agitated women, who founded organizations, lobbied for protective legislation, and left a legacy on which others could build."[56]

In its second decade Florida Audubon continued to pursue the objectives it had first set—education, public awareness, and increased protection. By 1911 almost every state in the nation had adopted the AOU Model Law and had an Audubon society. Florida had new legislation that outlawed target shooting of live birds. A New York state law forbade plume sales, hurting the millinery trade in illegal plumes, and in 1913 two federal laws—a migratory bird law and a non-importation law—went into effect as broader attempts to end the bird extermination business. Marrs worked for three months to secure the non-importation law, which drew some 200,000 letters and telegrams to congressional leaders. When it passed, the price of plumes, bird skins, and feathers in London and Berlin dropped dramatically, but sales did not cease. That same year Florida passed legislation creating a state fish and game commission, which used law enforcement officers as ex-officio game wardens. It was also the year that Tippetts's robin protection law was passed; unfortunately, both laws were repealed two years later, and the legislature decided game and bird enforcement were county issues. "There followed an orgy of lawless hunting and fishing and shooting under the system of county wardens appointed all too largely for political favors, which made the most optimistic Audubonist to lose heart and hope," wrote Blackman. "This is the sort of legislation under which and against which the Audubon Society had to work for the next decade." That all the birds were not "annihilated" was due to changing public attitudes that FAS had molded, she added.[57]

Tragedy struck in 1916 with the destruction of the Alligator Bay Rookery in southwest Florida, then the largest egret rookery in the state. Poachers shot an estimated eight hundred birds and torched the rookery to force the colony to move to more accessible grounds—all because there were not enough funds to pay for patrolling wardens to guard the nesting area. Not all Florida birds were lost, however, thanks in part to FAS help that had increased rookery numbers. By 1920 there were ten federal bird refuges in Florida in coastal nesting areas, and the National Association of Audubon Societies had preserved an additional island in Alachua County as a reservation. With a change in fashion—by 1917 prostitutes were using plumes in their hats, leading "respectable" women to stop wearing them—the demand for feathers diminished. Enclosed automobiles, introduced in the 1920s, also affected the feather fad as there was little room for passengers to wear extravagant hats. Still, numerous species were in serious peril.[58] The American involvement in World War I sapped some of the FAS strength from 1917 to 1919, but the group stayed active, developing a four-page publication for quarterly mailings to all FAS members.

The first two decades of the Florida Audubon Society were a remarkable time. From a small group of people in Clara Dommerich's living room, the group grew into a sophisticated organization that got laws passed and aroused the public to action. Women were critical to the success of Florida's first environmental group, using their talents to handle finances, keep records, communicate with different organizations, write brochures, deal with national leaders, and run meetings. They were the community connectors to schools, news media, and particularly women's clubs, where they rallied support from other progressive females for FAS initiatives at the local, state, and national levels. In turn, their involvement with Florida Audubon gave women the opportunity to work with men and prove their value as grassroots organizers and capable civic leaders. Although largely unseen, the tireless work—and accomplishments—of these community-minded women were felt well into the next century.

2

Conservation and Forests

Two centuries ago more than half of Florida was covered in tall, majestic pine forests. From its northern borders with Georgia and Alabama and south to the upper shore of Lake Okeechobee, the state was home to massive stands of long-leaf pine, a slow-growing tree that can reach fifty to sixty feet in height and five hundred years in age. Walking through a longleaf forest is akin to visiting to an outdoor cathedral; the thick-barked trees shoot heavenward, breezes play a high-pitched hymn through the thin, spiky leaves, and the clean, piney scent is nature's incense. Early visitors to the nation's Southeast thought the 60 million acres of longleaf forests growing there would last forever. Pioneers marveled at the extent of the forests while alternately complaining about their monotony and the difficulty of traveling through them.[1]

These trees became settlers' homes, fences, and in some cases their liveli-hood, as demand for turpentine and wood products from them increased with development and transportation. Longleaf pines grew with other pine and tree species on an additional 30 million southeastern acres—all resources that sup-plied a growing nation where, for a while, citizens were firmly convinced that the superabundance of American forests would never end. For them, trees had become not only shelter but also commodities that brought personal wealth.[2]

At the end of the nineteenth century, however, it was clear that this was the delusion of a populace that had placed its faith in an American myth. Forests across the nation were disappearing with little thought given to replenishing them for future generations—a problem that worsened into the next century. As they had with the Audubon movement, women in Florida and throughout the United States worked together to address this enormous problem. They sounded alarms, educated the public, and pushed industry and government to improve forestry attitudes and practices. They did this because they loved the beauty of trees as well as the birds and wildlife that lived in them, but they also saw the natural resource as vital to national economic health and independence.

"The time has arrived when the people of Florida must awake to the fact that beautiful forests of timbered land, pine trees and cypress swamps must be conserved if the picturesque landscapes of Florida count for anything in the welfare of the state," Veola Ezell of Leesburg warned members of the Florida Federation of Women's Clubs (FFWC) in a 1923 article that predicted a national wood famine because of forest depletion. She added her own Florida emphasis: "Forests prevent cold winds from devastating orange groves and temper the cold waves from the north and the northwest."[3]

By 1880 an estimated 75 percent of the country's forests had been hewn, and by 1930 only 13 percent still existed; in the next sixty years, half of these disappeared as well. Prior to the Civil War wood provided most of the nation's fuel, replaced by coal only near the end of the nineteenth century. Nowhere was the devastation of America's forests more apparent than in the Midwest, where most people "understood that settling the western prairies meant cutting the northern forests," writes historian William Cronon. The prime focus was white pine, which ranged from New England to the Great Plains and also floated, meaning that it could be cut in one place—such as the upper Midwest—and moved a great distance through water systems to markets such as those in booming Chicago. "What might happen to that landscape if and when the white pines finally gave out was not at first a cause for much concern: after all, providence would see to that" was how area boosters rationalized these practices. By the 1890s pines that were once plentiful in Michigan, Wisconsin, and Minnesota began to disappear, and fires often followed as farmers claimed lands for agriculture that never became productive because the clear-cutting and fires had reduced soil fertility.[4]

Longleaf forests, treated with the same carelessness, were disappearing by the late nineteenth century. Longleaf pines also floated; many were cut and rafted down Florida's waterways to railroad lines and sawmills. By 1996 only 2.95 million acres of longleaf remained in the Southeast, and almost all the old-growth areas were gone. This 98 percent decline made the loss "among the most severe of any ecosystem on earth," writes historian Lawrence S. Earley.[5]

"Need, greed, and mismanagement," were the culprits, Earley avers. "People cut the forest, burned it to farm and make spaces to live, exploited its resources, and changed the natural processes that had evolved with it and maintained it." The guilty included farmers, turpentine extractors, lumber and paper companies, foresters, and others who "made their livings from the forest and tried to shape it for their own ends." He tells the story of a "lumberman in 1893 who forthrightly stated that the cut-and-run loggers then beginning to pillage the great bald cypress and longleaf forests throughout the South were entirely indifferent to their fate, and rightly so." These loggers treated forests as inexhaustible mines "from which loggers extracted the trees and left the land" for another use while they moved on to the next forest. Those watching the devastation left in the wake of such practices advocated new forestry principles that called for treating trees as a crop, which meant that they needed to be grown, harvested, and regenerated—an "enlightened metaphor" compared to previous practices.[6]

European colonists, particularly the seafaring English, greatly valued Florida's plentiful forests. Since ancient times, pinesap, known as resin, had been used to create tar and pitch that made ships watertight and protected ropes from salt air. Trees also supplied vital masts, planking, and ropes. In 1782 Francis Philip Fatio, who built three plantations on the lower St. Johns River to grow indigo and citrus, raise sheep, and tap turpentine from pine trees, reported to the British government (then Florida's owner) that the area produces "the best naval stores in all America. . . . The forests on these lands will produce any quantity of tar, pitch and turpentine." At the same time Fatio praised Florida's forests, he warned that timberlands needed protection from destructive practices, including fires. He believed young trees should be left to restore the forest cover. "Experience has taught us how to remedy that vast destruction of timber, and proper provincial laws should be made to prevent setting on fire the pine-bearing lands, to regulate the boxing of trees for turpentine, to prohibit the extirpating of the young saplings, and to fix the number of trees that should remain on every acre." By the early twentieth century it was clear that his advice had fallen on deaf ears, as timber companies continued to harvest forests without replanting them.[7]

In 1860 Florida's forests were valuable commodities, and lumber products amounted to big business for in-state and out-of-state companies. The state, with a population of 140,424, had 87 sawmills that yielded products valued at $1.47 million annually. Within the next two decades, Florida had ten naval stores plants, and its 135 sawmills were producing 248 million board feet of products annually. The state's lumber production peaked in 1909 at 1.25 billion board feet. Historian Albert E. Cowdrey writes that southern forests were the center of the South's environmental history during the Gilded Age, exhibiting "the upheavals of a tumultuous time" in their change from "reservation to ex-

ploitation to the beginning of scientific forestry." Huge tracts of public timberland were sold in the late nineteenth century to largely non-southern lumber
companies benefiting "northern owners, processors, and speculators." In 1882 a
Florida lumberman reported that the woods were full of similarly minded men
from Michigan. Lumber transport was a very wasteful practice. In Florida, as
well as in other southern states, timber often was floated by river to mills or to
railroad spurs, but cut logs often were left rotting on riverbanks or sunken on
river bottoms.[8]

This visible wreckage, left in the wake of the nation's rapid industrialization
and urbanization, awakened Americans in the late 1800s to the idea of conservation of natural resources. Conservationists advocated for wise, scientific,
efficient use of resources so that they would be available for future generations.
This meant replanting forestry acres that in the past had been logged over and
left barren or smoldering from fires. The conservation movement reached its
peak in the early twentieth century, embraced by scientists, politicians, professionals, and, importantly, women. And forestry issues were at its forefront.[9]

Some of the earliest alarms about disappearing trees were sounded by
George Perkins Marsh in his groundbreaking 1864 book, *Man and Nature: or
Physical Geography as Modified by Human Action*. Marsh warned that human
destruction of the natural world could have tragic consequences: "Man is everywhere a disturbing agent. Wherever he plants his foot, the harmonies of
nature are turned to discords. The proportions and accommodations which in-
sured the stability of existing arrangements are overthrown." Marsh, who had
traveled extensively outside the United States, believed that great civilizations,
including the Greeks and Romans in the Mediterranean area, had collapsed
because of their abuse of natural systems and resources. Deforestation caused
erosion and water pollution and hurt soil fertility, ultimately causing economic
and social destruction. Marsh optimistically believed, however, that all was not
lost, that "geographical regeneration" could be achieved through "great political and moral revolutions in the governments and peoples by whom those
regions are now possessed," writes historian Char Miller.[10]

Marsh's book was an appropriate twenty-first birthday gift for Gifford Pinchot, who became America's preeminent expert on forests and a proponent for
their conservation. Pinchot's love of Marsh and of the outdoors led to his becoming the first career forester in the United States, having trained in France.
A friend of President Theodore Roosevelt, Pinchot in 1905 became the first
director of what would become the U.S. Forest Service, where he emphasized
the utilitarian "wise use" of forests in the national interest. For Pinchot, this

meant recognizing the limits of resources and using them "for the benefit of the people who live here now" without waste. "The outgrowth of conservation, the inevitable result, is national efficiency. In the great commercial struggle between nations, which is eventually to determine the welfare of all, national efficiency will be the deciding factor. So from every point of view conservation is a good thing for the American people," he wrote.[11]

The federal Forest Reserve Act of 1891 acknowledged the importance of the nation's timber and empowered the president to set aside such public lands. President Benjamin Harrison used this to protect 13 million acres in eleven forest reserves, where no commercial lumber removal was allowed, and in six timberland areas, where supervised logging was allowed. Pinchot believed it was the most important forestry legislation in the country. During Roosevelt's presidential terms from 1901 to 1909, the two worked to set aside more forested land, developing a national policy that gained public support. At the time Roosevelt took office there were forty-one forest reserves of 46.4 million acres. By the time Roosevelt left office, those numbers had increased to 150.8 million acres in 159 national forests. What had been an industry of exploitation—of cut and move on with little regard for the devastation and waste left behind—now turned into long-term planning and promotion of "sustained-yield forest management."[12] The management of these forests, however, would not resemble the biodiverse woods of the past. Now they would be planted and replanted with specific species desired for their quick growth and commercial success. It was an improvement on past practices, but still with an eye toward nature as a commodity.

Women's groups across America, including the national General Federation of Women's Clubs (GFWC) and the Daughters of the American Revolution (DAR), supported this new conservation model. Writes historian Samuel P. Hays: "A leader of the National Conservation Association wrote that three women leaders in these two organizations had 'done as much in the legislative field for conservation as any three men I know of.'" It helped that Pinchot's mother, Mary, was DAR conservation committee chair for several years. "And Pinchot himself declared that the Daughters of the American Revolution 'federated and organized spells only another name for the highest form of conservation, that of vital force and intellectual energy.'" Like their Audubon sisters, GFWC members were "particularly active" in organizing campaigns to save the nation's forests.[13]

Women, freed from the constraints of business ties, were horrified by the aesthetic toll of clear-cut logging but also moved to act by its collateral damage: erosion, watershed pollution, and forest fires. They rallied together in all-female groups, expecting that the power of their numbers would gain public and political attention and force change. In Minnesota Lydia Phillips Williams, of that state's clubwomen federation and GFWC forestry chair from 1904 to 1906, organized members to seek the repeal of a timber act that threatened the Chippewa Forest Reserve. They traveled to Washington, D.C., to threaten their congressmen, saying they had a state membership of "between six and seven thousand," which represented an equal number of husbands and "a few thousand sons who will possibly vote as their fathers vote." These nonvoting women used their male relatives to exert ballot pressure on male representatives—an interesting electoral twist. In California Laura White, president and founder of the women's California Club, led the campaign to save the Calaveras Grove of Big Trees. In Massachusetts women published a directory listing the state's historic trees and fought to exterminate moths that threatened trees. Philadelphia women organized the Pennsylvania Forestry Association and worked to create forest reserves and the Pennsylvania Department of Forestry. The GFWC also supported and coordinated efforts to create national forest reserves in the southern Appalachians and New Hampshire and backed the passage of the federal Weeks Bill to protect stream watersheds. In 1910 some 283 clubs sent letters and petitions pressing for forestry reforms.[14]

The GFWC created a forestry committee in 1902, as did many state and local women's groups, to educate members and the public about better forestry practices. They invited professionally trained foresters to their meetings to gain information and appealed to state governments to create forestry departments, set aside forest reserves, create parks, and force better lumber practices.[15]

Local women's clubs often took the initiative to save forests, an effort that led to working both with and against members of the opposite sex. To rescue a grove of redwoods from logging, clubwomen in Humboldt County in northwest California worked for two decades with members of the chamber of commerce, the Sons of the Golden West, and other prominent men. Women valued the trees for their beauty and their importance in ensuring a quality watershed, the latter being of great importance to health in the arid West. They also fought to save an area that had been a favorite local camping and picnicking place. Although they went up against logging, a male-dominated industry, the female and male groups converged to support the effort, engaging in the shared vision and hope that saving the trees would benefit the state economically. Women's groups eventually raised money to match state funds to buy the grove and create a park in 1925.[16]

Without the ability to vote until 1920, women used their organizing skills and moral authority to gain political power and to support the conservation cause. Perhaps nowhere is the difference between the sexes more apparent than in a 1908 article for *Forestry and Irrigation*, written by Lydia Adams-Williams, a conservation writer and GFWC forestry chair. She argued that women's "integrity, resourcefulness, genius and capacity for endurance" accomplished great work. And to Adams-Williams, conservation clearly was women's work. She said it fell to her gender "to educate public sentiment, to save from rapacious waste and complete exhaustion the resources upon which depend the welfare of the home, the children and the children's children. This is the inevitable conclusion for to woman has the practice of saving, of conserving, even been a paramount issue." Adams-Williams saw the sexes as vastly different in their attitudes and actions toward natural resources. Women's interests and talents focused on building home, family, and community, while male ventures addressed economics, causing the destruction found across the country. Men, she wrote, were too busy "building railroads, construction [*sic*] ships, engineering great projects, and exploiting vast commercial and financial enterprises, to take the time necessary to consider the problems which concern the welfare of the home and the future." She noted that the GFWC, with a membership of 800,000, had long worked to preserve forests. "It is conceded that the almost universal sentiment in favor of preserving forests is due to the interest taken in the subject by the women's clubs and the work done for them."[17]

Initially women were welcomed to the forestry movement by the American Forestry Association (AFA), which included them at its annual meetings and published their articles and poems in its journal. The GFWC was invited to submit reports on their forestry activities in 1906. But the welcome door to women closed in the 1910s when "AFA leadership decided that the continued participation of women would harm the association's reputation," writes historian Adam Rome, noting a 1910 editorial in *American Forestry* warning that "too much of the work of women's clubs was unsound and unhelpful" and questioning women's knowledge of the topic. GFWC reports were no longer published as of the following year. The AFA "decision to marginalize women was tied to a campaign to professionalize the organization," and women, few of whom had professional credentials, were seen as "unprofessional" because they concerned themselves more with the "beauty of forests than the resource value of trees." In Pennsylvania Mira Lloyd Dock transcended this prejudice because of her training in botany and her reputation as a public speaker; her admirers "said she did more for forests than any other woman in America."[18]

Florida's women also received different treatment from state forestry leaders, largely because one of them was a politically powerful and adept woman.

Like their national clubwomen sisters, Florida women were alarmed by the state's disappearing forests. The FFWC, a member of the GFWC, advocated for better logging practices by publishing articles about the value of forests from various perspectives. In 1905 the FFWC forestry committee issued a report quoting Roosevelt, who cautioned that if the "present rate of forest destruction is allowed to continue, a timber famine is obviously inevitable." Roosevelt warned that a lack of lumber resources could hinder U.S. industry, a common sentiment that appealed to male and female sensibilities.[19]

The most powerful Florida woman in the forestry conservation movement— perhaps the most powerful *person*—was May Mann Jennings, the "vivacious and charming" wife of a former governor, and a committed conservationist born into the political life. Her father, businessman Austin Shuey Mann, was very involved in Florida politics, helping draft the state's 1885 constitution and serving in the state senate. Her husband, William Sherman Jennings, was Florida governor from 1901 to 1905, representing a period of progressive politics in which his administration achieved a variety of innovative social and conservation legislation, including protection for birds and timber. After her husband's gubernatorial term (he died in 1920), Jennings, who was her husband's "intellectual equal" and similarly enthused about politics, became increasingly active in club work, serving in a variety of leadership roles at local, state, and national levels. She also served on the Florida Chamber of Commerce and worked on forestry conservation initiatives, earning the title "Mother of Florida Forestry." According to her biographer Linda D. Vance, by age forty-two Jennings, with her unanimous election in 1914 as president of the FFWC, "had become the most politically powerful woman in the state." She also was well versed in the politics of the era, equally able to address men's and women's groups comfortably and to appeal to their differing or similar concerns.[20]

Jennings's love of nature drew from her childhood in rural Florida—an area of perfuming citrus groves and abundant wildlife. There she developed a kinship with nature that sparked her lifelong love of the state's natural beauty. As an adult, she belonged to a family with large timber holdings and therefore had a personal interest in their wise management. Jennings often worked with her son, Bryan, on forestry matters. In 1919 she spoke before the Conference of Southern Foresters, arguing that the state needed a department of natural resources to oversee forestry and conservation programs. As a result she was appointed to a committee whose work led to the creation of the Florida Forestry Association (FFA). Bryan was named vice president, and Jennings was named the group's "special consultant on legislation," indicating her legislative power and prowess—something particularly notable since it was one year before female suffrage. The new group had several tasks: saving forests, preventing wildfires, setting up county forest fire protective associations, pushing the creation of a state forestry board, and publishing pamphlets to educate the public. The FFA's first president remembered Jennings as "'a public spirited woman [who] realized the loss occurring the way forests were being handled. She at the time . . . conceived the idea of getting together a group to develop it into the forest service and she really sparked the flame that developed into the FFA.'"[21]

Although the FFA's attempts to get a state forestry board failed initially, Jennings's hard work paid off with legislative approval in 1927. She wrote: "I handled the Forestry law entirely myself except for several days work done at different times during the session by my son, who is the author of the law. We are very proud of this big step in conservation for Florida." Jennings was lauded by news media and national forestry officials for this achievement, which merged with male interests in promoting state growth and economics. A friend wrote: "I wish Florida had a half dozen of you."[22]

Like the women of California's Humboldt County, Jennings was a model of how female interests could meld with those of male bastions of "progress" and development in an attempt to remedy natural resource problems. In doing so, she flexed politically strong muscles while also claiming the hearth and home and promoting the idea of municipal housekeeping. In a 1924 newspaper interview Jennings used a matriarchal tone, stating, "All good clubwomen should be, first of all, good home-makers," an "industry combining all that is greatest in art, science and profession. The most wonderful function of woman is motherhood." Jennings also voiced support of conservation and suffrage, but not in a militant fashion, advising that "much more can be done by tact and diplomacy." No doubt her espousal of the traditional female societal role earned favor with men from whom she sought and gained cooperation, despite the fact that she was often more politically astute. Ironically, given her wealth and social status, Jennings likely did little or no housework her entire life, but her words, couched in the language of old-fashioned femininity, promoted clubwomen's causes that extended far beyond their homes into the community.[23]

Jennings and clubwomen put their energies into what were essentially grassroots actions in response to disappearing wildlife and natural systems. They invoked their moral authority as mothers, wives, and citizens to justify their work. Men had created the mess—or so it was understood—and in Florida, women were there to try to clean it up or repair it, as they did at home, especially when it threatened the health of their children, neighbors, and community. As a consequence of their work—whether intended or not—Jennings and Florida clubwomen expanded the boundaries of the female experience and influence. In gaining the endorsement and cooperation of men on these issues, the women effectively elevated the female profile in new areas of public and civic concern. And they also carved out individual identities for themselves. Jennings was not just Mrs. William Jennings—she was *May Mann Jennings*, a person in her own right with a reputation that endured long after her husband's death. It was new territory for women who, until the 1970s, typically identified themselves by their husbands' first and last names rather than by their own given names.

In later years Jennings received an FFA citation for "outstanding contributions to forestry"—treatment far removed from the way the AFA had shunned the nation's women. The 1954 award states: "Mrs. Jennings' specialty was legislation. When Stetson University awarded her an Honorary Doctor of Laws degree in 1931, the University President commented jovially that he knew of no one who deserved the honor more, since Mrs. Jennings had 'doctored more laws than any person he knew.' Mrs. Jennings has been actively and energetically connected with many other worthwhile movements in conservation, beautification, and good citizenship." Whether she was known as Mrs. Jennings or May Mann Jennings, she had distinguished herself not only as a woman but also as an important Florida leader.[24]

Florida clubwomen enthusiastically joined Jennings in the campaign to save Florida's forests, producing pamphlets about fire prevention and tree planting to raise public awareness. Their interests also meshed with concerns about the state's bird populations at a time when the Audubon campaign was in full swing. Saving large stands of timber was commensurate with protecting birds and wildlife, providing additional impetus to the movement to conserve trees. The women fought for forests, habitat, and wildlife, using a many-pronged approach to appeal to both sexes.

"It is idle to talk of game and bird protection if the forests are to be destroyed," wrote Maud Neff Whitman, FFWC conservation chair, noting in 1922 that some states had begun saving swamp and forest lands for wildlife. "Without forests in a land having no mountains or sheltered haunts for wild life there can be no birds or game."[25] Whitman, of Orlando, railed about devastation caused by lumber interests and forest fires and called upon women to change things, using reasoning that incorporated conservation and economic messages:

> It is useless to expect the average man financially interested in timber to heed any altruistic appeal. He is not concerned with the beauties of Nature, is indifferent to an appeal to sentiment but is quick to listen to sound financial argument. If he can be shown that his business and his children's business will come to financial loss unless it can be assured a continuous supply of timber he will at least give some attention to the conservation question.
>
> Without her forests Florida would lose her lumber industry and thousands of acres of land, unfit for other use, would become a barren waste.
>
> Without her forests Florida would have no game and would present no attractions to the hundreds of sportsmen who come here each season and whose value in dollars and cents can hardly be estimated.
>
> Without her forests Florida would lose much of the beauty and mildness of climate that are such factors in bringing desirable citizens among us.[26]

Whitman reflected the GFWC's conservation message disseminated to its national member groups. It included arguments designed to appeal to male and female sensibilities—economic and sports reasons for men and beauty for women. Florida's female activists were demonstrating that they grasped all the pertinent issues that concerned women and men and were ready and able to counter them in their efforts to protect forests and wildlife, a natural extension of the female sphere of influence.

As conservation issues involving the natural world captured the nation's attention, women became politically adept in their activism and often were courted by industry groups who sought their participation. By the 1920s the AFA, in a turnaround from its stance a decade earlier, sought women's club cooperation in the movement to conserve forests and prevent fires; GFWC leaders in turn suggested that clubwomen present programs on the topic, work with forestry commissions about state needs, press for school instruction on the issue, and write new club programs and literature. It should be noted that in the 1930s Lura Reineman Wilson of Jacksonville served as vice president of the AFA, perhaps because she had served as the FFWC representative to the Florida State Chamber of Commerce, was GFWC chair of Conservation and Natural Resources, and was active in state Democratic politics. Her husband had owned a mill and lumber company. Here was a woman with a wealth of connections, not only through her women's work but also through politics and business, making her a strategically valuable addition to the AFA.[27]

Articles regularly featured in the *Florida Bulletin*, the FFWC publication, demonstrated a sensibility about the state's agriculture, forestry, and economics as well as a plea to aesthetics. During World War II Susan Floyd Fort Jeffreys viewed the state's pinelands as weapons in the country's defense. "As I look at a Florida forest of planted slash pine I feel that here are trained soldiers, soldiers in God's own living green. These planted pines are great factors in our defense program. These trees are patriots and ready to aid us when needed," she wrote in 1948, noting that Florida had 38 million acres of land, of which 23 million acres were forests. She bemoaned forest fires that she reported had caused $8 million in damage the previous year—fires of which only 1 percent were started by lighting, the rest being human caused. "Let us give thought to the beauty and the healing balm of the forests. This would be a dreary and cheerless land without forests. While we are battling for economic stability let us with our minds and hearts and souls battle for beauty. Let's keep Florida green."[28] It was an argument appealing to patriotism, male and female alike, while also invoking the largely female aesthetic appeal.

Forest fires that blackened wooded areas and destroyed wildlife habitat were another concern for the state's women. The fires were destructive and ugly, the women loudly proclaimed in their efforts to stem the blazes. Unknown to them was the fact that many of Florida's habitats, including longleaf pine, need fire to be healthy. Thunderstorms and lightning are regular summer events in the state, and a variety of native trees are adapted to the resulting fires. Fires clear the forest floor of debris and shrubs, allowing the growth of grasses and the germination of pine seeds. With its thick bark, the longleaf easily survives fires. However, without regular burns, plant detritus builds up and fuels high-temperature fires that can be catastrophic to trees and their ecosystems. As Earley notes, "fire in longleaf pine forests is like rain in a rain forest." Thus regular low-intensity forest fires in Florida are positive events—but in the decades before fire ecology became widely understood in the mid-twentieth century, women saw them as evil and unsightly. And, as Jeffreys claimed, they believed humans were the cause of most of the infernos.[29]

One mostly female group involved in fire prevention was the Florida Federation of Garden Clubs (FFGC), founded in 1924 with the mission of protecting the state's trees, shrubs, flowers, and birds; five years later it counted 2,180 members, many of whom were also women's club members and community activists. Like the FFWC, the garden clubbers supported the FFA, even giving the forestry group the FFGC membership list to help it raise funds. At their 1932 annual meeting the FFGC adopted a resolution supporting the FFA's educational work in hopes "that the prevention of woods fire shall become State-wide." The resolution explains their reasons: "The wide-spread practice of woods burning in Florida is denuding our woodlands and killing baby trees by the million, and . . . the shelter and food for wild game and bird life is being destroyed by wild-fire, resulting from the common practice of light-burnings, and . . . wild flowers and plant life are being driven from our woods and fields thereby destroying the natural beauty of our state."[30]

Concern about wildfires was more urgent in 1935 when the FFGC adopted a new resolution that pledged a stronger focus on forestry conservation: "Whereas, there are annually on an average of 15,000 forest fires in Florida, and Whereas, Florida has the largest burned over area of any state and that these fires have been more prevalent and devastating this year than ever, destroying our scenic beauty and wasting our material resources to a ruinous extent, and, Whereas, no beautification is possible while such fires continue. Therefore, be it resolved by the FFGC . . . that the Federation shall make conservation its main objective for the coming year and shall urge all member clubs to work for county wide fire prevention units and other measures of fire control and educate public opinion through the schools, press, radio, speeches, exhibits, and all other ways possible." The FFGC later embraced the national Smokey Bear wildfire prevention campaign, launched in 1944 by the U.S. Department of Agriculture's Forest Service and advertising executives. The group continues to sponsor annual poster contests featuring Smokey for children to promote his message about stopping human-caused fires.[31]

With this commitment, garden club members, like their sisters in women's clubs and Audubon societies, offered their talents and energy in getting the public's attention through a variety of methods that included education, displays, political pressure, and the ever-widening world of news media. These were female foot soldiers of Florida conservation.

Their general was May Mann Jennings. Although she spent much of her energy on Florida's trees, Jennings also worked with clubwomen on other conservation projects. In 1925 she joined forces with Audubon leader Katherine Bell Tippetts to convince the state legislature to protect a variety of state plants that were in peril from over-collection, especially native hollies that were much in demand during the Christmas season for home decoration. That year Jennings also pushed legislation to create a Commission of Game and Fresh Water Fish, hoping that government intervention would help manage Florida's wildlife. In a 1925 article in the *Christian Science Monitor*, she lauded the state's recent steps to establish the commission as well as the creation of fish hatcheries in conjunction with the federal government and a law for a new system of state and county parks. Jennings wrote: "When one is a conservation enthusiast, keenly realizing the great need of conservation along all lines, it is difficult to choose that which would be most far reaching in a State's development, but I can say with perfect safety that the Florida Legislature made long steps in the right direction and the friends of the State need not be surprised to see her stand shoulder to shoulder with her sister states in the matter of the conservation of natural resources after the next regular session of the Legislature."[32]

In later decades, as Florida's growth penetrated farther into its natural systems, Jennings and sister conservationists would advocate for city and roadside beauty, for creation of state and national parks and forests, and for restoration of natural systems. With time they came to understand the importance of forest fires and to see the evolution of thinking from utilitarian conservation to big picture environmentalism. They would be critical in teaching others to care about wetlands. For now, however, they tried to teach a developing state to love and value its vast woodlands—of which only a remnant exists today.

3

Creating Parks

Mary Barr Munroe was worried. For decades, scientists and naturalists had hiked and slogged through South Florida's Everglades to explore its exotic landscape, flora, and fauna. The seemingly endless sawgrass, the jagged marsh plant found through much of this freshwater wetland, dominated the area, but there also were luxuriant orchids, brilliant wading birds, and animals seen nowhere else in the world.

Of special concern was Paradise Key, a lush hammock island that supported a variety of vegetation, including more than sixty varieties of trees, orchids, ferns, vines, and tree snails. Its centerpiece was almost a thousand royal palms, majestic native trees that towered a hundred feet or more in height. Also known as Royal Palm Hammock, the area arose forty-six miles south of Miami and a dozen miles southwest of Homestead. Its location seemingly should have left it isolated and safe from the development that was starting to consume the state, but by the 1890s efforts to save it had begun. Botanists Charles Torrey Simpson and John Kunkel Small, who fretted early on about the future of Florida's natural areas, suggested it might be preserved as a national monument, but that proved difficult because of land title issues.[1]

Munroe, however, was a feisty woman accustomed to taking on big challenges. Having embraced the Audubon cause, she castigated any woman who wore bird-plumed hats. An active Coconut Grove woman's clubber, the fifty-four-year-old Munroe also knew the potential power of women in Florida to get things done. Using her authority as Forestry Department chair of the statewide women's club organization, the Florida Federation of Women's Clubs (FFWC), she revived efforts to preserve and protect the key. Joining Munroe was Edith Gifford, a clubwoman from Coconut Grove, whose husband John was a former Cornell University professor and forestry expert. At their urging, in 1905, the FFWC adopted a resolution calling for the creation of a federal forest reservation on the key, noting that Royal Palm Hammock was the only place in the United States where the palms grew naturally. Without protection, they feared the palms would be poached for landscape ornamentation or plowed under for agriculture. It was a reasonable request—as earlier noted, U.S. President Theodore Roosevelt was actively creating forest reserves, which totaled almost 151 million acres when he left office in 1909.[2]

Soon Gifford and Munroe "were both assaulting" state legislators to protect Paradise Key. It took almost a decade before their efforts and those of FFWC bore fruit. The key to their success: May Mann Jennings's election in 1914 as president of FFWC, then nine thousand members strong. Jennings was well versed in conservation and forestry issues; now she turned her considerable talents and connections toward protecting the hammock key. Her decision to make this a priority "was to have historic and far-reaching consequences for Florida, launching her upon a political, economic, and public relations struggle that would span thirty-three years," writes biographer Linda D. Vance.[3]

Their actions came at a crucial time. By the century's second decade the area was being mapped for future development, which included a railroad extension from Miami to Key West planned by Henry Flagler, whose development and transportation projects already were lining parts of the state's east coast. The next year a road opened to the key from Florida City, wrote historian Charlton W. Tebeau, creating the "possibility that the vegetation might be removed to clear the land for farming."[4]

Jennings set about this new mission with a fiery ardor, calling upon the aid of up to one hundred FFWC members who had links and family ties to prominent men, including governors, judges, bankers, government leaders, and college presidents, providing access to "the state's highest circles of power." It was an "old-girl network" of clubwomen who used the "cult of southern womanhood" to gain male support for their projects, observes Vance. They were southern "ladies," but they wanted their way and knew how to get it. The women were aided in their quest by Flagler's wealthy widow, Mary Kenan Flagler, an FFWC and Audubon member who offered 960 acres of land on and around the hammock. Munroe, through her relationship with James E. Ingraham, president of Henry Flagler's Model Land Company, conveyed news of the promised donation to Jennings. Their hope was that the state, which held ownership to the rest of the land through the Internal Improvement Fund (IIF), would donate it for a park. This was bold thinking and doing—no women's club had ever established and run a state park in the United States.[5]

Early on, FFWC members often perplexed legislators when visiting their Tallahassee offices to demand community improvements. Lucy Worthington Blackman, a former FFWC president, recalled that her sisters faced the "old Adam war-cry, 'Woman's place is in the home,'" which "reverberated through the pines and over the rivers and lakes and ocean from Pensacola to Key West." Women were "reviled" for getting involved in the movement. "Thanks be, there were enough women with spinal cords starched stiff, who raised their undaunted eyebrows and said, 'Ah! indeed!' to this masculine mandate—and then went forth and did as they saw fit." These women had the "annoying habit of . . . talking back at the legislators after they had been told politely to go home and tend the babies—this pesky, unreasonable, feminine pertinacity," Blackman wrote. By 1940 the FFWC no longer came to the legislature with numerous proposals; the list was shorter "because, as a result of their sandspur tactics, the lawmakers finally succumbed and cleared the women's calendar by passing the legislation so persistently demanded of them." Women were belittled and ridiculed by politicians and the state's news media, but a funny thing happened on the way to Tallahassee: their strategy of sticking to a thorny issue en masse and never letting go had gained political attention and legislation even without the power of the vote. Instead of having the insider "good old boys' club" to rely on, they utilized their own female network to press lawmakers, shift public opinion, and carry the day.[6]

No one exercised greater political agility in the female network than Jennings, Florida's former first lady. And nowhere is this better illustrated than in her 1914 strategy to persuade state leaders and Governor Park Trammell to create the park and to nudge the legislature into funding its maintenance at $1,000 per year. She could not vote or stand on the floor of the legislature to seek help. But she could—and did—turn to her cadre of influential clubwomen for behind-the-scenes assistance. Florence Cay, a clubwoman married to a former legislator and Tallahassee businessman, contacted Virginia Trammell, the governor's wife, on Jennings's behalf. As a result, Virginia Trammell promised to "speak to the governor"; better yet, Jennings was invited to stay at the governor's residence during her trip to the capital—quite cozy quarters for a woman who was lobbying for money and land. On December 23, as Jennings hoped, IIF trustees gave Dade County the authority to stop hammock trespassing; a day later they agreed to the park, but it needed approval and funding from the legislature. It was going to be a struggle, so Florida's women leaders readied for it. On December 28 Munroe led a trip to the verdant key—the first time Jennings had seen it. Accompanying them were Jennings's husband (the former governor) and son and two women's club leaders who experienced the "bone-shattering" fifty-mile car trip on a rough, unpaved road that took hours.[7]

The IIF trustees' decision to donate the property, according to Vance, "marked a quiet but dramatic change in state government." This was a vital step toward creation of Florida's first state park, increasing its size to four thousand acres; eventually it would become the nucleus of the state's first national park. Jennings was the fulcrum of it all. She got her husband to draft a bill for the needed legislative approval for the proposed Royal Palm Park, mobilized clubwomen across the state, encouraged publications, and began an extensive speaking tour to garner backing. "Instead of contacting an official or legislator directly to ask for his support," writes historian Polly Welts Kaufman, "she first interested the official's wife in the project; if the wife was not already a club-woman, although many of them were, Jennings found another clubwoman who could introduce her to the wife." Jennings also used a strategy that perhaps only the state's clubwomen could implement—threatening the withholding of dessert—according to a 1947 article written by FFWC past president Mildred White Wells. "Unique in the annals of legislative lobbying was Mrs. Jennings' pressure on individual legislators. It became a question of 'Pie or Park,'" Wells wrote (seemingly humorously) in a history of the park. "In a letter to each club president, Mrs. Jennings urged them to write to their members and relatives in the legislature that 'if they don't get that bill through for Royal Palm Park, they won't have any pie for two years.'" Perhaps by invoking *Lysistrata*—the ancient Greek play in which women withhold conjugal favors as a tactic for persuading men to end war—the Florida women were ready to apply—or threaten to apply—imaginative forms of pressure to get men's attention and cooperation.[8]

The FFWC included the park in its bills for the 1915 legislature—proposals that also pressed for compulsory education, a girls' industrial school, a state tuberculosis hospital, a law allowing women to be on school boards, and land for Seminole Indians. What Jennings had not expected were problems for the park posed by some of her fellow women. She later learned by letter that the $1,000 request for park operations had been eliminated by Tallahassee clubwomen, who did not want to support funding for an aesthetic project. She also ran into problems created by another formidable clubwoman, Minnie Moore-Willson of Kissimmee, a prominent advocate of Seminole rights, who felt the FFWC should be fighting for an Everglades Indian reservation rather than a park; she threatened state officials with reprisals if they failed to do just that. Moore-Willson wrote to other FFWC members espousing this view and claiming that the Jenningses were "Everglades speculators" who would personally benefit from a park because they owned thousands of acres of nearby land. Moore-Willson threatened to expose Jennings as part of a land scandal but never did.[9]

When time became critical for passage of the park bill, Jennings wrote to Moore-Willson on May 12, 1915, assuring her of FFWC support for the Seminoles and trying to stop the attacks that might incur negative reactions from the all-male legislature. "As I have mentioned to you before, antagonism never accomplishes anything, and as the Federation has a splendid standing with the officials in the State, we cannot afford to jeopardize that standing by any antagonism, and I could not permit an attack on the officials to be made in the name of the Federation, and of course if you still persist in taking that course you would have to do it as an individual, and could not use our Federation pages for that purpose," Jennings wrote. "I have always found that even if I disagreed with officials that it was best to use a great deal of policy, and women had had to use a great deal of policy in their work to get the men to listen to them at all, as a great many men still think that women are carried away by sentiment, enthusiasm and hysteria."[10]

Jennings's words indicated that female unity and calm behavior, as opposed to aggressiveness—which risked being interpreted as hysteria, allegedly a trait of women—were an absolute necessity to get anything accomplished in Tallahassee in view of its track record of masculine mockery of FFWC proposals.

After a trip to Tallahassee in which the $1,000 appropriation was restored to the bill, Jennings, exhausted and sick at home in Jacksonville, enlisted her husband and son to go to Tallahassee to promote the proposal. Its fate had become critical because publicity about the park and its valuable flora had inadvertently led to more poaching of the hammock's exotic palms. Two days before the legislature's scheduled June 4 adjournment, the House passed the bill; the Senate did so at midnight the next day. The appropriation was not passed. However, Florida's clubwomen became the first in the United States to create a state park that they also managed—an achievement that would be an inspiration for like-minded women.[11]

When Royal Palm State Park was dedicated in 1916, a motorcade of 168 cars, many with clubwomen, led the way to the ceremonies. The keynote speaker was Mary Belle King Sherman of the 2-million-strong General Federation of Women's Clubs (GFWC), who pronounced the event proof of the "power of the clubwomen's network to preserve 'national scenic areas.'" At the same ceremony Jennings declared the park to be "God's Own Garden" and called it the "only jungle of its kind in the United States and the only one owned by a Federation of Women's Clubs." It was a new precedent set by women.[12]

Sherman, writes Kaufman, changed the mission of GFWC's Conservation Committee from "that of emphasizing conserving natural resources to one of protecting scenic landscapes, a concept she termed 'the conservation of natural scenery.'" Sherman pressed for the 1915 creation of Rocky Mountain National Park, telling Congress that it "would benefit its millions of visitors 'physically, mentally, and morally.' She cited support from the ten thousand members of the Colorado State Federation" and the Denver Daughters of the American Revolution (DAR). That same year Sherman used the GFWC to create a "natural scenic area survey," asking each state conservation chair to "name the parks in her state and suggest areas that should be protected." Sherman argued that children and communities needed contact "with things of beauty and interest in the outdoor world." Nature was "a splendid antidote for the ills of our complex civilization," she said, adding that national parks should "become great outdoor nature schools, splendid travel centers, common meeting grounds, where the people of all sections will get acquainted and come to appreciate one another"—in other words, a great act of democracy that could affect the lives of many generations. Sherman also supported the creation of the National Park Service in 1916, the same year the Florida park was dedicated.[13]

Royal Palm State Park signified the state's rising participation in a park movement that was sweeping the nation and redefining conservation to include preservation of landscapes. And women such as Sherman, Munroe, Gifford, and Jennings were integral to its success. The first national park in the United States—and the world—was Yellowstone, established in 1872 in an effort to protect the park's unique geological features. It also heralded the rising consciousness of disappearing wilderness in the United States. Thirteen years later New York created the Adirondack Park and Forest Preserve, setting aside 5 million acres to remain wild—and to ensure that water resources were safe. Historian Roderick Nash states that wilderness was "preserved unintentionally" in these two places, since their main purposes were natural oddities and watershed, but it was this type of preservation that would be "one of the most significant results of the establishment" of these parks. Impetus for state and national parks also was spurred by the reality of America's disappearing wild lands and creatures. The ultimate example of what might otherwise happen was the commercialization of Niagara Falls, which left the wondrous area a tacky, dirty scene for tourists who traveled to view its splendor but instead found fences with operators charging fees to look through holes to see the falls.[14]

The first national park consciously created to preserve wilderness was Yo-

semite in 1890, the same year General Grant and Sequoia were established. Cra-
ter Lake, Glacier, and Rocky Mountain national parks came in the next twenty-
five years. Historian Samuel P. Hays writes that these "were lands of spectacular
geological phenomena," the protection of which was promoted by "explorers,
big game hunters, archaeologists, and naturalists who had ventured westward
for purposes other than settlement. Private ownership and development, they
felt, would deprive the nation of assets that would be increasingly prized over
the years." The extensive media and governmental debate over flooding the
Hetch Hetchy Valley, part of Yosemite National Park, and the 1913 congressional decision that allowed it to be dammed for hydroelectric power and water
supplies for the city of San Francisco, aroused the country's interest in its national parks. Women were integral in the grassroots effort to try to save Hetch
Hetchy—a cause led by noted author and Sierra Club founder John Muir. The
GFWC rallied its almost 800,000 members to stop the dam, and many women's
groups petitioned Congress for the same. Their actions challenged masculine
authority, leading to a cartoon depiction of Muir wearing a skirt and using a
broom as ridicule for his association with female conservationists.[15]

Although the valley was lost, the public, with women firmly part of the
conversation, had debated for the first time what national parks should be and
how they should be used—and never again in the twentieth century would one
be dammed for utilitarian reasons. Congress created the National Park Service
to oversee the lands and the growing movement that would bring national
parks to the East Coast in 1926 with Great Smoky Mountains, Shenandoah,
and Mammoth Cave, and with Acadia in 1929—all of which began with private
or state donations of land that sparked federal participation. Like Royal Palm
State Park, the East Coast parks started with private ownership and led to bigger acreage and prominence—and Florida's clubwomen would come to have
equally grand plans.[16]

The creation of Royal Palm State Park left the FFWC with a preserved site
but no money to maintain and operate it or to build a planned lodge. Jennings
tackled the problem by making financial appeals to groups, news media, and
wealthy and influential notables such as John D. Rockefeller, Andrew Carnegie,
Charles Deering, and Thomas A. Edison (the latter two had winter homes in
Florida). To hire a caretaker at a cost of $1,200 annually, and to cover other
expenses, the FFWC held a "mile of dimes" campaign, trying to raise $6,000
through various fundraisers. Some of the land was rented to area farmers to
raise additional funds. Again the clubwomen's connections helped when the
wives of several Dade County commissioners obtained a one-year $1,200 grant

from that agency. That grant and loans from FFWC funds dedicated to other purposes funded the eventual improvements. The old-girl network continued to be invoked for the next two decades as the women sought and received funding and legislative support for the park. After 1920 they could also leverage their election votes. In an undated report to the Housekeepers Club of Coconut Grove, affiliated with the FFWC (and Munroe's creation), Eleanor H. Sollitt related an enlightening story she heard at the March 1938 FFWC annual meeting. Although there had been a regular annual appropriation for Royal Palm State Park that had been "gingerly and grudgingly" doled out by the legislature, the FFWC's lobbying in the prior year had increased that appropriation to $4,000. However, the actual money was not forthcoming until shortly before the 1938 state convention, when an unidentified clubwoman's husband, in a not-so-subtle threat, "told the men at Tallahassee that there were approximately 9,000 women in the State of Florida who had something to say about whether the Royal Palm State Park should receive what had been appropriated toward its upkeep and that representatives of the 9,000 women were convening in West Palm Beach in March and with the primaries so near at hand these women might be ready to do something about it." The day before the convention, "at the eleventh hour," the FFWC received a check from the state for $2,000. The legislature understood the strength of the FFWC, its members now empowered with the vote, and succumbed to their pressure.[17]

Florida's first park was no model of wilderness preservation. Its female creators had very definite ideas of what they wanted the park to be, and much of it involved manipulation of the landscape with little care about saving the neighboring wetlands; indeed, most favored the long-standing state policy of draining the adjacent Everglades for agricultural production. A year after the park was created, Jennings suggested that a dike and canal be constructed on 160 acres west of the park to grow coconut and lime trees to generate operating revenue. This view was in line with the progressive conservation ethic of wisely and scientifically taking what appeared to be "useless" land and making it productive for people while also preserving a few spots of aesthetic beauty. States Vance: "Floridians still live with both the positive and negative results" of these visions.[18] Without knowledge of the ecological value of the Everglades— the term and concept of ecology did not come into general use until the second half of the twentieth century—drainage promoters had little idea of the toll their schemes would take.

As historian Jack E. Davis notes, Jennings "believed parks should be created not for 'protective purposes' alone but 'because of some choice natural beauty' and for 'public recreation.'" To improve the beauty of the park, Jennings planned to move royal palms to line the road into the park, cut trails, and create a bird sanctuary, botanical park, and game preserve. She was little concerned about the neighboring Everglades, having long shared views with her husband that the seemingly useless wetlands would be a boon to the state if they could be drained and put into fertile agricultural production. She visualized "a land of milk and honey rising out of the swampy vastness of South Florida," writes Vance.[19]

Perhaps out of funding concerns, there was talk early on of making the new park part of the national system of parks and monuments. In 1916 David Fairchild, who held the title of "agricultural explorer in charge" for the U.S. Department of Agriculture, sent his congratulations to Jennings about the park and asked if she had "ever considered the possibility of having this park taken in executive order" by the president to become a national monument. Fairchild wrote that he had met with George P. Dorr, who was working on the proposed Acadia national park project, leading Fairchild to wonder, "why should it not be possible for the women of Florida, if they manage adroitly, to have the Royal Palm Hammock taken out of politics entirely and put where it will be forever a permanent national park?" On a separate page he wrote an endorsement of the park: "It should not be difficult for anyone familiar with the changes which have transformed the wonderful hammocks about Miami into residence sites for the wealthy, to imagine the popular approval which the next generation will bestow upon the foresighted women of Florida who have saved Paradise Key for the eager-eyed botanists and nature lovers of America. It should be made a National Monument."[20]

Jennings replied that she was not in favor of turning the park over "just at present":

It may be that if we get the botanical garden well started [the] making of the Park a National Monument, might be considered. If we could be assured that our plans would be continued. I had known of course that these Monuments were made by executive order, but I had not gone into the detail of the proceedings. I should be very glad if you will give me the information of just how to proceed in detail, as of course it might be possible we could not carry the expense of keeping the Park and would have to appeal to the Government for aid in this way.

Jennings hoped to turn the acreage donated by Flagler into botanical gardens that "may rival the famous botanical gardens of Java. Of course, we have not

hope of the scenic beauty which is found in the Java gardens, such as mountains and waterfalls, but we can construct water ways, and have a very wonderful collection of plant life." Other ideas for the park included raising and
selling tropical birds and creating an amusement park; Jennings vetoed the
latter, suggesting that Miami Beach would be a better site for such activities. A
decade later Jennings was still exploring ways to manipulate the park, which
by 1929 had grown to nearly 12,000 acres and since 1921 had received a $2,500
annual legislative appropriation. Her latest idea was to use part of the park to
raise deer and, perhaps, whooping cranes and sandhill cranes to repopulate the
state. Jennings said she was inspired by a 1911 trip to Queen Wilhelmina's deer
park near the Hague in the Netherlands, "and ever since have been anxious to
bring such an attraction to Royal Palm State Park." But first, the deer nursery
would need to be "properly drained," she wrote.[21]

Jennings's work for parks did not end with Royal Palm State Park. She
hustled tirelessly to get more state parks and enlisted help from the Civilian
Conservation Corps (CCC), a federal work-relief program developed during
the Great Depression to put young men to work. It would be a conservation
army, focused, in President Franklin Roosevelt's words, on "forestry, the prevention of soil erosion, flood control and similar projects." Jennings saw that
as completely compatible with the creation of state parks. Now she enlisted the
forestry board, headed by her son, with the prospect of federal funding and
increased tourism; and naturally she made sure Royal Palm State Park, still
owned by FFWC, gained the first CCC camp in the state. The CCC had two
fronts in Florida: forestry, which included tree planting and fire protection, and
parks.[22]

With the CCC involvement Florida finally got a system of state parks—the
first seven stretched through the state and covered a variety of habitats. As
with Royal Palm State Park, there was little mind given to preserving wilderness. These new parks were built environments that managers eagerly acted to
change to suit their definitions of natural beauty; one described it as the "work
of a creative artisan." Jennings embraced this idea. The CCC sent two hundred
men to a camp near Royal Palm State Park, where they repaired the FFWC
lodge, built a power house for electricity and water, created a lily pond, cut
new roads, built hiking trails, and planted trees. After more than seven months
there, the crews headed north to the Highlands Hammock area near Sebring.[23]

Highlands Hammock, with hundred-foot trees and its virgin hammock, had
long been on the local residents' wish list for park status. Deemed too small
for a national park, it needed to be funded with money raised locally. In 1930

Margaret Shippen Roebling, the wife of a wealthy bridge builder who owned a nearby estate, donated $25,000 to buy the original 1,000 acres and then another $25,000, challenging the community to raise $5,000. Almost every citizen contributed, with amounts ranging from $1 to $1,000. After Roebling died that October, her husband John spearheaded the project, building its infrastructure. The 1,280-acre park was dedicated in 1931, and in 1935, with the establishment of the Florida Park Service, it became one of seven state parks.[24]

In 1934 the CCC began working on a botanical garden planned on 1,500 acres of adjacent land. Supporters of the Florida Botanical Garden and Arboretum, among them the mostly female Florida Federation of Garden Clubs, hoped it would complement the park or become part of a proposed DeSoto State Forest, and they lobbied Tallahassee to make it a reality. At a 1934 meeting the FFGC's executive board discussed a report from Conservation Chair Clara I. Thomas, who served as contact member for the Special Committee of the Highland Hammock. The report expressed appreciation for FFGC's securing of a master architect's plan for the project, intended to help the state forestry department direct CCC work. In the meantime, Thomas urged all garden clubbers to visit the hammock "so that each and every garden club member may consider herself an agent to see the idea of a State Forest Park, Botanical Garden, and Arboretum in her community." Thomas described the arboretum plan, based on one in Belgium, as "naturalistic" to show "the relationship of trees to each other; those things which grow naturally in harmony with each other." Serving on the arboretum's advisory council were Fairchild as well as noted national landscape designers and planners John Nolen and Frederick Law Olmsted, the latter of whom designed New York City's Central Park. Thomas reported that the group was working on a state plan that would connect parks and reserves in Florida by a system of scenic highways. In 1935 the arboretum and park projects merged to become Highlands Hammock State Park, but the botanical garden project ended after World War II.[25]

The need for a far-reaching plan for state parks and highways was evident as Florida underwent rapid growth and transformation. With the arrival of trains and then the automobile, more people were moving to or visiting the state, notes Mark Derr, driving Florida "into a period of unprecedented growth culminating in a buying frenzy that left the nation's bankers breathless and the state bankrupt" three years before the Great Depression. To naturalists such as Simpson, the "collapse of the real estate market was a disaster that came too late"—much damage to the natural world already had been done. Schemes began to build a shipping canal across the state, increase acreage of exotic fruits, build sea walls, flatten mangrove forests, and get rid of problematic wetlands. Developers and state leaders had done their best to drain and reclaim the state's wetlands, with 3.5 million acres disappearing between statehood and 1920. Still, the U.S. Department of Agriculture determined that in the early 1920s, the state had 16.8 million acres of land that needed drainage for agriculture.[26]

The state's booming population was to blame. In 1925 alone, some 2.5 million people visited or relocated to the state, where the population had risen from 188,000 in 1870 to 968,470 in 1920 and then leaped to 1.8 million in 1940.[27] These growing numbers did more than anything else to reshape the landscape and send the state's women worrying about saving natural places for the future. Around them were disappearing forests, dirty streams, miles of new roads, ugly billboards that seemed to sprout up overnight, and fires in the woods and wetlands that could not be ignored.

Florida's clubwomen foresaw a bleak cultural and aesthetic future if agricultural and urban development continued in this pattern, which likely inspired their push for parks. In her 1923 annual report as FFWC parks chair, Veola Ezell stated that parks were "of inestimable value to the health of individuals in any community" and argued that "no money was ever more wisely spent. We Americans are a busy, pushing people. Let us push for parks in our communities and do all possible to arouse interest and enthusiasm for the state parks not forgetting our own Royal Palm Park." She warned that by 1940 or 1950 the state might be "one vast orange grove and vegetable farm" with great swaths of forest removed. Countering this by advocating for parks was a job for the state's women, who held the moral authority and know-how to get it done. "Public sentiment will go a long ways to preserve beauty spots not yet despoiled," wrote Ezell. "And nowadays women help make public opinion, so the Florida Federation of Women's Clubs have a great work before them, especially so when prominent men tell us 'We look to the ladies of the state to create that sentiment of preserving Florida's natural beauty spots.'" It is interesting to speculate about the source of Ezell's concerns. Although she lived in the relatively rural Lake County, Ezell was well aware of the potential impact of agriculture on the state. Citrus there was becoming an important crop, rebounding from two devastating freezes in 1894 and 1895 that killed 99 percent of the area's citrus trees. By 1923, however, groves covered an estimated 30,000 acres of land that had once supported old-growth pine forests.[28]

At the same time Ezell had to be aware of plans to convert large areas of wetlands to agriculture—actions that would change the state's complexion. Yet there was abundant rural land in the state, and Lake County was not in danger of urbanization. Perhaps she was simply clairvoyant, with a keen concern about where the state was heading. Or she may have been borrowing a template argument about the importance of parks that was being disseminated regularly by GFWC and FFWC. That message was spurred by the undeniable loss of natural scenery in the country's urban areas, particularly in the Northeast. Ezell may also have been inspired by a conservative impulse, not just regarding natural resources but also from a desire to keep parts of Florida unchanged. As a leader of various historical groups, including the Daughters of the Confederacy and the DAR, Ezell participated in revering the past as expressed in the nation's wars. Her call to create more parks, then, may have been a way of preserving not only the state's landscape but also its heritage from change.[29]

The crowning achievement of the Florida women's conservation movement remained Royal Palm State Park, which by the 1920s was beset by new problems. In a 1927 article FFWC leader Katherine Bell Tippetts extolled the park's importance and compared it with other clubwomen's preservation projects in California, Nebraska, and Washington: "And thus moves along the work of conservation, through the united effort of clubwomen." FFWC members implemented new schemes to support the project, including selling postcards of the park and planning a nursery to generate revenue. A lodge had been built on the property to house visiting scientists and tourists, and the FFWC hoped it would make money, but it suffered extensive hurricane damage in 1926 as well as a fire that burned fifty acres. The legislature approved $5,000 for park aid, while FFWC members raised money by collecting rent from tomato growers, selling plants, giving chicken dinners, and seeking donations from member clubs and individuals. Two years later another hurricane damaged the lodge, which may have led the park oversight committee to reconsider becoming part of a proposed Tropic Everglades National Park that the women voted to endorse.[30]

By the 1920s problems in the neighboring Everglades were becoming apparent as newly drained and reclaimed soil oxidized, literally disappearing as fires erupted in the organic soil and salt water intruded into Miami's supply of fresh water. It was during this decade that Ernest Coe, a Miami landscape architect whom some regarded as a "man obsessed," began his crusade to create a national park in the lower Everglades. Miami journalist Marjory Stoneman Douglas described him as "a man on fire with the passion of the idea that would possess him for the rest of his life. No one ever wrote more letters, paralyzed more people with his insistent talk, was considered more a fanatic than Ernest Coe." As he worked feverishly during the next two decades to bring his dream to reality, women were there to support the project at almost every step along the way—and their Royal Palm State Park would become the nucleus of this grand venture.[31]

As Davis notes, "Coe had his work cut out for him" in convincing leaders in Washington, D.C., to establish a park in southern Florida. Since the inception of Yellowstone, more than five hundred proposals for national parks had flowed in, with only twenty-five created by 1931. In 1930 the National Park Service sent a delegation to see the proposed park, and these visitors were joined by a number of naturalists as well as Douglas and Ruth Bryan Owen, Florida's first congresswoman. Owen, elected in 1928, was the daughter of noted politician and orator William Jennings Bryan, and she was a key factor in the creation of what would eventually be named Everglades National Park. Douglas was filled with hope after the visit and wrote in the *Miami Herald*: "It really looks as if this were going to be true. It really looks as if, through the wisdom of the national park service, we in our time were going to see great pilgrimages of people along the marine highways of the Everglades park, to those remote fastnesses where the white egrets soar in their thousands and where in the lovely air of some stained sunset hundreds of quiet people can make their peace again with sea and vast sky and brooding land in the inexpressible sound of wings."[32]

Several months after the tour, which included bird watching and a dirigible ride, Owen cosponsored a bill to create the park. According to Davis and the lore surrounding the effort, when House opponents argued in a hearing that the Everglades were "good for nothing more than slimy vermin," the tall, stately Owen made a gutsy move: she picked up a large nonpoisonous king snake that a surgeon had brought and dangled it from her shoulders. "That's how afraid we are of snakes in the Everglades," she calmly stated, neglecting to mention that she had never before picked up a snake. In late December a Senate delegation spent a week in the Everglades, leading to Senate approval of the park bill in early 1931. Owen lost her election that year; despite the fact that her successor supported the bill, the national economic downturn took its toll, and the House of Representatives refused to approve the park.[33]

Coe was not to be stopped, however, and he turned to women for help in publicizing the project. Douglas, along with Department of Agriculture scientist Ralph Stoutamire, penned a brochure titled *The Parks and Playgrounds of Florida*, in which they argued that the "impressiveness, the sheer greatness and power of primeval earth which this region will hold forever intact, will be felt inevitably by tens of thousands of visitors. Its vast and untouched age has still the youth of the sea-ooze in it, the youth of the great salt winds over it, and of the imperial snow-bursts of the clouds which hang in airy dazzling turrets at its horizons. A nation will come here and be silent and go away and never forget."[34]

In 1934 the House finally passed a bill, and Coe agreed to Senate restrictions—no funding until 1939. As a result the park was approved in 1934, and federal lands within its proposed boundaries were removed from sales or settlement. Unable to promote the park for scenic values, as in the preservation of Yellowstone and Yosemite, and with only limited promise for recreational use, Coe won the "near-universal support" of scientists and naturalists, who agreed that the biological wealth of the unique wetlands merited a national park designation.[35] For the first time Americans would have a park deemed important simply for the plants, wildlife, hydrology, and geology it contained.

Prior to the federal approval, in 1929 state leaders created a Tropic Everglades National Park Commission, with the authority to acquire lands for the park; Coe was elected director. Joining him on that commission, which was revived in 1936, were two prominent clubwomen—Jennings and Mary Sorenson Moore of Miami, wife of a developer and former legislator. Moore reported back to the FFWC in 1936 that much needed to be done, including land acquisition, improvements to the lodge, and more salary for the Royal Palm State Park warden. The next year the commission sent Jennings to lobby for $87,000 in funding from the legislature, an acknowledgement of her political skills. In a maneuver by Governor Fred Cone, whom Jennings later described as a "double-dealer," the entire commission resigned (including Coe) to get gubernatorial approval of the funding. Vance writes that Cone appointed a new chair of the commission and allowed it to "remain in limbo," and this "effectively stymied the movement to establish the park, which was opposed by some recalcitrant local landowners and by many of the state's hunters and fishermen." When Governor Millard Caldwell revived the commission in 1945, Moore and Jennings were included in its membership. Jennings was specifically designated to represent area landowners and, in a gesture of support, immediately deeded her acreage near Flamingo to the park.[36]

The year 1947 was to be a watermark in Florida's conservation history. In the spring Everglades National Park became the twenty-ninth national park. It was dedicated on December 6 at a gathering of more than eight thousand people, including prominent supporters and politicians, with a keynote speech by President Harry S. Truman. Jennings, who appeared on the program, and Florida's clubwomen had spent thirty-three years saving Paradise Key and then lobbying for the park. In an editorial the following day the *Florida Times-*

Union, the newspaper in Jennings's hometown of Jacksonville, called the park a "permanent monument to the Florida Federation of Women's Clubs" and stated that "all who are familiar with the work of Mrs. Jennings will agree that a large measure of credit is due her for determination and persistence which at times bridged wide gaps of disappointment in the progress of the program."[37]

Florida had a national park, but public sentiment was still firmly entrenched in the conservation ethic of utilitarian management of resources. In his speech Truman reiterated these values, decrying the processes that destroyed natural resources and calling for wise use of minerals, forest, water, and soil.[38] This was no call for preservation of wilderness for preservation's sake; the emphasis remained on use of resources for human betterment. Despite their desire to save the park area, Jennings and Douglas and many other clubwomen were in full accord with this view of nature. Now that the park was safe, it was perfectly fine, in their eyes, to continue large-scale drainage and manipulation of the rest of the Everglades under the auspices of improvement.

This thinking would change in coming decades as the concept of ecology and the toll of environmental crises became evident. But for now, women had propelled the state in a new direction that led to a series of state parks, one of which became Florida's first national park. Munroe had sparked it with her concerns about Paradise Key; she lived to see the state park but died in 1922, long before the national park's creation. Today the original park site houses a visitor center, nature boardwalks, and a sprinkling of swaying royal palms that survived modern hurricanes. Guests from around the world learn about the area's rich biota and view wading birds and lolling alligators. It is part of the vast expanse of Everglades National Park, recognized as a World Heritage site—a legacy that Munroe could not have foreseen but a fitting tribute to her vision and that of Florida's clubwomen.

4

The City and State Beautiful

Stinking garbage in the streets. Pigs and cattle roaming through town. Cemeteries and vacant lots overgrown with brush. Stark, treeless roads lined with advertising signs. Slums with dilapidated housing and open sewers.

These were the facts of urban life for many Floridians in the first half of the twentieth century. Although most residents relocated to the state for its Edenic qualities, rapid growth left numerous cities unprepared to deal with resulting problems that affected the quality of life. As a result concerned Florida women took action to address these ills, working through clubs, garden groups, historical associations, and local agencies to counter civic ugliness. Using their collective political power—and later their ability to vote—they fought proliferating billboards, planted thousands of trees, helped create parks, and pressed local governments to enact city planning and to improve or remove slums. They wanted to save natural areas while at the same time bettering the urban landscape. That work often started in their own back yards.

Fed up with their town's condition, women in Green Cove Springs in 1883 organized a village improvement association—Florida's first women's club—to spur city action. In their first year members petitioned the city to stop tree cutting and to make street improvements, consulted agriculture professionals about the proper type of shade trees to plant, and paid $45 to spread clay and sawdust to tame dusty streets. The women removed weeds, planted flowers, and hired and supervised a man to clean streets and collect trash. Six years later the newly created Crescent City Village Improvement Association went to work "grubbing out dog fennel and coffee weed from the streets, making shell walks, crossings and a few roads, trimming trees on the streets," and tending the cemetery, wrote historian Jessie Hamm Meyer. The card-playing ladies of the Palmetto Club of Daytona Beach turned their attention to such matters as ridding the streets of cows and pigs and insisting that city officials improve streets and lighting and abolish billboards. Across the state, women's groups arose, offering labor and funds to clean streets, provide trashcans, install horse hitching posts, and encourage cemetery cleanings.[1]

City beautification even inspired a public demonstration. To save a large live oak that stood in the path of a road-paving project, two Madison women in the 1920s staged what may have been Florida's first sit-in protest. The women, whose homes were on either side of the tree, determinedly sat on chairs near the oak and refused to budge until the town agreed to spare it. To this day, the great oak stands, dividing the road around it.[2]

These Florida women were reacting to the problems of their everyday lives, but they also were part of the City Beautiful Movement, a national crusade that arose in the 1890s and continued into the next century as part of the Progressive Era's reform agenda. It was an effort by middle- and upper-class Americans to improve their cities by imposing order, beauty, and harmony. Believing beautification would create order in cities, clubwomen embraced the movement and, as they did with birds and forestry, claimed moral high ground as justification to promote a number of improvements, including better housing, education reform, and the building of parks and playgrounds. While men emphasized "street improvements, architectural merit, and public statuary," writes historian Julian C. Chambliss, females stressed "cleanliness and environmental protection," addressing these issues through their clubs.[3]

A woman gave the national movement its name. In 1896 Mira Lloyd Dock of Harrisburg, Pennsylvania, joined the efforts of the Civic Club of Harrisburg to clean up the city's dirty, unpaved streets. Nearby rivers were essentially sewers. An active women's club member at the state and national level, Dock pressured male leadership to make changes, using her writing and speaking skills to disseminate her message. In December 1900 she spoke on "The City Beautiful" to the Harrisburg Board of Trade, charging that the city had abused its beautiful setting. She appealed to social consciousness, arguing that working-class families needed natural beauty and recreation—an argument designed to appeal to a wide spectrum of citizens and leaders, including both sexes and different economic groups. This tactic had been employed successfully by clubwomen addressing different issues across the country, and now it worked in Harrisburg, where city officials quickly began drawing up a comprehensive beautification and improvement plan for the city that included paved roads, sewage treatment, and water purification.[4]

The City Beautiful movement was promoted by the *Ladies' Home Journal*, a leading women's magazine; its influential editor, Edward Bok, became a winter resident in Florida. Bok promoted beautifying cities, eradicating billboards, and preserving Niagara Falls, which had been overrun by commercial interests. Bok envisioned the magazine as an aid to homemakers and a way to guide women's clubs. To instill an aesthetic sense in his readers, Bok asked J. Horace McFarland, president of the American Civic Association and a friend of Dock, to write a regular magazine column. From 1904 to 1907 McFarland's column, titled "Beautiful America," exhorted women to join in his call to improve and beautify the nation's cities—nothing less than asking women to remedy the mess rendered by male-run industry and development. Through the City Beautiful movement women put a new face on their communities and on themselves.[5]

McFarland, a preservationist, publisher, and horticulturist from Harrisburg, used his public forum to describe the beauty of the country, point accusing fingers at its ills, and urge women to instigate change, often including photographic examples of his subject matter. "The natural beauty of America is scarcely a thought in the lives of millions of our people," he penned in his first column in January 1904. "We accept the ugliness of our home premises, the filth of our streets, the monotony of our highways, as necessary, and have little thought of the natural outdoor beauty we are entitled to." McFarland believed "women must start this work if it is to be done. Men are well enough to come in later, but it is the mothers, wives and daughters who have the courage, inspiration and faith to attempt and to do the apparently impossible." One query, he noted, was from Florida, asking, "How shall I make our sluggish councilmen pass a law to keep hogs off the streets?" Dock observed the same problem in Harrisburg.[6]

Southern cities during this period often were portrayed as backward, with unpaved streets, epidemics, excessive poverty, and a segregated populace that was "victimized by white supremacist businessmen and politicians," writes historian James B. Crooks. "Unfortunately, at times all of these portrayals were true." These cities lagged behind owing to post–Civil War poverty and racism, which kept them from competing with northern urban areas until the mid-twentieth century. Florida was largely a rural state in this period, and its largest cities in 1900 were Jacksonville with a population of 28,429; Pensacola with 17,747; Key West with 17,114; Tampa with 15,839; Orlando with 2,841; and Miami with 1,681. Despite the small urban numbers, females across the state championed City Beautiful issues, configuring them to fit the problems of their own communities. They could not sway municipal leaders through elections, but they did effect change by lobbying the male power establishment and sometimes by simply conducting it (or paying for it) themselves.[7]

Jacksonville's Woman's Club responded in like fashion to problems in the state's largest and most urban city, accomplishing a great deal by "persuading male-dominated organizations to respond to their agendas," writes Crooks. When McFarland came to Jacksonville to speak, Francis P. Conroy of the Board of Trade proclaimed, "'I cannot speak too highly of the position taken by the Woman's Club of this city in the matter of civic improvement. They have always been leaders in anything looking to the betterment of our streets, parks and public buildings.' He could have added, schools, health care, the environment, and any community institution that worked to improve the quality of life in the city."[8]

The formation of the umbrella organization Florida Federation of Women's Clubs (FFWC) in 1895 united women's concerns and political savvy to address issues on a statewide basis. The FFWC's first business was to promote a petition asking that the state legislature rescind an act allowing cattle to roam freely in towns. The petition was ineffective, and it would be more than five decades before the state legislature ended the open range, mostly as an act of safety to prevent collisions with cars. By 1898 the FFWC affiliated with the General Federation of Women's Clubs (GFWC), and the group's initiatives expanded to those promoted by its national sister.[9]

By affiliating in these larger umbrella organizations, Florida's female activists increased their political clout, though they still lacked the ultimate power of the vote. By 1919, sixteen Florida towns had granted suffrage to women, but the state refused to do the same. Dr. Anna Shaw, a national suffrage leader who visited Florida, predicted that gaining the female vote would further beautification efforts: "When I think of Florida clubwomen having to do things like fixing up parks, cleaning streets, and setting out trees by your own club contributions and donations, it makes me furious, when, if you were part of the government, it could be done and kept done. It is maddening and we have got to make men see it, and women see it, but neither men nor women will see it until we can vote."[10]

Florida women were proven leaders in the state's parks movement and continued to press for more refuges for recreation and wildlife. Local parks also sprouted around the state, often due to women's work. In a 1924 FFWC report Veola Ezell noted that a new Wekiwa Park was dedicated that year, with Seminole County women's club members in attendance. "The civilized man needs the wilderness. Behind the present day civilization, there lies the immeasurable background of time when man was largely an out door animal, so this inheritance, this love of Nature—God's own work—lies deep in the nature of us all," she wrote, adding, "Let us work for more Parks where man and the coming generations may enjoy nature, not artificial Parks, but the real natural Parks of Florida, which offer the real taste of nature which man's inner being craves."[11]

Although Seminole County was a rural region during this period, its clubwomen were sounding alarms and taking action to preserve natural areas. A number of people in the spring-fed Wekiva River basin, which includes Lake, Orange, and Seminole counties, recognized its importance in supporting wildlife and recreation and tried to preserve areas along its path that had been heavily logged by timber companies. With so much attention focused on conservation and forestry issues, Ezell and the FFWC likely were aware of the potential for devastation of this unique resource.[12]

Many women also were wary of the impacts of Florida's booming growth. By 1920 the state population reached 968,470, almost doubling in the prior decade. That number jumped to almost 1.5 million in 1930; since then, the state has been mostly urban, with 75 percent of the population living on 6 percent of the land. In 1930 Jacksonville had exploded to 63,000 inhabitants; Miami had 78,000; and Tampa had 91,000. That surging growth led to inevitable environmental decline, particularly since most people flocked to the coasts, lakes, and rivers to build their new homes. By supporting park systems, even in rural areas, Florida's clubwomen protected some portions of forests and natural systems from the development that was beginning to devour parts of the state.[13]

Garden club members strove to protect Florida's natural spaces and to defend the ones already set aside for the public. Upon learning that the State Board of Parks and Historical Memorials had approved timber leases in Torreya State Park, the Florida Federation of Garden Clubs (FFGC) board at its October 1953 meeting adopted a resolution to "vigorously protest the proposal of cutting of timber for commercial purposes, the sale or lease of timber or timber rights for any purposes, or any processing of timber for use in any and all state parks." The FFGC sent copies of the resolution to the governor, the attorney general, and the state parks director, noting that their membership was twenty-one thousand strong. Unlike the clubwomen who founded Royal Palm State Park in 1916, garden clubwomen could now say they were voters, giving their views added political clout. The resolution declared that state parks are "dedicated to posterity, have been set aside for the preservation of plant and wild life," and serve as "museums of horticultural history, education and pleasure for all citizens and visitors of Florida." Garden clubs also promoted

Florida's nature by awarding free scholarships for college-age women for week-long nature study courses at different state parks. By immersing women in wild areas and extolling the importance of natural systems, the FFGC exposed the state's educated youth to the park system and created future leaders.[14]

Florida women found a variety of ways to support park projects. In 1948 FFGC President Madira Bickel donated a tract of Manatee County island property to the state. The spot, now known as the Madira Bickel Mound State Archeological Site, features an important ceremonial Indian mound where researchers found evidence from three periods of native culture. Gertrude Rollins Wilson, whose family owned a plantation on Fort George Island, Florida, near the mouth of the St. Johns River, donated one hundred acres of the heavily forested land in 1940 to Rollins College, founded by her relative Alonzo Rollins. The property, known as the John T. Rollins Bird and Plant Sanctuary in honor of Wilson's father, now is part of the U.S. National Park Service's Timucuan Ecological and Historic Preserve. Wilson, an artist, was a founder of the Garden Club of Jacksonville, former president of the FFGC, and an author of two garden books and a gardening column for the *Florida Times-Union*. Margaret Dreier Robins of Brooksville also made sure her family's property would remain in public use. In 1932 Robins, a former women's labor leader, and her husband donated their home, known as Chinsegut Hill Plantation, as well as the 2,080 acres of groves and forests that surrounded it, to the U.S. Department of Agriculture to become a wildlife refuge and an agriculture and forestry experiment station. Today it is home to the Chinsegut Conservation Center and is managed as a wildlife education complex.[15]

Maud Neff Whitman was integral in beautification and park development in the city of Orlando, which claims to be "The City Beautiful," a motto adopted in 1908 after a citywide contest won by a woman. The city strove to meet this description by planting more than "5,000 live and water oaks, and hundreds of palms, azaleas, and flowering shrubs." As the only female member of the city's first park board—and the first woman in the state appointed to any city board—Whitman served as its secretary-treasurer and did "much of the planting and gardening herself" to save money. She "redeemed" the grounds around Lake Eola, the city's centerpiece, from "an unsightly waste; this park stands as a monument" to her "indomitable spirit and good taste." For eleven years Whitman chaired the Orlando Park Board, and she subsequently served on park, recreation, and charter boards while also holding leadership roles in the Orlando Garden Club, FFWC, and the Florida State Chamber of Commerce.[16]

While Whitman gained political appointments for her beautification impetus, Lena Culver Hawkins used the same to acquire elected office. In 1913, two years after moving to Brooksville, Hawkins joined the city's women's club and soon became involved as volunteer secretary to the local chamber of commerce. In 1928, using a platform of city beautification, she ran unopposed to become Brooksville's mayor. After that term Hawkins ran unsuccessfully for the state legislature and later was honored as one of the state's "Great Floridians." Through their work on city beautification, Whitman and Hawkins not only stimulated change but also placed themselves in municipal leadership positions typically held by men. Whether they intended it or not, they had helped elevate their sex into new tiers of society, winning the acceptance and, more important, the endorsement of male leadership.[17]

Although heavily burdened by Jim Crow segregation laws, poverty, poor schools, and a lack of social services, some African American women in Florida also were able to secure parks and playgrounds—but with an eye to serving their youth, not to preserving nature. On July 4, 1918, residents of the east Jacksonville community of Oakland formed a joyful patriotic parade to celebrate the opening of Oakland Playground—the city's first for black children. The park, touted as a path to uplift the community, resulted from years of efforts by Eartha M. M. White, an African American activist who helped establish numerous social service agencies for the city's minorities. A black woman (initially paid by White from her own funds) was hired to serve as director of the park's playground and recreation, and within a week two hundred children were enrolled in its programs. A local newspaper proclaimed that the playground "is small, entirely too small to accommodate all but it is a happy beginning which, let all trust, will be followed up until reasonable provision will be made for all." By 1946 the city had seven segregated play areas for its youth of color, four with professional staffs.[18]

In West Palm Beach, Alice Mickens, president of the Florida Federation of Colored Women's Clubs, used her connections to press for community reforms. After a decade of diligent effort she secured a playground for African American children on the city's Fifteenth Street. "White children had nine or ten playgrounds and athletic fields; colored children had none. And playgrounds reduce crime," wrote historian Lottie Montgomery Clark. Mickens, like White, also fought for improved social services that included better schools, day nurseries, and boarding homes for girls. Today a verdant park with a children's climbing structure in the city is named in her honor.[19]

Tree planting was a major activity for clubwomen, who adorned cities, parks, and roadsides with thousands of trees—some out of a conservation impulse, others for beautification. Why plant trees? In her 1926 report to the Florida Daughters of the American Revolution (DAR), Nellie Watrous Semonite Hill explained in this poem:

A Tree for Every D. A. R.

What do we plant when we plant a tree?
We plant the ship which will cross the sea.
We plant the mast to carry the sails;
We plant the planks to withstand the gales—
The keel, the keelson, the beam, the knee;
We plant the ship when we plant the tree.

What do we plant when we plant the tree?
A thousand things that we daily see;
We plant the tower that out-towers the crag.
We plant the staff for our country's flag.
We plant the shade, from the hot sun free;
We plant all these, when we plant the tree.[20]

As did their national sisters, Florida's DAR members planted trees to commemorate special dates and occasions, acts that also served to beautify highways and parks. Across the country DAR groups planted trees: in California, thirteen trees, each from one of the original thirteen states; in Tacoma, Washington, a DAR group created a "grove of historic trees." One of the Florida DAR's biggest projects was a twenty-five-acre forest of twenty thousand pine trees planted in 1940 by the Civilian Conservation Corps at Hillsborough River State Park near Tampa. The venture was carried out in conjunction with the golden jubilee celebration of the national DAR and was called the Penny Pines Project.[21]

In 1932 Florida DAR members planted trees to participate in national commemorations of the two-hundredth anniversary of George Washington's birth. In Tampa they put palm trees on the site of a historic schoolhouse. A "Washingtonian palm" was dedicated with special services in Daytona Beach. The DeSoto Chapter in Tampa reported that it helped finance a fourteen-mile "Road of Remembrance" that featured fifteen hundred oak trees alternating with the same number of oleanders, a flowering evergreen shrub.[22]

Oleanders were not native to Florida, but that was not a concern during this period, when a variety of plants were imported and planted for their beauty, with few concerns about how they might interact with indigenous species. The science of ecology and the harmful effects of non-native flora were not understood or appreciated. Newcomers often tore out local plants in order to plant fruit trees or to create landscapes similar to those of their home states. As a result Florida came to have more than a thousand alien plant species, many of which created environmental nightmares. Eliminating these plants—or getting them under control—subsequently cost agencies millions of dollars. But none of this was anticipated in the early twentieth century, when the main consideration was how a plant or tree might make the state *even more* attractive.[23]

Women's club members also joined in tree planting efforts. The FFWC's Forestry Department published a pamphlet encouraging clubs to plant trees on roadsides and in schoolyards and "wastelands," while also celebrating arbor days and supporting forestry legislation. Laura Hensley of Tampa, FFWC chair of the Division of Parks and Natural Scenery, decried developments that removed trees: "How many times in the past few months have we seen beautiful jungles of native palms and spreading oaks give way to the ruthless invasion of some enthusiasts trying to lay out a site for home makers and thus increase the beauty and comforts of life?" Hensley worried that the "rapidity with which these places are disappearing in many sections is alarming. The members of this organization favor progress along every line, but how we can build cities and develop our rural sections and still preserve the parks and nature's growth that will take a century to replace is the burning question? Are we creating a sentiment for these in proportion to our development?"[24]

These worries swept across the state. The Garden Club of Jacksonville focused much energy on protecting the city's live oaks in a project to "Save the Trees and Make Jacksonville an Evergreen City." With the aid of Jacksonville philanthropist Jessie Ball duPont, the group rescued the historic Treaty Oak, an ancient live oak located in the city's Jessie Ball duPont Park. Garden club members also helped preserve the state's oldest tree—a bald cypress that dated back an estimated 3,500 years. Dubbed "The Senator," it became the centerpiece of a park in Longwood; the FFGC helped provide iron fencing to prevent defacement of the tree.[25]

Designating the proper state tree was also a priority, and the FFGC persisted for five years before finally succeeding in getting that status for the sabal palm. It was a matter of saving the tree—and of accuracy; the state seal featured a sabal palm but listed it as a "cocoa tree." The sabal palm, a native tree that can grow to a height of eighty feet, was a good candidate for Florida's state tree because it was widely dispersed throughout the state and had inspired early visitors, including noted author and preservationist John Muir. During his 1867 trek across the state, Muir, an avid botanist, saw a sabal palm along the St. Johns River and wrote that "whether rocking and rustling in the wind or poised thoughtful and calm in the sunshine, it has a power of expression not excelled by any plant high or low that I have met in my whole walk thus far." After the 1953 legislature agreed with the tree designation, the FFGC focused on other species. A year later, the FFGC board approved spending $5,000 to help purchase 160 acres of bird-filled virgin cypress trees in Collier County, and "thus the Corkscrew Swamp Sanctuary," now an Audubon sanctuary, became "a part of the Federation's heritage."[26]

Harmony, in the eyes of numerous women in Florida and across the United States, was a landscape without the visual pollution of billboards and street signs that sprang up across the rapidly industrializing country and had been regulated in some European countries. McFarland railed about their proliferation in his columns and admitted to a friend that he had torn signs down. At his urging, Harrisburg passed an ordinance to regulate and restrict billboards, an action that women across America emulated. "Billboards stand much in the way of Beautiful America and if we are to return to our Eden they must be either eliminated where offensive, or very materially modified in character and appearance where they seem to be permissible," McFarland wrote in July 1904. After offering numerous examples of signage blight, McFarland advised his readers to use persuasion, through letter-writing campaigns to advertisers and others, and compulsion, such as restrictive laws, to battle the problem. His column often featured photographs of signs and recounted stories of billboard battles in different areas of the United States.[27]

Florida women found plenty of evidence to confirm McFarland's assertions and worked for decades to fight signage they viewed as ugly and dangerous. Removing the billboards did not create beauty in Florida; rather, it "de-uglified" the visual blight beginning to accumulate along roads that women worked so hard to line with trees and pleasant landscaping. Different groups formed committees, passed resolutions, and sought local and state legislation to deal with the intrusive signs along the state's rapidly growing network of streets and highways. In the July 1929 edition of the FFWC publication *Florida Clubwoman* an article featured photographs of billboards along roads near Daytona Beach and Jacksonville. The article's unnamed author wrote: "It is not too much to say that the ubiquitous billboard has made a mockery of our outdoors. It has smeared a once verdant landscape with trash, has made of our noblest trees nothing but hitching posts for vagrant advertising ideas, and has condemned those who ride our highways to drive between staggering lanes of blatant paint and grammatical errors." The author continued: "It has been said that this is an era of outdoor advertising, as the motorist cannot protect himself. But the woman can, and it is up to them to rid Florida of that many-headed monster which coils along our roads and snorts forth its brazen commands at every turn."[28]

Florida's sign blight was particularly troublesome, according to Elizabeth B. Lawton, chairman of the National Roadside Council, a group that fought billboards across the country. In February 1935 Lawton wrote, "You will go far to find a State which has more billboards than Florida or a State where they are more obnoxious," adding her estimate that she saw one sign every seven seconds on a drive from Jacksonville to Miami. Lawton reported that 3,700 signs were found on 300 miles of highway, not counting additional signs at filling stations, road stands, or on trees. She asked, "Can anyone explain why every landscape in Florida must be tagged for example with a six hundred and sixty-six patent medicine sign on tree, fence, barn or billboard? Or why a state which promises to restore health and youth should be plastered with signs for ambulances and undertakers?"[29]

Her suggested antidote: a state billboard law to replace a 1929 law that she deemed to be "entirely inadequate." The current law required annual license fees for billboard companies, but she preferred that the state require permits for individual signs.[30]

Garden clubwomen were equally concerned about Florida's growing billboard problem, which came at a time of rising automobile use and highway construction across the nation. In 1919 Americans had 6.7 million passenger cars, a number that jumped to 23.1 million in 1929. As historian Dorothy M. Brown notes, the Federal Highways Act of 1916 produced a "network of roads" that brought with it jobs and roadside businesses. Someone had to point out where those businesses were—the job of billboard advertising. At the same time, the automobile changed the nature of tourism in Florida. No longer was it a destination for the rich and elite—mass-produced cars now gave middle-class families the opportunity to come to the state. Tourists in this new group, nicknamed "tin can tourists" for the canned food they brought with them, were more mobile and demanded affordable lodgings and campgrounds. Governments scurried to improve roads to facilitate visits by these new travelers and connect the state's large cities to federal highways. Signs sprouted up to direct visitors to local restaurants, hotels, attractions, and shops. Before the Great Depression of 1929 Florida had 3 million annual visitors—more than three times the total state population; during the Depression that number dropped to 1 million—still a large influx for the state and its roads to handle.[31]

At the 1930 annual meeting of the FFGC, President Cora Scott Riggs announced that she had appointed a chair for a Roadsides and Billboards Committee to deal with the issue. She stated that "several of our clubs" had local committees to address the problem, with the result "that more than 50,000 signs" were removed from highways. Whether women tore down the signs is unclear, although highly possible; at the very least, they urged local governments to do so and supported stricter regulations and taxation on signage.[32]

In their publications, women's and garden club members discussed laws enacted in other states and urged members to work for local and state regulation while also contacting advertisers to ask them to control their industry. "Blessed are they who swat the sign and banish the bill board along the rural highway, for they shall be called protectors of roadside beauty and landscape scenery," wrote Margaret Pryor of Haines City, FFWC chair of state beautification, in her update of the biblical beatitudes. "Blessed are they who stand against friend and relative in the protection of nature's gifts to Florida for they shall be recognized as true patriots of Florida."[33]

Several FFGC members served on the national council, where billboards and city beautification were the regular focus of their actions. The Billboard and Roadside Committee was one of the first committees created by the National Council of State Garden Clubs, founded in 1929. "The powerful outdoor advertising industry viewed with scorn the early efforts of the garden clubs as merely an annoyance," wrote Eleanor R. Crosby, National Council historian. "But garden clubwomen were undaunted and set out to do something about the deplorable situation." Almost a decade after gaining suffrage, women had the power of the vote, but in fighting billboards they continued to rely on the collective power of their organizations to try to force changes in outdoor advertising blight.[34]

Bolstered by knowledge of actions in other states, women's and garden club members regularly endorsed different laws at public meetings and at their annual conventions as a way of galvanizing their membership and throwing their considerable collective weight into the political arena. For example, in January 1935 a large number of St. Petersburg women, representing a variety of groups including women's and garden clubs, endorsed a city tax adopted by councilmen in an effort to curb roadside signs. Flora Wylie, a garden club leader, emphasized eliminating street advertising, declaring it a matter of civic pride. Lawton, of the National Roadside Council, also attended the meeting and endorsed Wylie's sentiments, noting that other communities with sign taxes were still experiencing blight. That laws were being adopted is evidence that billboard blight was not solely a "women's" issue. City planners, City Beautiful advocates, and a number of lawmakers—most of these positions held by men—also tried to curb signage abuses. However, for the next three decades the loudest voices on the issue would be those of women, who were better organized and less likely to feel any economic pressure to stand down from their demands. They could not and would not be ignored.[35]

The advertising industry was forced to respond. The Outdoor Advertising Association of Florida distributed a multi-page pamphlet at the FFGC's March 1935 annual meeting, defending itself and declaring its agreement to voluntary billboard restrictions. "Has it ever occurred to you that the Garden Club members possibly are being used by selfish interests as a means to destroy the Outdoor Advertising industry?" the pamphlet asked in a rather condescending tone. "Now 'beautification' is a fine and worth-while thing. 'Beautification' is a fine slogan, but it certainly should not unwittingly become the cats-paw of any greedy interest." The brochure stated that billboard companies employ "approximately 1,500,000 people"—an important point during the Great Depression—and suggested that opposition might have been fomented by other industries that wanted outdoor advertising dollars. Employing an economics versus aesthetics argument, the brochure stated, "beautiful thoughts do not fit in with thoughts of destruction; and what greater destruction is there in life than to take work away from people when it is so hard to find."[36]

The FFGC members were not swayed. Four years later they passed a resolution encouraging their members "by word and deed" to put an end "to this misappropriation of highway space for advertising purposes and the serious interference thereby with highway safety and beauty." The resolution declared: "We maintain that the use of public roadsides for advertising purposes should be prevented by state legislation and enforced in the courts, and by public sentiment against this abuse." A year later, as the group considered introducing a bill further restricting state billboards, two advertising executives appeared before the FFGC executive board to suggest that the groups work together, stating that the industry would not oppose legislative controls and asking to see the bill before it was introduced to the legislature. The advertising businessmen were well aware of the clout held by the FFGC, which could rally its members to demand legislation.[37]

Advertising interests tried to counteract National Council campaigns as well, offering free billboard space "for fund drives and even to garden clubs to pub-licize their projects," writes Crosby, adding that these "attempts met with chill-ing response from garden clubs." Garden clubbers in some areas countered by urging their members and other consumers to write to the companies and manufacturers whose goods were being advertised on the unsightly signs. Such practices, notes Crosby, "seemed to hit the manufacturers *where it hurt* as they recognized the resentment building up against them." The billboard companies promised to increase self-regulation, and their powerful lobby defeated any bills for national control.[38]

By 1951, as a result of garden club work and a 1941 signage law that the FFGC had worked for eighteen years to get passed, more than 300,000 unlicensed signs had been removed from state highways. Two years later garden clubbers still worried about roadside debris and signage and advised members to look for problem intersections and properties and then contact landowners for help in getting them cleaned. Members were advised not to fight to get rid of all signs, noting that companies and landowners profited from them.[39]

As with various other Florida issues, May Mann Jennings of Jacksonville played a large role in Florida highway beautification. Through her work as an officer of the FFWC as well as the Duval County Federation of Women's Clubs, the twenty-year chair of the Beautification Committee of the Florida Chamber of Commerce, and a leader in the Duval County Highway Beautification As-sociation, Jennings pressed lawmakers and businesses for decades to improve the appearance of Florida's roads. In 1931, after several years of hard work and through the support of numerous groups, Jennings gained passage of a state law that required landscaping, hundred-foot rights-of-way for roads, setbacks for wire-holding poles, and the appointment of a beautification expert to the state road department.[40]

Jennings's arguments for roadside improvements included the economic and the aesthetic—a savvy melding of interests to appeal to male and female alike. At a 1933 beautification conference held by the state chamber, Jennings "urged the immediate need of increasing the conservation and beautification work in a score of urgent directions in Florida." Understanding her audience, Jennings "reminded the Sarasota convention with a tinge of humor that all ef-forts of this nature, whether for parks, highways, or whatever related interests, had long been adjudged 'women's work' rather beneath the dignity of club hus-bands and city fathers," according to an article in the *Christian Science Monitor*. "But present-day competitive business methods, she declared, have brought out clearly the fact that beautiful cities, country sides, and highways, are among our soundest investments, drawing in throngs the travelers and helping mold youth to good citizenship."[41]

As the century progressed, state and national garden clubs continued to press for billboard restrictions, which were enacted nationally in 1958 and 1965, the latter law requiring a state to give up 10 percent of its federal highway funding if it failed to comply with federal regulations that dictated sign sizes, setbacks, and placements along roadways. The federal rules were the first to attempt nationwide control of signage; while they did eliminate some eyesores, they did not solve the problem. Advertising signs evolved to meet and sidestep the federal rules, which were regularly amended until the end of the century to address new issues of the day. Noting that highway beautification was a top issue in the 1950s and 1960s, culminating with the federal acts, authors Charles F. Floyd and Peter J. Shedd maintain that the legislation has been the movement's greatest failure, damaged by "crippling amendments," legal loopholes, exemptions, "a lack of national standards, and general indifference among former supporters."[42]

When plotting how to beautify Florida's cities and roadways, the state's women increasingly came to view governmental planning and zoning as necessary to urban quality. In her 1925 "Beatitudes," FFWC beautification chair Pryor offered this benediction: "Blessed are the towns and planning boards, for great beauty, prosperity and peace shall descend upon them."[43]

The planning movement in the United States arose out of concerns about the ills of rapid urbanization, particularly in the Northeast. Frederick Law Olmsted led the movement in the late nineteenth century, and his son Frederick Jr. took planning to a more professional level, becoming the planning movement's leader. Women offered "substantial contributions" to city planning, writes historian Eugenie L. Birch, not only as planners but also as community activists, especially through their club connections. Women also were active in a number of other organizations, all of which propelled them into public affairs. There remained a "clear division" between men's and women's activities, Birch adds, with women claiming "certain urban problems" that reached into sanitation, cleanliness, and beauty.[44]

The FFWC supported city planning, which reinforced other club efforts that included sanitation, hygiene, playground construction, and child welfare. In 1912 the GFWC's Civic Department chair Alice Davis Moulton called on club members across the country to bring planning to their communities. Women argued that their "impartial views on planning and other reform issues were untainted by selfish motives and therefore more impressive," writes Birch. In various municipalities, including Los Angeles, St. Louis, and Boston, women's clubs "frequently stimulated profession efforts to replan an area," often in consultation with designers, among them noted planner John Nolen.[45]

Although Florida did not suffer from all the urban ills of the large cities, its women, many of whom had relocated from northern cities, saw enough problems to take action, especially during the land boom of the 1920s and the ensuing decades, as growth mushroomed. The Woman's Club of Winter Park is a prime example—in 1924 it successfully petitioned the city to create a planning and zoning commission; to this day the city is considered a model of exemplary design. Earlier, the club had secured municipal garbage collection and put up signs declaring Winter Park to be a bird sanctuary. Clubwomen also pressed for creation of a city Parks and Planning Board.[46]

Nolen recognized that Florida's development would be unlike that in the northeastern cities—electricity and automobile transportation "had quickened the pace of urbanization, and the gaps once separating cities from their hinterlands were fast closing," writes biographer R. Bruce Stephenson. In the past century transportation had gone from horses to railroads; by 1930 Florida had more than 3,200 miles of paved roads. Nolen believed regional planning was essential to address the impending impact on natural systems, water supplies, and land use. In 1922 he used these ideas to develop a plan for St. Petersburg, Florida's first municipal plan. Ten years earlier the city had joined with Pinellas County officials in hiring the Olmsted Brothers, a company operated by Olmsted Sr.'s two sons, to create a county park plan, which resulted in a public waterfront that paid big dividends in tourism. Nolen now foresaw a city that could be "a model for the 'bound and permanent development of Florida,'" Stephenson writes. The St. Petersburg plan included a greenbelt with barrier islands along the coast of the Gulf of Mexico, transportation routes, neighborhoods, tourist areas, commercial districts, and farmlands. Nolen's plan was defeated in a city referendum in 1923, but the city did adopt some of his ideas. He and his firm would go on to consult for more than twenty Florida communities, including West Palm Beach, Clewiston, and Venice. Women's club members were among the early proponents of planning in West Palm Beach, employing the moral and aesthetic grounds promoted by the City Beautiful movement.[47]

Perhaps no woman was as important to the cause of Florida planning as Jessica Waterman Seymour, who had been involved in planning issues in St. Paul, Minnesota, before her move to Miami after World War I. In Florida she became involved in local and state women's and garden clubs and was a leading proponent for Miami planning. Seymour also became a friend and mentor to Miami journalist Marjory Stoneman Douglas, and the two espoused the idea of regionalism—Seymour through her advocacy and rallying of community groups, and Douglas through her daily column in the *Miami Herald*. They believed that although Miami was not an industrial city, its rapid growth combined with its lush natural palette made city planning imperative. Seymour and Douglas, according to historian Jack E. Davis, incited grassroots activism by clubwomen who called for "zoning ordinances, public parks, tree planting, landscaped boulevards, waste recycling, and managed growth."[48]

When Miami was under consideration for the 1926 National Conference on City Planning, Seymour wrote to Nolen that the city and South Florida needed planning, adding that "'most of the men in charge of affairs here are small town men, consequently the right kind of preliminary education work is necessary,'" according to Stephenson. She hoped that holding the conference in Miami would propel the city into taking action. She told Nolen that the "opportunity for Florida unquestionably lies in regional planning, if the distinctive and natural features of the state are to be preserved at all," adding that Florida would be his land of opportunity. Their give and take suggested mutual respect and reliance, all geared toward improving the urban landscape.[49]

Planning leaders held the 1926 meeting divided between St. Petersburg and Palm Beach. At the conference Seymour delivered an address titled "A State Plan for Florida," in which she related her club work that led to travels and studies of planning in different states. Seymour also presented the idea of a state plan to the FFWC, where it was "received with great commendation," largely because it relied on the ideas of Nolen and other notables in the planning movement, she stated, reminding the assembled group that with 1.5 million people, Florida was still in its pioneer phase. "Again, when you look at Florida it is flat, of course; it cannot compare with California or Colorado or the Great Lakes or North Carolina or many other places in the matter of picturesqueness. It is a place that cries aloud for engineers and artists and landscape architects who will work together on the whole state, so that counties and cities may co-operate in order that the entire state can be considered a part of the plan and each part of the state have its own character." Seymour viewed Florida as a place that needed improvement and called for professionals to help reshape the state, making it more attractive.[50]

In closing, Seymour chastised the male-dominated planning professionals for discounting the influence of women in such matters:

I think you possibly made a mistake in leaving women too much out of your conferences because women nowadays are going to decide where they shall live; they are going to decide which town they will bring their family into; they are going to decide what those children are going to do; they are going to decide whether they shall be horticulturists and botanists and scientific men and women, or whether they shall entirely go over into business and industrial life.

We are just beginning; we are just born; we are infants in this thing, but we are very lively infants, and we intend to grow and expand, and we intend to take the finest, the most ideal, the most splendid thing from any home that any one of us has ever known. We intend to take that thing out into the community, into the county, into the state, as our work. It is not political work, it is artistic, scientific work, it is democratic work, and we believe in it.[51]

Through the first three decades of the century, Seymour pushed for planning and for beautification. She served several years as FFGC Beautification Committee chair, developing an agenda favoring the use of native plants, highway planning, garden design, and city and regional planning. Seymour created the FFGC program called "Landscape Gardening and Landscape Art," which was used by California garden clubs and distributed by the National Council to its member groups. "We are trying to change the indifference of towns, counties, and the state, as well as individual members of garden clubs, to an active interest in the necessity for a better understanding of plant material and its proper use, whether in the small garden, the large estate, parks, on the highway or in a general city or regional plan," she wrote in a 1933 FFGC report. Two years later, the FFGC unanimously adopted a resolution endorsing a state bill that would "authorize cities and towns to provide and prescribe zoning regulations and to provide for planning boards and zoning commissioners."[52]

In Jacksonville, women had a great influence on city planning, particularly through club activist Grace Wilbur Trout, chair of the city's planning advisory board. In a 1929 FFWC article Trout lauded St. Petersburg for developing a plan and lamented that if Jacksonville had done the same "much valuable property would have been protected and its commercial value maintained if the people who then were building expensive homes could have been assured that this property would remain residential." City planning had "stood the test of time," attracting residents, which provided more customers for businesses and the construction industry, Trout wrote, adding that "city planning which goes hand in hand with city beautification enhances and stabilizes real estate values."[53]

Trout, a women's rights crusader in Illinois, and her husband, George, bought a holiday home in 1914 on the south side of the St. Johns River in Jacksonville. They moved permanently to the city in 1921, and four years later Trout was elected president of the Garden Club of Jacksonville, a title she held until 1927; she also served as second vice president of the FFGC. During her leadership the Jacksonville group created a Men's Advisory Committee with which they met annually to seek advice—a savvy step for a women's group that had larger interests in the community. "Jacksonville was growing like a proverbial weed, in a hit-or-miss fashion, so the Garden Club felt the need of a survey and a city plan," according to the group's self-published history. Trout, Ninah May Holden Cummer, and Ella Ecker Alsop (wife of Jacksonville's six-term mayor) were appointed to the City Planning Commission, and in 1928 George W. Simons Jr. became Jacksonville's first city planner.[54]

From its inception, according to Simons, the Planning Board advocated saving park areas that developers eyed for projects. Board members also worked to draw plans for the city that would "be helpful not only from a utilitarian standpoint but plans that would contribute to aesthetic development," and they were ably guided by Trout, whom Simons described as "a master in political strategy." A city plan, adopted in 1929, helped guide waterfront improvements and a street system; a year later the City Council approved a planning board–inspired update of zoning regulations that "checked the wanton invasion of residential areas by undesirable uses."[55]

Approaching the mid-twentieth century, women's groups across the state continued to urge stricter zoning and planning laws in their effort to fight roadside blight created by fly-by-night roadside stands and billboards and to make their communities more attractive. They were very effective fighters. In a 1949 article in the *Florida Clubwoman* titled "Never Underestimate the Power of a Woman," Judge Webber Haines, of Winter Park, highlighted the persistence and power of women in civic affairs. "In many zoning hearings, I have seen the men objectors gradually quieted by legal terminology, or argued into silence, or acquiescence, by the seeming expediency of the action to be taken," Haines wrote. "But the women remain adamant. They don't attempt an argument on any other level than that the proposal is right, or wrong, and you can depend on them to maintain their position until the last word, and they usually have it." Still, he noted, few Florida women served on city councils, "and they have something to contribute."[56]

Miami and its environs had exploded since the early part of the century and were experiencing urban problems, including ghettos of poverty like those with which northeastern cities had been coping for decades. By midcentury Miami had a half-million residents and was the most segregated city in the country. Coconut Grove, part of the Miami metropolis, suffered from a lack of plumbing and electricity, uncollected garbage, vermin, and ramshackle buildings in its segregated black enclave. It was a job for the community's women. In August 1948 Elizabeth Landsberg Virrick, a feisty, well-educated woman who owned a Coconut Grove apartment building with her Russian-born husband, joined Reverend Theodore Gibson, rector of the black Christ Episcopal Church, in calling a meeting that drew two hundred people, leading to creation of the biracial Coconut Grove Citizens' Committee for Slum Clearance. It was a brave step for Virrick, who risked being ostracized by a white community steeped in segregated housing areas and Jim Crow laws.[57]

The group set out initially to investigate sanitary conditions, to work for rezoning of the "Negro" area, and to publicize high rents and other problems that plagued tenants in that area. The group proposed two ordinances—requiring that households be connected to city water and that every household have a flush toilet, septic tank, and sink; the ordinances were approved in October by the city of Miami. The committee, recognizing the financial difficulty involved in forcing these actions, established a fund to help defray costs that residents could repay in small monthly payments. For two years the group tried to get the area rezoned to favor single-family residences and duplexes rather than apartments and commercial and industrial buildings, which also were allowed. Frustrated with the city, the committee gathered petition signatures and forced a referendum that was approved in November 1949. A history of the group states that the committee "had carried through the first successful initiative petition and referendum in the State of Florida. It is also the only case known in the United States of an area's zoning being accomplished by an initiative petition and referendum." In coming years the committee, chaired by Virrick, publicly opposed variances in the area and pressed for improved garbage service. The biracial group cleared a dump to create a playground and get rid of nuisance vermin. It also helped get African American police for the area and raised $35,000 to establish a children's nursery.[58]

Virrick presented a plan to the city of Miami to eliminate slums in the next decade or two. Her plan, however, was not intended to remove blacks from Miami, as some suspected was the motive in other urban slum clearance plans. Rather, Virrick believed that eliminating the ghettos would end segregation—

and vice versa. Virrick "was driven solely by compassion," writes historian Laura Brackenridge Danahy, and she believed in raising the standard of living and ending segregation of the black slum population. Through her persistence and willingness to challenge Miami's status quo, writes Danahy, "Virrick's militant campaign for improved housing and slum clearance became a watershed even in Miami's grassroots urban reform movements."[59]

"Virrick was the gadfly, the crusader, the militant watchdog, operating outside the official power structure, badgering city commissioners and planning and housing officials into action," writes historian Raymond A. Mohl. "Politicians learned that to cross swords with Virrick might shorten their careers in office. Slumlords, builders, and attorneys for the local real estate lobby hated to see her show up at hearings and meetings. She often made public officials squirm at those open forums, as she demanded full public accountability."[60]

With her work to improve the living conditions of fellow Miamians, Virrick carried on the work of Florida's activist women in addressing community problems. Women had found greater freedom through suffrage and now used their growing political clout to help others burdened by poverty and slum life. It was an inevitable outgrowth of women's outreach that began with worries about cattle and trash in the streets but matured to include parks, sign regulations, and city planning. They wanted a more "beautiful" Florida and, while their vision was largely one of artificial aesthetics and not of true wilderness, it did include livable, landscaped communities in harmony with some forms of nature and with human needs. They used a number of tactics, from pressuring governmental leaders to donating land for parks to simply pulling the weeds and planting trees themselves. In doing so, women blazed new, broader paths into the public arena, expanding their influence in ways still felt today.

Part II

Operating in Female-Male Groups

5

The Three Marjories, Rachel, and the Rise of Ecology

When it comes to saving natural Florida, one name outshines all others: Marjory. Or Marjorie. It depends upon which of three exceptional women is concerned: author Marjorie Kinnan Rawlings, whose storytelling taught a nation to love the state's rural scrub lands; Marjorie Harris Carr, who proved that a group of scrappy activists could halt big government boondoggles that threatened sensitive areas; or Marjory Stoneman Douglas, a long-lived writer-advocate who, though diminutive in size, could instill fear in a roomful of developers or politicians with whom she disagreed. Taken together, their work, infused with fervor, intellect, and immense quantities of talent, spanned the twentieth century and changed attitudes about Florida's wildlife and landscape.

The latter two inspired generations of activists as well, setting the stage for a new way of approaching environmental issues through groups that included men and women working side by side to address crises. Employing the principles of ecology, a new term for most Americans, they used science to understand, explain, and defend the complex relationships of plants, animals, and resources in the natural world. They also led efforts that included grassroots uprisings and proved the power of many voices to defeat the financial and political gain of a few.

Marjorie Kinnan Rawlings and her husband Charles made the adventurous move to Florida from Rochester, New York, in 1928 to pursue the literary life. The couple bought seventy-two acres in the rural hamlet of Cross Creek that included a white wooden cottage flanked by orange groves. The fruit, they hoped, would supplement their writing incomes. As an increasingly unhappy Charles worked to produce magazine articles about the state, Rawlings explored the people and landscape around their home, finding inspiration for her writing. Two years later Rawlings sold her first story, which led to novels and the 1939 Pulitzer Prize for fiction for *The Yearling*, the tale of a young boy, a pet deer, and his family's struggle to survive in the sandy scrub lands that Rawlings visited. In 1942 Rawlings published *Cross Creek*, a meditation about the hardy folk she now called her friends and the terrain that shaped them.[1]

These books were enormously successful and opened the eyes of Americans to the wonders of Florida's nature. Rawlings described bear hunts, fishing trips, backwoods folk, and the stress and beauty of rural living "with something akin" to what famed nineteenth-century nature essayist Henry David Thoreau "realized at Walden Pond," the setting of his most famous work, writes Anne E. Rowe. "Although Rawlings' Florida was not a garden of Eden—it was replete with ants, skunks, and snakes—it was, nevertheless, a place where one could live in close accord with nature, attuned to the changes of the seasons, in complete harmony with the surroundings. For Rawlings life at the orange grove at Cross Creek was as close to an idyllic life as is possible on earth. Her Florida of groves, scrub, and rivers was a largely unspoiled paradise."[2]

Rawlings's Edenic view of Florida flowed freely from the beginning of *Cross Creek*, the first chapter of which is titled "For This Is an Enchanted Land." It reveals a spiritual connection that fueled her writing and passion for her adopted state. "We cannot live without the earth or apart from it, and something is shrivelled in a man's heart when he turns away from it and concerns himself only with the affairs of men," she warned. "Who owns Cross Creek? The redbirds, I think, more than I. . . . It seems to me that the earth may be borrowed but not bought. It may be used, but not owned. It gives itself in response to love and tending, offers its seasonal flowering and fruiting. But we are tenants and not possessors, lovers and not masters. Cross Creek belongs to the wind and the rain, to the sun and the seasons, to the cosmic secrecy of seed, and beyond all, to time."[3]

Rawlings died in 1953 at age fifty-seven, before major problems in Florida's natural systems were apparent. Even so, she made some observations in *Cross Creek* that show a growing environmental awareness. She noted that several species of wildlife were becoming rare, including the limpkin, a wading bird, and the Florida panther, which is now critically endangered. In *Cross Creek Cookery*, Rawlings acknowledges that black bears, once plentiful in Florida, "are becoming scarce. I see no reason for destroying the remaining ones, since they live so far from any domestic clearing that they are no longer a menace, as formerly, to stock." And yet she proceeded to offer three recipes for bear meat to her cookbook's readers. Today Florida's black bears are protected by law and no longer hunted.[4]

Although she was not part of the corps of conservation-minded activists, Rawlings's books were steeped in descriptions of the rural North Florida environment, home to some of the state's largest forest stands, and she worried about wasteful forestry practices. In 1942, the same wartime year that *Cross Creek* was published, Rawlings agreed to write an article for the U.S Forest Service for *Colliers*, a national magazine, to raise conservation awareness. In the 1943 article, "Trees for Tomorrow," she objected to the clear-cutting of southern longleaf pine forests by timber companies, justified "at the time by the need to support the war effort." She asked a question similar to that of *Cross Creek*'s final page: "Whose trees are these?" and answered that 13 million Americans were reliant not only on the wood industry but on the erosion prevention, flood control, and water quality that intact forests provided. "They are my trees and your trees. They are our trees. No selfish minority, no careless majority can continue to jeopardize our common interests." Her response also claimed patriotism: "We are fighting today for many valuable things. We must fight also at this critical moment to preserve the God-given forests without which we should be helpless atoms on a sterile earth."[5]

After the article was published, Rawlings was solicited to write more about the topic. She declined, writing to her second husband, Norton Baskin, then serving overseas: "I feel if I could be of help in such a critical matter, perhaps I ought to. My literature is painfully likely not to be deathless, but I might go down in history as the gal who saved the nation's trees!"[6]

As historian Florence M. Turcotte notes, Rawlings's awakening was the realization that the "Florida that she had fallen in love with 20 years earlier was being transformed by a population explosion and human attempts to 'improve upon paradise.'" Today, Rawlings's home is preserved as a state park, and she is honored as a "First Floridian" who helped Americans discover the splendor of Florida's landscape. Saving it would be the job of other women who shared her passion. One of them would be Marjorie Harris Carr.[7]

Since Florida's earliest days, settlers had dreamed of building a canal across the state, linking the Atlantic Ocean with the Gulf of Mexico. It would shorten shipping times and avoid treacherous trade routes at the peninsula's southern tip. Several schemes came and went until a cold day in 1964, when an explosion of dynamite hailed the project's final incarnation: the Cross Florida Barge Canal. What enthusiastic promoters could not anticipate was that less than ten years later the project would die, largely through the efforts of Carr, who led a spirited and determined group of academics and outraged citizens in Florida's first large-scale grassroots environmental battle and a victory that resonated across the United States.[8]

As a biologist who held a master's degree, and the wife of internationally renowned sea turtle researcher Archie Carr, Marjorie Carr was uniquely qualified and positioned to stop the canal. Born in Boston in 1915, Carr moved as a young girl to Bonita Springs in southwest Florida, where she reveled in the natural beauty of the area while simultaneously witnessing human abuse of the state's flora and fauna. Along the river banks there were no living things "because it was the custom for men to come down, hire a boat, take a gun and stand up in the front of the boat and shoot anything that made a moving target," she recalled. "Alligator, red bird, heron, what have you. Anything that moved was the sport. That outrage, that stupidity of killing every, anything called attention to the plight of the wildlife." It was the same anger that spurred early Audubon members and clubwomen, and Carr was well aware of their contributions, noting that the rise of conservation in Florida was "closely connected with the garden clubs and with the women's clubs." She said, "It is very important that these groups got started. They weren't hunters. They were either garden clubbers or women clubbers who had a sense of the need for caring and they fought hard for it."[9]

Unlike many women of her era, Carr attended college, receiving a zoology degree in 1936 at the Florida State College for Women in Tallahassee. Although she was an honors graduate, inducted into the Phi Beta Kappa honorary society, Carr was denied admission to graduate programs in zoology and ornithology at Cornell University and the University of North Carolina because of her gender. She was fortunate to find jobs in science, working in a fish hatchery and then a laboratory. In 1942 she received a master's degree in zoology from the University of Florida for her research on the breeding habits and embryology of the large-mouthed black bass. While working at the hatchery as the nation's first female wildlife technician, Carr traveled to the University of Florida for laboratory work and met her future husband Archie. Theirs was a loving, collaborative relationship that opened many doors for Carr and greatly influenced her environmental work.[10]

Although Carr had never studied ecology specifically in college, historian Margaret F. Macdonald notes that Carr's professors were some of the first to employ ecological theories as they applied to Florida. In her botany classes, Carr also learned how to "read a landscape," a skill that would be important in her future activism. Archie Carr had studied animal ecology as early as 1931 at the University of Florida, where the emphasis in the biology department was on the complex study of biota in their ecological contexts. He had a distinguished career as a biologist, naturalist, writer, and herpetologist, receiving the Eminent Ecologist Award from the Ecological Society of America in 1987.[11]

In the early twentieth century, however, ecology was not a science understood by the American public. The term derives from *Oecologie*, promoted in the late nineteenth century by German zoologist Ernst Haeckel. He described it as the study of the relationship between living organisms and their world—essentially how they act as a family unit. Haeckel was an advocate of British naturalist and evolutionist Charles Darwin, considered by many scholars to be one of the founders of this field. By the late 1800s the term was coming into use, and it began to be formalized as a discipline in Europe. Researchers in the United States helped pioneer ecological studies during the conservation movement, when the complexities of natural resource degradation forced Americans to seek solutions through this new science, applying it largely in botany to studies of plant adaptation.[12]

The ecological message came to Florida—and its activist women—through academia, popular literature, and personal contacts as its principles were applied to the problems affecting the state's unique natural systems. Botanist John Kunkel Small used ecological descriptions in his 1929 book *From Eden to Sahara: Florida's Tragedy*, warning that "reckless, even wanton, devastation has now gained such headway" that Florida's tropical paradise could become a desert. "Not only are Fauna and Flora threatened with extermination, but in many places the very soil which is necessary to their production and maintenance is being drained and burned and reburned until nothing but inert mineral matter is left."[13]

Charles Torrey Simpson sounded similar alarms. A friend of Small and Miami clubwomen (and an ally in securing Royal Palm State Park despite his misgivings about some of the women's planned "improvements"), Simpson spent thirty years studying South Florida's plant and animal communities and writing books about his discoveries, including observations about the intricate relationship between land, plants, and animals. By 1932 the naturalist mourned the destruction of the state's natural systems by dredges, development, and overhunting. "If things go on here as they have done in the past few years this can only end in the destruction of all that is lovely and of value that nature has bestowed on us," he wrote. "Mankind seems to be almost crazy to destroy, claiming that what is done is necessary in order that food and the necessities of life may be produced and that money may be gained."[14]

As ecology seeped into American academia and literature, a number of crises provided vivid examples of its principles. The Dust Bowl in the 1930s, during which millions of tons of topsoil in the arid, drought-plagued southern Great Plains literally blew to the eastern U.S. coast, forced the federal government to act, creating agencies and policies that reflected new ecological thinking. During the same period, government-sponsored removal of predators, intended to protect cattle and improve deer numbers for hunters, proved disastrous as deer surged in numbers, damaged habitats through overgrazing, and ultimately died of starvation when food supplies were destroyed. Aldo Leopold, a Yale-trained forester and author, observed this first-hand, an experience that led him to reject the utilitarian conservation idea and argue instead for an ethic based on ecological values. In his 1949 posthumous masterpiece, *A Sand County Almanac*, Leopold argued that humans needed to develop a new "land ethic" that "changes the role of *Homo sapiens* from conqueror" to a member of the land community. Leopold's work was widely acclaimed and influenced public thinking about the role of humans in the natural world.[15]

It took a female writer-scientist, however, to bring ecology to mainstream America. Rachel Carson's best-selling 1962 book *Silent Spring* awoke the country—and the world—to the dangers of uncontrolled chemical and pesticide use in the environment, refuting claims by the chemical industry and federal and local governments that newly developed technologies would improve lives. Of particular focus was the widespread use of the chemical DDT (dichloro-diphenyl-trichloro-ethane) to control insects. As Carson showed, relying heavily on research from noted scientists, DDT remained in the environment for long periods of time and was stored in plants and animals. Eventually the accumulated chemicals moved through the web of life, causing toxicity and reproductive problems, particularly in avian raptors, including the bald eagle. The book's title conveys Carson's concern that unregulated use of pesticides might create a world where songbirds no longer existed.

She documented widespread fish kills (including one in Florida's St. Lucie County), animal deaths, and threats to human health posed by DDT and other pesticides, and compared them to the dangers of nuclear arms and detonations. In discussing health problems posed by chemicals, she wrote that it was "a problem of ecology, of interrelationships, of interdependence." The book created a huge uproar, in part because of attacks organized by chemical companies, and it fueled debates in the media and Congress, eventually leading to the 1972 U.S. ban on DDT. Carson was attacked as a "female alarmist" and a "fearmonger"—criticisms leveled at her simply because she was a woman.[16]

Carson's book, however, struck a deep chord with Americans, especially women. Letters to the editor had more female than male authors, and as biographer Linda Lear notes, they were concerned about "a spectrum of pollution and contamination issues: fluoride in the water, food additives, thalidomide, radioactive fallout, government secrecy, and corporate deception. They linked their concern with their primary roles as housewives and mothers and with the protection of future generations. Their outlook was not so much economic as humane." Ironically, Carson's attackers used her status as an unmarried woman with no offspring to discredit her. They demeaned her first as a mere woman, too squeamish to be logical, and then belittled her expressed concern for future generations by claiming she lacked the greatest of all female authority and influence: motherhood. (In fact, she was raising her nephew).[17]

Ultimately Carson's meticulous use of facts and experts won over the American public, and the publication of *Silent Spring*, now seen as a classic in ecological literature, is often hailed as the beginning of the modern environmental movement. Former U.S. vice president Albert Gore, a Nobel Prize laureate, wrote that when the book was "first published, 'environment' was not even an entry in the vocabulary of public policy." Without Carson's work, "the environmental movement might have been long delayed," Gore wrote. "She brought us back to a fundamental idea lost to an amazing degree in modern civilization: the interconnection of human beings and the natural environment. This book was a shaft of light that for the first time illuminated what is arguably the most important issue of our era."[18]

Established conservation organizations, including The Nature Conservancy and the Audubon Society, joined in the growing environmental movement by midcentury, espousing ecological views. Some conservation-era groups had stagnated for years, their numbers hurt by World War II. Now, as new issues arose in the public's consciousness, these groups were positioned as leaders in the cause and served as "breeding grounds for more radical groups," according to Luther P. Gerlach and Virginia H. Hine, two of the first scholars to study what they called the ecology movement, including campaigns in Florida. No longer was this field "some type of esoterica studied by specialists in their ivory towers or the name of the game in Walt Disney's nature films." Scientists and grassroots activists united to expose the country's environmental problems and to demand action—one of the many fights waged across the country in the 1960s as social unrest swirled around the Vietnam War, the Civil Rights movement, and the demand for women's and gay rights. Protesters, reflecting a distrust of government inspired by *Silent Spring*, insisted that government reform itself with interventions to solve issues such as water and air pollution, nuclear radiation, oil spills, and abuse of natural resources. They demanded new laws and governmental accountability in efforts to counter the damage already inflicted on the natural world.[19]

Nowhere was this better illustrated than in the Cross Florida Barge Canal project, which greatly influenced the nature of environmental controversies in the state and across the United States. Ecology was a centerpiece in that conflict, and Carr knew how to wield it with deft accuracy.

Carr's early environmental skirmishes, including saving trees in her town, stopping a highway path through the University of Florida, and helping preserve a large savannah area outside Gainesville, armed her with the latest tactics of the modern protest movement. She appreciated the importance of working with established organizations to achieve her goals, including a local garden club and the Alachua Audubon Society, where she was co-chair. Unlike the female garden club, Alachua Audubon was composed mostly of professional men, including businessmen and University of Florida (UF) faculty. The group's focus was not just birds but also ecological issues. In a 1990 interview Carr noted that many women conservationists who had previously put their efforts into garden club work moved to organizations "specifically focused on conservation," such as Alachua Audubon.[20]

In 1962, the year of *Silent Spring's* publication, Carr talked with a Jacksonville woman who served on the board of the Florida Federation of Garden Clubs (FFGC), the only group that questioned the wisdom of the massive federal canal project that would damage the Ocklawaha River. Carr and her Alachua Audubon co-chair, David Anthony, put the canal on the group's agenda for discussion on November 2, 1962. Anthony was a UF biochemist with an activist bent; he was related to suffragist Susan B. Anthony and had worked on the Manhattan Project, which led to his unsuccessful fight for the creation of an international agency to control nuclear weapons. At the meeting, Anthony recalled, Alachua Audubon members realized they were "probably the closest conservation type group" to the federal canal project. When they questioned what the project meant to the environment, none of the academics around the table, many of them trained ecologists, could answer the question. After another inquiry, the U.S. Army Corps of Engineers (hereafter referred to as the Corps), the construction agency for the canal—replied that the river would be relatively undisturbed, a characterization greatly at odds with the project's formal description. The river, extolled for centuries by poets and writers for its beauty and well loved by Carr, would be largely destroyed, along with 27,000 acres of adjacent wetlands and forests.[21]

Seeking better information, the suspicious Alachua Audubon members contacted state officials but were frustrated by their inconsistent answers and were angered into action. The Corps, however, had little reason to suspect there would be serious opposition. For decades the agency had been welcomed to the state, with hopes that its experts would find ways to drain and control Florida's waters, while also bringing in jobs and federal funds. The Corps also was lauded nationally for its extensive dam-building projects in the American West. In a 1991 speech Carr noted that waterways construction was a major engineering focus of the era, supported by human-centered beliefs that river systems could and should be altered. By the early twentieth century, Carr said, "an entire waterways construction industry had developed in the nation—an industry complete with powerful political support and skillful lobbyists." The projects were funded with federal dollars and carried out by the Corps. "And in our arrogance—born of ignorance—the prevailing thought was what is the *use* of a river other than transportation or sewage disposal?" she asked. "A river as a complete entity—as an ecosystem—from its head waters to its estuary, was an alien concept."[22]

In Florida the Corps was responsible for flood control projects and canals spiraling out from Lake Okeechobee, the channelization of the Kissimmee River (begun in 1961 and completed ten years later), and the development of an Intracoastal Waterway system along the coast. Historian Raymond Dasmann described the Corps as the "great 'pork barrel' agency of government," supported by Congress members who wanted federal money and jobs for their home districts. The Corps was "involved with many of the most environmentally destructive projects in the United States," he wrote. "Once they are involved, they are hard to beat, since they are devoted to their objectives and pursue them with a persistence and single-mindedness that their opponents seldom have the time or the capability to turn aside. So it was to be with the Cross-Florida Barge Canal."[23]

But times were changing. Dams had been stopped in the Grand Canyon. Coastal residents were opposing Corps dredge-and-fill projects. And Alachua Audubon was not a group of flighty birdwatchers. Many members were trained scientists from the University of Florida, the state's preeminent institution of the period. And there was Carr. "An open, friendly person, Carr is committed, energetic, and, she would concede, politically naïve enough to lead an unpromising cause," wrote historian Luther J. Carter. Although many people, male and female, were involved in the anti-canal campaign, Carr became the face of the effort, and many credit her energy, humor, intelligence, and force of will as essential to the cause. She also came into her own as a bioactivist, applying her scientific training with crusading to fulfill her moral obligation to save the river and its biota. As a result Carr and Alachua Audubon headed for unavoidable collisions with the Corps, the Florida Board of Conservation, the cabinet, the governor, and the Canal Authority, an appointed body that oversaw this project for the state. Carr's group initially did not expect to stop the barge canal but hoped to reroute it away from the river to "Save the Oklawaha," the name the campaign first adopted.[24]

To oppose this Goliath, anti-canal activists armed themselves with facts. They studied maps, traveled on the Ocklawaha, and demanded information about the river and the canal project. Carr and company, Macdonald writes, had begun an intense "'get the facts' strategy that utilized scientific, economic, and legal research; expert testimony; a grassroots letter writing campaign; and public education." One source of information was Margie Bielling, a high school science teacher and UF-trained biologist. Bielling shared her knowledge of the geology and hydrology of the Ocklawaha River Valley, particularly how the canal might affect underground water reservoirs known as aquifers, and helped create brochures to teach the public about the canal's potential ecological damage. Their efforts gathered steam; by the fall of 1965 Alachua Audubon had support from the Federated Conservation Council, which represented sixteen groups, including garden and women's clubs, Audubon chapters, and sporting groups.[25]

By 1966 the canal project was well under way, with eight miles of construction finished on the eastern leg and a $10 million annual appropriation from Congress. But the tide turned after a January hearing at which more than 350 river supporters traveled to Tallahassee to voice their concerns, only to learn later that state officials had voted to continue the project *before* the hearing. The deception angered Carr's group and woke up the complacent news media. "We got angrier by the mile," Anthony said, adding that this fury transformed the group into tough-minded apostles: "They were John Browns. It was a catalyst." The anti-canal forces went into overdrive.[26]

Carr turned her kitchen into the campaign's command center, complete with a whirring Xerox machine. She and her staff of volunteers contacted news media as well as numerous scientists, seeking support. "Marjorie—she made arm twisting into an art form," recalled Anthony. He was never certain that the canal could be stopped, but the ever-optimistic Carr was. "That's where Marjorie played a role—she gave us backbone," he said. "She was never daunted, never. And she kept saying, 'Well, we're right. We're right.'"[27]

In formulating her strategies Carr used a variety of tactics. Although she had formal science training, she willingly played the "housewife" persona if it caught politicians and engineers unawares and garnered public sympathy. In a very real sense, she shrewdly used biases long held by men as a weapon against them. The housewife image also opened many doors for publicity, recalls JoAnn Myer Valenti, who helped in the media effort. The group, with Carr's cooperation, "sold" the story to the media about Carr as a "little old lady in tennis shoes" or a Florida homemaker (which she was) fighting against all odds. "I think she probably relished that because it made her less threatening," Valenti said. And it paid off. The news media embraced the idea of a housewife and mother versus the Corps. In reality it was a myth, since Carr did not act alone, having the support of many like-minded men and women. But it was an image that sparked the public's imagination: a confrontation between a powerless domestic and a monstrous, seemingly faceless military bureaucracy. The gendering also applied to the Ocklawaha River. In January 1970 *Reader's Digest* published an article titled "Rape on the Oklawaha," describing the canal venture as a "boondoggle." The article title was shocking, likening the project to a sexual crime. This media attention elevated the controversy into the national spotlight, an important turning point.[28]

Carr's group, which eventually adopted the name Florida Defenders of the Environment (FDE), shifted gears from trying to reroute the project to aiming to halt it outright. They did it with facts, aided by the shifting politics of the 1960s. The Vietnam War had tightened the federal budget, and crises had aroused public environmental awareness, heightened in Florida by problems in the Everglades and the visible damage caused by canal construction between 1966 and 1968. In 1967 Florida's legislative districts were redrawn, removing the power base long held by rural politicians, known as the Pork Chop Gang, and giving more representation to urban areas and South Florida. "Gang" members had long supported the canal, but now different eyes evaluated its political capital and found it less compelling. There was another huge political shift in Tallahassee as well in 1967 as Claude Kirk became Florida's first Republican governor in ninety years; two years later, in 1969, the Republicans would take the presidency and begin to see the Cross Florida Barge Canal as a fiscal waste caused by Democrats.[29]

In 1969 anti-canal forces met with the Environmental Defense Fund (EDF), a New York group that advocated lawsuits to halt ecological damage. In September EDF sued the Corps in federal court in Washington, D.C., asking to stop the canal, an action that sparked additional national publicity and angered canal supporters, who already had spent $50 million on the project and needed an additional $100 million in federal funds to complete it. Carr recruited professionals to write about or refute different aspects of the canal. She found botanists, biologists, geologists, economists, historians, English professors—many from the University of Florida—whose studies showed not only the value of saving the river but also that the entire canal project would be a grave mistake. "Marjorie Carr's opposition to it was utterly fantastic," said Nathaniel Reed, Kirk's environmental advisor. "Her opposition to it was partly built on science, and environmental action and reaction." The experts gave FDE credibility with the press, which started to rethink its previous endorsements of the canal project.[30]

FDE also took lessons from another state conflict surrounding efforts to stop a jetport larger than the city of Miami from being built in the Big Cypress Swamp that bordered the Everglades. Kirk broke ground on the project in September 1968. A few months later concerned groups, including the U.S. National Park Service, the Sierra Club, and the Corps, convened to discuss the jetport and its impact on the nearby national park. The U.S. Department of the Interior, charged with the well-being of Everglades National Park, decided to conduct a study. Art Marshall of the U.S. Fish and Wildlife Service—and a friend of Carr's—coordinated the effort. Other wheels also were in motion; in the spring of 1969 Senator Henry M. Jackson of Washington announced hearings about the jetport's ecological impact. Jackson, chair of the Senate Committee on Interior and Insular Affairs, was developing the National Environmental Policy Act of 1969 (NEPA), which would require environmental impact studies for all major federal projects. The jetport study concluded in 1969 that the project and its support facilities would "lead to land drainage and development for agriculture, industry, housing, transportation, and services in the Big Cypress Swamp which will inexorably destroy the South Florida ecosystem and thus Everglades National Park." That autumn U.S. Secretary of Transportation John Volpe, whose office funded the project, and U.S. Secretary of the Interior Walter Hickel announced their opposition. Kirk joined in, spurred to a change of heart by his advisor Reed's intervention. On January 15, 1970, federal, state, and local representatives signed the Jetport Pact along with Kirk, officially abandoning the site in favor of finding a new location. To date the jetport has not been built, although a runway used for training flights still exists in the wetlands.[31]

Following EDF's advice and Marshall's lead, FDE leaders assembled their own barge canal environmental impact statement, completed in January 1970 (the same month the jetport was halted) and published in March of that year. The report attacked the canal on many fronts, projecting that it would cause wildlife destruction, water pollution, and saltwater intrusion into the aquifer. The report also torpedoed the Corps' calculations of the canal's cost-benefit ratio, which assessed the economic benefits versus the cost of the project. Economist Paul Roberts argued that the numbers were subjective and failed to account for a number of costs; he also proposed that the Ocklawaha River system had value simply by its existence—something that had not been considered by the Corps but reflected the rise of ecological thinking.[32]

The passage of NEPA added further fuel to the fire. FDE amended its lawsuit to argue that the Corps was proceeding with a project with undetermined impacts. On January 15, 1971, two weeks after NEPA became law, a federal judge issued a temporary injunction to stop the canal project on the grounds that the Corps did not have a NEPA-required environmental impact statement. Four days later President Richard Nixon halted it by executive order—the first time a U.S. president had terminated a public works project so far in progress. The jetport had cost the Dade County Port Authority $14 million and the U.S. DOT $700,000, but this was nothing in comparison to the magnitude of the barge canal, the "sunk cost" of which was an estimated $71–77 million. Whether he realized it or not, writes Carter, Nixon was challenging a host of pro-canal federal and state agencies and "their make-believe economics, their single-minded concern for economic development and token regard for esthetic values and biological diversity, and their habit of catering to narrow economic interests." Nixon's order was overruled by a judge in 1974, but by then the project had been shelved. Two years later the Florida Cabinet and Governor Reubin Askew withdrew their support for the canal. In 1977 the Corps' chief delivered a report recommending termination of the project; seven years later Congress formally de-authorized the western portion of the canal, finally de-authorizing the entire project in 1990 and transferring the land to the state.[33]

Kenneth H. "Buddy" MacKay Jr., a former state legislator later to become Florida's lieutenant governor and governor, worked with Carr to de-authorize the canal during his first term in Congress. Freshly elected in 1983 to a new district that included Alachua and Marion counties, MacKay received a surprising telephone call from Carr. "I'd been in Washington six weeks and Marjorie called up and said, 'Well, you've been there six weeks. Why isn't the barge canal de-authorized?' I said, 'Marjorie, you've got to be kidding.'" She was not, and stated: "'You don't have anything to do. You can spend full time on this.'" Taking her advice, MacKay set out to visit the 434 other members of the House to convey his belief that the canal was a boondoggle, with the added authority that it crossed his district. In his autobiography, *How Florida Happened: The Political Education of Buddy MacKay*, he relates how he followed her demand: "I advised almost every single member of Congress of my vehement opposition to the canal." However, senior congressmen who had long supported the canal in part because it was linked to other national public works projects resisted MacKay. In his efforts, MacKay relied on Carr and FDE leaders for facts and media contacts. In 1984, unable to win the congressional vote, MacKay forged a compromise that de-authorized the canal from Palatka west to the Gulf of Mexico—an act that for all intents and purposes ended any possibility of barge traffic.[34]

Until her 1997 death from emphysema at age eighty-two, Carr led FDE in its new missions to de-authorize the canal and then to restore the parts of the Ocklawaha River that had been damaged and flooded in early canal construction. She remained a formidable force, getting media attention for her cause. But she never saw her dream of restoring the river realized, and to date legislation and funds to restore the Ocklawaha River have not been secured. Lands set aside for the project instead were used to create the Cross Florida Greenway, a 107-mile recreational path that traverses the state and was named posthumously for Carr as a tribute to her work. At her funeral, pallbearers dressed in uniforms that represented different government agencies related to Florida nature carried her simple pine coffin. Mourners wore buttons stating "Free The Ocklawaha River"—the same sentiment proclaimed by a sticker on the back window of her hearse.[35]

At the same time Carr was fighting to save the Ocklawaha, Marjory Stoneman Douglas was doing the same for Florida's "river of grass"—the vast freshwater Everglades that spanned the peninsula's southern tip. Her 1947 book had given the wetlands that moniker and taught the nation how to understand and appreciate them. "There are no other Everglades in the world," she declared in the first line of *The Everglades: River of Grass*. For Douglas, becoming an Everglades activist in 1969 was a fresh act in a long life that spanned decades of journalism and fiction writing. But now the plight of the damaged, polluted wetlands "promised to become a reason for things, a central force in my existence at the beginning of my 80th year. Perhaps it had taken me that long to figure out exactly what I was able to contribute, and for me to marshall my forces," she wrote.[36]

By the time of her death three decades later at age 108, Douglas was the state's preeminent environmental activist and the patron saint of all things Everglades. Presidents, governors, and political hopefuls flocked to her side, seeking her hard-to-gain approval. Those who hoped to capitalize for themselves by destroying or degrading the Everglades bemoaned her presence at public hearings. With her trademark floppy hat and thick glasses, the petite Douglas looked the part of the sweet grandmother, but her soaring elocution and dogged determination made her a powerhouse.

"She was the matriarch of conservation in Florida and among the giants of conservation in the history of this country," said Clay Henderson, former president of the Florida Audubon Society. "She lived to see restoration of the Everglades rise to the top of the national agenda. Her success was a factor of her sense of history, her ability to communicate effectively, and her focus on a single problem over a long period of time. She was the embodiment of the great lure of conservation: that one person can make a difference."[37]

And what a difference she made. Fleeing a bad marriage, Douglas came to balmy Miami from the Northeast in 1915. She began writing for her father's newspaper, the *Miami Herald*, soon becoming its society editor and writing general interest articles. Miami was a small town then, with a population of less than five thousand people—no more than "a glorified railroad terminal" for the line built by tycoon Henry Flagler, she recalled. Even then she could observe damage to the environment, including the silting of the Miami River caused when its rapids were dynamited and the removal of Indian mounds and live oak hammocks for development. Douglas was amazed by the natural beauty that remained—the "magnificent" Biscayne Bay with its lush marine life and flocks of wading birds. After a stint in the Red Cross during World War I, she returned to a booming Miami, where she became a regular newspaper columnist and editor.[38]

Her friend Jessica Seymour, an advocate for city planning and regionalism, steered Douglas "toward the Everglades, which changed my life much later on," she recalled. Using her journalism, Douglas supported early efforts to create Everglades National Park and served on the park committee. She learned to love the wetlands and the rich flora and fauna to be found there. In the Ten Thousand Islands at the area's edge, she saw "great flocks of birds, amazing flights of 30,000 to 40,000 in one swoop"; she visited Royal Palm State Park and watched birds sitting on bridge railings; bald eagles soared above her on one trip deep into the area. But Douglas was realistic about the impenetrable sawgrass and swarms of bug life, particularly mosquitos: "Let me say right away that knowing the Everglades does not necessarily mean spending long periods of time walking around out there. Unlike other wilderness areas, where the naturalist is a hiker, camper, and explorer, the naturalist in the Everglades must usually appreciate it from a distance."[39]

While working on a novel, Douglas was approached by an editor of a Rivers of America series published by Rinehart and Company. The editor was interested in a book about the Miami River, but Douglas convinced him that the Everglades, from which the Miami River flowed, were the real story. She had not been in the park more than twenty times, and her knowledge was limited mostly to her belief "that the birds were spectacular, that it should be a national park, and that it shouldn't be drained, that there were millions of acres of it." So, like all good writers, Douglas dug into the facts about the long-maligned wetlands. In talking with state hydrologist Garald Parker, Douglas learned that the Everglades were not stagnant swamps but a "subtle flow of water." After mulling it over, she asked Parker if the Everglades could be considered a "river of grass." And with that idea, Douglas found three words to "change everybody's knowledge" and explain the Everglades to the world.[40]

It was a vastly different image from that long held by Florida politicians and developers. For most of the past century governors had been elected on their promises to drain the Everglades, to change the "wastelands" into arable land for agriculture. This was the refrain of the Progressive movement and conservation—to use natural resources wisely and scientifically for the best results for humans. Unfortunately, this was often achieved in ignorance of the long-term effects, as demonstrated by the Dust Bowl and predator control. Even Douglas had agreed with this idea, penning a 1925 article in which she envisioned a bright future for the Florida Everglades—as a drained farmland of rich black, muck soil that would be "the great tropic agricultural center of the world"—perhaps the home of future orchards of mangoes and other fruit-bearing plants.[41]

After several years of research, however, Douglas found a new appreciation for the Everglades and its cultural history. Although the science of ecology was not a part of her book, it was reflected in her examination and explanation of the interconnections of Everglades hydrology, geology, and biology.[42]

In November 1947 her book was published; a month later more than eight thousand people gathered to celebrate the dedication of Everglades National Park, with President Harry S. Truman as keynote speaker. In his speech Truman reiterated utilitarian conservation values, railing at processes that destroyed natural resources and calling for wise use of minerals, forest, water, and soil—a call in line with the thinking of most of those in attendance. Douglas and many other clubwomen were in full accord; now that the park was safe, it was perfectly fine in their eyes to continue large-scale drainage and manipulation of the rest of the Everglades under the auspices of improving it.[43]

Douglas—although she warned in her book that the "Everglades were dying" from destruction wrought by development, saltwater intrusion, fire, overdrainage, and soil misuse—did not believe the area should be left alone. Instead she advocated greater water management planned by the federal government that she expected would suit park, agriculture, and humans alike. As biographer Jack E. Davis notes, Douglas's "trust in federal water management as beneficent panacea came back to haunt her." Within months of the national park's dedication, the Corps launched a massive flood-control and water management project largely for the benefit of agricultural expansion. The multi-million-dollar construction plan would span many years and include the building of dikes, dams, canals, and water retention areas. Douglas supported the plan because she believed there was "room for both a park and farming," Davis writes. "She had no way of knowing at the time that in truth the corps put little importance in the park. She was not alone."[44]

Within two decades Douglas would come to understand her mistake, an about-face achieved through greater scientific information about the Everglades system from watching continuing crises, including droughts, fires, and pollution in the wetlands. It was a new era of thinking in the United States in which environmentalism and ecology replaced old conservation concepts of wise and scientific use of resources. The battle turned to cleaning up the mistakes of the past, preventing future problems, and preserving what natural lands still existed. It propelled Douglas into an unexpected role as advocate. And it all began with a trip to the grocery store.

In the twenty years following publication of her book about the Everglades, Douglas concentrated on her journalism and fiction writing, not imagining any activism beyond her support of the national park. She was aware of the fledgling environmental movement but considered herself a "sympathetic bystander." One night in 1969, Douglas, in need of cat food, ran into Amy Wilson, an assistant to Joe Browder, then leading efforts to protect Biscayne Bay and stop the proposed Everglades jetport. As Douglas wrote in her autobiography, *Marjory Stoneman Douglas: Voice of the River*:

I said, "I think you and Joe are doing great work. It's wonderful." She looked me square in the eye and said, "Yeah, what are you doing?" "Oh me?" I said. "I wrote the book." "That's not enough," she countered. "We need people to help us." To get out of the conversation, I casually mumbled some platitude like, "I'll do whatever I can."[45]

Browder was on her doorstep the next day and asked Douglas to issue a press release denouncing the jetport. When Douglas replied that such a message would be more effective coming from an organization, he challenged her to create one, noting that since Douglas was not connected to any specific group, she could "help unite the various individuals and organizations that had grown up around the cause of preserving it." After a trip to the jetport site, as had happened with many others, Douglas realized that it must be stopped. Then aged seventy-nine, she mulled over Browder's idea until November 1969, when, as she sat at a book-signing table at Fairchild Tropical Gardens, she talked to Michael Chenoweth, a friend from sailing events. What would he think about an organization, perhaps to be called the Friends of Everglades? Chenoweth answered by handing Douglas a dollar bill. Douglas recalled: "Now I had not only the idea of an organization to contend with, but also one member and an endowment." And she had a new role as an important environmental leader.[46]

From those synchronistic events sprang the Friends of the Everglades advocacy organization (FOE). Usually dressed in dark glasses and floppy hats that gave her the look of "Scarlett O'Hara as played by Igor Stravinsky," Douglas gathered members, at a cost of one dollar each, from the numerous events at which she spoke. The purpose of FOE, she wrote, was to include people in all counties in the Everglades region in a grassroots effort to "gain a better idea of the nature and future of the whole region, as the heart and life of South Florida." She hoped "to develop a body of informed and responsible people" to influence state and local conservation efforts and to create "a better climate for regional planning." Michael Grunwald writes that Douglas used her "moral authority as the grandmother of the Glades" to press her points, confiding that no one "can be rude to me, this poor little old woman," but she could be rude to them. As Davis notes, fifty years earlier, Douglas would have relied on women's club members to support such activities, but now FOE "epitomized the micro in the macro postwar transformation in institutional outlets for female environmental activists." Although women's and garden clubs supported Douglas, FOE resembled other issue-oriented groups around the state and country, such as the Audubon Society and FDE, where men and women worked together to oppose ecological ills. Even after the jetport was stopped, FOE thrived, soon turning "to the general predicament of water." In the Everglades, water was and remains a critical issue.[47]

Since 1947 the Corps had invested huge amounts of money, energy, and construction into re-plumbing the Everglades. But two decades later, the damage from the Corps' boundless determination to control the water flow was evident. The Everglades "was still in critical condition," writes Grunwald, "ping-ponging between too-wet and too-dry." In 1971 South Florida endured the worst drought on record, sparking fires and causing saltwater intrusion in drinking wells. Three water conservation areas, basically enormous retaining ponds, were built on the eastern edge of the Everglades, stifling water flow and leading to a buildup of what Douglas described as "polluted ooze." This "interrelated stupidity," she wrote, was crowned by another engineering feat—the straightening of the meandering Kissimmee River at the northern watershed of the Everglades. In the space of a decade the Corps had spent $35 million to undo the work of millennia, turning the river into Canal C-38. By its completion in 1971, it was clear to everyone that the project was a disaster that had ruined a river and its plant and animal life. Now the greatest threat to the Everglades area and the national park was water quantity and quality. Pollution from urban areas and agriculture, particularly the sugarcane industry and dairy farms, damaged the natural systems and, as Douglas pointed out, endangered the drinking water of all South Floridians. Until age 101, Douglas used FOE and her growing authority to fight for the Everglades.[48]

Nowhere was this better illustrated than in the creation of the Marjory Stoneman Douglas Act, a state act intended to spur joint federal and state cleanup and restoration of the Everglades. The bill, written in large part by sugar lobbyists, was heavily compromised, and Douglas would have nothing to do with it. A month after she was likened to Mother Nature by President Bill Clinton, the 103-year-old Douglas wrote to Senator Lawton Chiles of Florida insisting that her name be removed from the bill, a move Grunwald calls "the Everglades equivalent of George Washington demanding that his name be taken off the Washington Monument." It was renamed the Everglades Forever Act. "Mother Nature" Douglas was not happy with the machinations of the male politicians that had led to this disaster and would not have her name attached to anything less than a plan she truly thought would be successful. After all, she had been suspicious of male motivations and their environmental consequences since her columnist days, writing in 1923 that men "are chiefly interested in the material improvement of their part so the state . . . all related in some way to their earning capacities," while women instead focused on "the welfare and advancement of the people."[49]

In many ways, as Davis demonstrates in his all-encompassing Douglas biography, *An Everglades Providence: Marjory Stoneman Douglas and the American Environmental Century*, she embodied the learning and activist curve of Florida's women during the twentieth century. She arrived in Florida as an outsider, came to love the state's beauty and wildlife, and advocated for it in early conservation efforts. Once a proponent of Everglades water management and drainage (as were many clubwomen), Douglas learned through crises and ecology about the delicate nature of the system and the damage inflicted upon it, eventually becoming the greatest champion of its restoration. A suffragist who encouraged women to use their rights, Douglas was a friend to women's clubs but eventually founded FOE, a bi-gender group, to address problems in the vast "river of grass." Douglas had been booed and jeered as "an old lady in tennis shoes," but her passion and tenacity overcame sexist prejudices as she rose in prominence and power. Douglas adjusted her views and activism as evidence and scientific knowledge demanded, often relying on the advice of FOE member Marshall, whose biological knowledge helped stop the jetport. With these new resources and her growing persona, Douglas focused squarely on saving the state's natural areas.[50]

By the time of her death in 1998 Douglas had secured her place as the state's most important environmentalist. Through her book and FOE, she left an indelible print on the state's consciousness and its landscape. A year earlier, her name was placed on the Everglades Wilderness Area; it also is found on a Miami elementary school, a state building housing an environmental protection agency, and an education center on Key Biscayne that she helped secure. More important, she inspired future generations of activists to take up her mantle.[51]

Theodora Hayes Long relishes her memories of Douglas, to whom she read when the aged activist's eyesight started to fail. Douglas frequently urged Long to be environmentally active, to stay optimistic, and not to accept the word "no" when it came to an important project. Today Long is executive director of the Marjory Stoneman Douglas Biscayne Nature Center, a bright, cheery building on Key Biscayne that includes laboratory facilities and wildlife displays. The center exists because of Douglas's intervention—at her urging, the state legislature in 1976 designated 165 acres along the shores of aquamarine Biscayne Bay as an environmental study area. Nine years later, Douglas, then ninety-five, realizing that the site's struggling center needed help, approached the Junior League of Miami (JLM) to plead for volunteers and financial support. The three-hundred-member JLM was a natural ally, as Douglas had long engaged women's groups in her efforts, and the JLM had earned an eco-friendly reputation from its efforts to clean up the Miami River. The JLM helped raise $4 million to build the current center, and Long, a JLM member, took over its leadership in 1992. Building on Douglas's example, Long tells its youthful visitors that "one person can make a difference" to empower a new generation of passionate activists.[52]

This is the lesson of Rachel Carson and Florida's Marjories—that one determined, fact-obsessed, consensus-building person make can an enormous difference. And three Marjories can change a state. Through the writing, activism, and leadership of these women, thousands of Floridians and many more across the nation learned about the beauty and importance of the state's natural systems. Together they stopped a barge canal and started efforts to save and restore the Everglades. MacKay calls Florida's modern female environmental activists "Marjories." It is a name he bestows as a tribute to three of the state's most prominent figures: Douglas and Carr, whom he knew and with whom he worked, and the much-admired author Rawlings. "I call people a 'Marjorie' to mean a leader, a forward-thinking leader. Fearless. Very, very well informed. Highly persuasive. Energetic. So to me it's a compliment."[53]

6

Clearing the Air

Ah, the Florida life. Warm winters. Year-round greenery. Sunny blue skies with healthful balmy breezes.

True more often than not, this image had long drawn residents and tourists to the state, especially those from urban areas with skies darkened from industrial smoke. By the 1960s, however, it was clear that trouble was in Florida's air. Residents could see and smell it. In Jacksonville women's stockings melted from sulfur emissions. Polk County residents stayed indoors to avoid air pollution from nearby phosphate plants. Miamians gagged on fumes from jets, incinerators, businesses, and the newest offender—automobiles.

Air pollution was no longer confined to big northern cities that had long considered smoke and dirty air the price of "progress." It was damaging paradise, and Florida's women rolled up their sleeves to oppose not only the ugliness associated with air pollution but also the health consequences that threatened their families.

The "American woman is bound to make certain that the air her family breathes is clean," wrote Polk transplant Harriet N. Lightfoot in 1966. Tired of suffering from burning eyes, skin problems, and throat soreness that confined her to her home, she appealed for support from other clubwomen so all residents could partake of "our God given right to breathe clean air and enjoy clean water." That type of plea resonated throughout the nation and state, propelling more women into the budding environmental movement, where their long history of conservation, grassroots organizing, and growing political status made them powerful, effective advocates for the cause.[1]

This new idea of "environmentalism" was the outgrowth of post–World War II changes in American society and economics. For conservationists in the early part of the century, nature was largely a commodity that needed scientific management and efficiency for future use; environmentalists now became focused on "the quality of human experience and hence of the human environment," writes historian Samuel P. Hays. As a result the two groups often were in conflict. It was, in a real sense, the changing of the guard—from protecting resources from disappearing to protecting them instead from degradation that was equally destructive.[2]

In the postwar era, rising affluence, automobile ownership, and housing finance programs allowed many Americans to leave noisy, polluted urban areas for newly created suburban housing to achieve a better quality of life. Hays notes that "moving to the suburbs reflected a desire to enjoy a more natural setting, but it also evidenced the search for nature beyond the metropolitan area in the parks and woodlands of the countryside." This was echoed in the growing drive for parks that set aside much national and state acreage for recreation. But this new attitude and the resulting building boom that relocated people to the urban fringes also brought with it the loss of wetlands and floodplains, clear-cutting of lots, subdivisions without green space, energy-inefficient homes, and leak-prone septic tanks. Women who made their homes in these new suburbs faced these threats head-on. These new activists were largely white, in their thirties and forties, well-educated, and living in metropolitan and college towns, and they usually identified themselves as "housewives." The municipal housekeepers had become environmental keepers.[3]

By 1963 problems were evident across the United States. On the heels of Rachel Carson's *Silent Spring* came U.S. Secretary of the Interior Stewart Udall's call for Americans to make changes. In his groundbreaking book *The Quiet Crisis* Udall wrote: "America today stands poised on a pinnacle of wealth and power, yet we live in a land of vanishing beauty, of increasing ugliness, of shrinking open space, and of an overall environment that is diminished daily by pollution and noise and blight." This, he said, was the "quiet conservation crisis" of the period. Udall surveyed the country's woes, from disappearing species to poor planning, from litter to water pollution; the latter would require 10,000 treatment plants to remedy. His plea to action was endorsed in the book's introduction by President John F. Kennedy, who wrote that the "crisis may be quiet, but it is urgent." The country, Kennedy wrote, must "expand the concept of conservation to meet the imperious problems of the new age." He urged each American to make the preservation of the country's beauty and bounty "his personal commitment."[4]

If one were trying to escape urban chaos and find refuge, what better place than Florida? During World War II hundreds of thousands of service personnel were stationed at Florida's 172 military installations or traveled through the state. With the benefit of Veterans Administration–guaranteed loans, many ex-military personnel made it their home after the hostilities ended. From 1850 to 1900 the state population increased sixfold to 530,000 people. By 1950 residents numbered more than 2.7 million people—a number that doubled to more than 6 million by 1969. These were modern-day settlers with a new sensibility and a dream list that historian Gary Mormino writes "included a house, a car, and a vacation." He adds that "postwar prosperity and Social Security" made a move to sunny Florida "affordable, attainable, and acceptable to millions of Americans" at a rate second only to migration to California.[5]

Florida was vastly different from the places many new residents had once called home. Its geography, embracing subtropical and temperate climate zones, made the state's biodiversity unusually rich but also susceptible to tropical storms and hurricanes as well as freezing temperatures and droughts. The state lacked the visual majesty associated with other parts of the country—no mountains, canyons, glaciers, or roaring rivers to capture a sense of awe in its transplanted humans. Florida's beauty, instead, was subtle and unfamiliar. Often one had to be educated to appreciate its natural features, from its underground aquifers with vast amounts of fresh water to coastal estuaries that provided nurseries for saltwater species and wetlands such as the Everglades that were of immeasurable value to wildlife and humans alike in terms of habitat and water resources. At the same time many who came to Florida never fully transferred their affections and allegiances from their home states, a situation known as "the Cincinnati factor," referring to Floridians who moved physically to the state but "emotionally never left" places like Ohio.[6]

One thing they did expect, however, was clean air.

For more than a century, the state and its chambers of commerce had touted Florida as a spa-like mecca that promised well-being for those who visited. By the 1820s arriving steamboats brought travelers, many of them invalids, seeking what was touted to be a health-restoring climate. Several of those seeking Florida's tonic were quite famous. Author Ralph Waldo Emerson came to St. Augustine as a young man in 1827 to recover from a lung ailment. One of the founders of America's transcendental movement, Emerson wrote descriptive (and often unflattering) letters and poems about his visits and, after a winter in the mild climate, returned home in good health. Famed author Harriet Beecher Stowe came to the Jacksonville area in 1867 with her son, Frederick, who had been wounded in the Civil War. The next year, she bought thirty acres in the small hamlet of Mandarin on the lower St. Johns River, where she and her family wintered and tended a small orange grove until 1884. Stowe penned articles promoting the state for many northern magazines. In *Palmetto Leaves*, published in 1873, Stowe noted that many people came to Florida suffering from serious diseases. Some did not find improved health, she wrote, but "on the other hand, there are now living in Florida many old established citizens and land-owners who came here ten, twenty, and thirty years ago, given over in consumption, who have here for years enjoyed a happy and vigorous life." Florida's wetlands were a source of malarial fevers, but the same was true in New York. She wrote: "The situation of Florida, surrounded by the sea, and the free sweep of winds across it, temper the air, and blow away malarious gases." Two years later, poet Sidney Lanier wrote in his travelogue *Florida: Its Scenery, Climate and History*: "Consumptives are said to flourish in this climate; and there are many stories told of cadaverous persons coming here and turning out successful huntsmen and fishermen, of ruddy face and portentous appetite, after a few weeks." Sadly, although Lanier returned to Florida a year later, he was not cured of his fatal case of tuberculosis.[7]

Many people plagued with respiratory illnesses were the victims of dirty air breathed in the industrial north, where pollution in the late nineteenth and early twentieth centuries led to a rise in lung diseases, including tuberculosis and bronchitis. It was literally a man-made problem, since men ran the technology that created air pollution in male-dominated cities. The degradation of industrial cities resulted from public policies that encouraged "rapid, unregulated growth," writes R. Dale Grinder, adding that smoke pollution was considered a trade-off for industrial expansion. The few who were willing to suggest that it be stopped or controlled did so out of their own fiscal interests. The Smoke Committee of Cleveland reported that eleven department stores lost a combined total of at least $25,000 annually because of damage to "white goods"—clothing damaged by pollution. Women could attest to this: the Cleveland committee reported that air pollution produced household damage and forced constant home cleaning, laundry, and dry cleaning. If women were responsible for clean homes and healthy children, then they had to address community ills that affected these duties. In 1926 the Women's City Club in Cleveland successfully campaigned for the creation of a municipal Division of Smoke Inspection; as a result, air pollution waned until the Great Depression hit and factory regulations were lifted.[8]

From the outset women's clubs and organizations supported smoke abatement measures because their members were constantly exposed to pollution problems. Discarding the largely male-generated arguments that smoke was a necessary byproduct of industry, women used their moral authority in the battle, arguing that smoke destroyed the very fabric of society. Jean Sherwood, president of the Chicago Woman's Club, told her board of directors that the city's dark smoke was "responsible for most of the low, sordid murders and other crimes within its limits. A dirty city is an immoral city, because dirt breeds immorality. Smoke and soot are therefore immoral." This was a clear indictment of the companies and corporate boards producing the filth that women believed debased society and made housekeeping onerous. More than any other anti–air pollution group, Grinder writes, women "were the radicals in the movement as they sought immediate results." They had some victories; by 1912 most large metropolitan areas had smoke abatement laws. However, many anti-smoke efforts were futile in the face of a "pro-growth mentality that reinforced the idea that smoke was a sign of prosperity."[9]

Women in numerous areas of the country, including St. Louis, Boston, New York, and Philadelphia, took up the cause. In 1908 Chicago women of the Anti-Smoke League held a housework strike and announced an economic boycott in their efforts to support electric train lines that they believed would reduce smoke. Historian David Stradling contends that smoke abatement work, which began in some areas in the late nineteenth century, "was nothing less than an environmentalist philosophy," as it was "an effort to exert control over the ur-ban industrial environment, an attempt to place beauty and health along with prosperity and profit as the ultimate goals of civilization." It was an early step to clean up and mitigate the excesses that had turned Mother Earth into an increasingly polluted landscape.[10]

As the twentieth century advanced it became clear that filthy smoke was also a serious health risk. A series of crises, repeated in newspaper headlines across the country, made the consequences of unclean air evident as the vo-cabulary of the problem changed from an issue of smoke to that of air pollu-tion. This now included industrial wastes and lead-laden exhaust produced in an increasingly car-centered culture. And it was startling.

Residents in Los Angeles in 1943 thought they were victims of a "gas attack" caused by a chemical plant's air pollution. In reality their ocular, digestive, and respiratory ailments were caused by the first recognized episodes of smog. That the central culprit was car exhaust became clear when the plant was temporar-ily closed. Five years later a temperature inversion and fog in Donora, Penn-sylvania, pushed gases from industrial mills, furnaces, and stoves downward toward the ground in a poisonous smog. As a result twenty people died—and probably many more in subsequent years from lingering cardiac and pulmonary issues. In 1949 air pollution in Los Angeles County damaged almost half a million dollars' worth of crops; in 1961 it was estimated that California had $8 million in agriculture losses owing to pollution. In 1952 more than four thousand deaths were attributed to a deadly fog in London, England.[11]

However healthful Florida's air once had been, by the postwar years problems with its quality were evident, and Florida women, like their activist sisters elsewhere in the country, were quick to recognize and confront the issue. Historian Scott Hamilton Dewey writes that Florida women initially adopted the "traditional feminine role as protector of the home as a foundation for environmental activism and as an indirect challenge to male authority." But unlike female reform efforts across the country, which typically attracted middle-class members, Florida's anti–air pollution movement also attracted working-class women and senior citizens, who met roadblocks from largely male-run businesses and government in a perpetually pro-development state. This resistance slowed pollution control, but activist women rallied their communities to press for reforms, keeping the issue alive long before environmental constraints became national policy.[12]

In Jacksonville, air pollution spewed from local industries that included pulp milling, chemical production, phosphate production, oil reclamation, shipbuilding, and food processing. City incinerators, electric plants, home furnaces, and automobile emissions inflamed the problem. The city reeked of "noxious odors," and there was visible evidence: plant damage, skin disorders, soot, and corrosion to metal, windows, and paint. One morning in 1949 sulfuric acid–laden soot from an unidentified industrial boiler dissolved the nylon stockings worn by women. When asked about the problem, the city's male health officer, in a confusing and not-so-soothing comparison, said the situation was similar to that of Donora but added that the Jacksonville soot particles "could not be inhaled," as had happened in Pennsylvania. He said Jacksonville would probably never experience a similar tragedy because of "dilution" in the local air, a response that was meant to be comforting—unless your stockings had been ruined. Certainly the Donora reference was a chilling one.[13]

Many simply hoped that Florida's offshore breezes would sweep it all away. Dilution as the "solution to pollution" was a concept many supported, according to South Florida activist Ross McCluney. "The idea is that if we can just spread the offending pollutant uniformly over a large enough area, it will be dispersed and diluted to a relatively harmless concentration." But that resolution, which was applied to air and water pollution in Florida, had its own problems, requiring vast enough host resources to achieve proper dilution. He noted: "For some pollutants the whole ocean is not a big enough place." Even though pollutants were invisible through wide dispersal, science proved that they remained problematic. McCluney surmised: "Until we can find economically acceptable methods for rocketing our unwanted (and non-recyclable) pollutants to the sun, we on earth will have to learn to solve these problems."[14]

By the 1960s Jacksonville's air problems led to a joint federal-state-local study that found "significant levels" of automobile and industry pollutants in the northern Florida city's air. As the problem grew, citizens, particularly those in the working-class neighborhood of Talleyrand, pressed the city for action. Leading the group was Ann Belcher, labeled "the crusading mother from Talleyrand," who presented to the city council a petition signed by more than a thousand people and was accompanied by a hundred women from her neighborhood, described by Dewey as a "legion of angry housewives." To illustrate her point Belcher brought "a badly stained sheet and a sickly potted plant as exhibits." Edna Taylor complained that her furniture, as well as her husband's health, had been seriously damaged. The group included men and representatives of black and white neighborhoods. Belcher also wrote to Governor Farris Bryant and U.S. Senator Edmund S. Muskie, whose subcommittee on air and water pollution held hearings in Tampa in 1964 to consider Florida air pollution as part of its fact-finding to implement the groundbreaking federal Clean Air Act of 1963, which provided funds to combat the problem. She told Muskie that she had asked for help from everyone she could but had only gotten the runaround from officials. Belcher and two other women asked Muskie to hold hearings in Jacksonville but were unsuccessful. Tampa was the only Florida site for a hearing. The next year the Duval County Air Improvements Authority was created by the legislature, but it did little more than conduct research. It was not the first or last time that women tried to get Muskie's attention on the issue—one woman in Cicero, Illinois, angered that he did not bring air pollution hearings to her town, scraped black soot off her window and mailed it to him in a fat envelope.[15]

Pollution released into the skies from phosphate plants in Central Florida brought more women into the movement for improved air quality. For decades, phosphate had been an important state industry centered in Hillsborough and Polk counties, mining minerals used for fertilizers and detergents. By the 1950s, Polk County was the leader in national phosphate production, with Florida providing 86 percent of the U.S. industry and 30 percent of the world's phosphate. However, the public costs of phosphate increased when the industry went from mining to also processing lawn and agricultural fertilizers, in huge demand in Florida, releasing fluoride and sulfur oxides into the air from

1948 to 1970. As early as 1958, Polk leaders were concerned about the issue, with several attending a national conference on air pollution held by U.S. Surgeon General Leroy E. Burney. At that conference of 900 people, including civic, medical, and social groups (among them the General Federation of Women's Clubs), air pollution, "the nation's colossus of possible calamity was attacked on all sides." The group agreed that the key to resolving the issue was scientific, including medical research and knowledge sharing. The Florida legislature, following the election of Governor Claude Kirk, who became pro-environment after his election, addressed the issue in 1967, when it created the Florida Air and Water Pollution Control Commission. At its first session in November of that year, the commission cited some sixty industries and many cities for failing to meet pollution control standards, and gave each a timetable to correct the problems. Among the polluting industries were sugarcane processors, pulp and paper mills, citrus packers and canners, and the phosphate industry. It was a bold step, but it did not resolve the problem.[16]

By 1969 the air in Central Florida was so noxious that *Life* magazine included it in an article featuring photographs of heavily polluted areas of the United States, including steel mill output in Indiana, car fumes in Washington, D.C., and pulp mill discharge in Montana. The article described how the phosphate industry burned wastes, producing fluorides that contaminated soil, hurt the growth of citrus trees, and sickened cattle, with an estimated $14 million in damages during the previous twenty years. Ironically, Polk County was also the center of citrus production with 16 percent of the U.S. crop—a huge business conflict. Phosphate also created human health problems. "People living there are reluctant to grow vegetables because of this rain of chemicals," wrote journalist Richard Hall. "Many of them go around all day with sore throats."[17]

Women were among the most vocal protesters of the phosphate plant pollution, especially Harriet Lightfoot, a senior citizen who came to Florida for her health after her husband's retirement. She chaired a local women's club committee and, in 1954, led the newly created Polk County Citizens' Committee on Air Pollution's Division of Health. Bi-gender and issue-specific, attuned to public health and quality of life, the Citizens' Committee was an example of the makeup of the new, postwar generation of environmental organizations. Lightfoot nevertheless inaugurated her role by doing what women activists had done for generations: she wrote letters. She complained to state officials about public health problems that included burning eyes and skin requiring medical attention—symptoms that she first thought were caused by pollen, only to discover that they resulted from phosphate emissions. "I came here nineteen years and some months ago to enjoy the fresh air and sunshine; but for the past eight years I have been forced to stay indoors when the wind comes from the phosphate processing plants," she wrote to state officials in 1963. "I must insist upon your cooperation to stop this evil which descends upon our unsuspecting citizens from the phosphate processing plants." In a later letter to Governor Farris Bryant, Lightfoot played the tourism card, noting that she had dissuaded friends from visiting the state until controls were placed on air pollution. Her appeals to federal officials were for naught; she was told that under the Clean Air Act of 1963 federal authorities could only intervene with permission from the state. Working with the committee, Lightfoot recognized the need to engage different members of the community and used her clubwoman ties to gain backing. Although all-female groups were not as prominent in environmental work as in the past—many had refocused on social service issues—they still offered a network of activists with ties that bolstered the committee's work. As Water and Air Pollution Chair for the Florida Federation of Women's Clubs (FFWC), Lightfoot appealed for support, noting in an article for the organization's magazine that women's groups across the country viewed air pollution as "a special and economic problem of very formidable dimensions." She asked clubwomen to distribute a petition demanding that state officials increase air pollution controls. The "excessively polite" wording of the petition, Dewey notes, "reflected the uncertain position of women acting in the still largely male-dominated realm of public policy, as well as the frustrating situation of ordinary citizens relying on technical experts to define and address a scientifically complicated issue." Still, the petition gathered five thousand signatures within a few weeks.[18]

Lightfoot also appealed to the news media. In a 1966 Associated Press article that appeared in newspapers across the country, she described waking up in her lakefront home "feeling that a strangler's hands were at her throat" and then falling to her knees retching from phosphate pollution from a nearby plant. She discussed Jacksonville and Miami air quality, noting that Florida was a state "to which millions of people have been lured from dirty climes by the promise of pure air and water." Jane H. May of nearby Plant City joined the action, complaining to the U.S. Department of Health that phosphate pollution had damaged her orange grove and put her under a doctor's care for breathing issues. Several of her neighbors participated in her letter campaign seeking federal help. Their issues were not resolved, Dewey writes, until 1970, when lawsuits and federal government pressure forced the state and phosphate industry to lessen and regulate emissions—a victory that "had taken a painful fifteen years of unending public activism" to achieve.[19]

Despite the emergence of environmental groups in the 1960s and 1970s that had male and female members and focused on specific and often local problems, women's organizations continued to press for nature protection, expanding their interests to include issues that had not been concerns fifty years earlier. For example, a report from the FFWC's 1968 convention noted that group members had planted 62,016 trees in the previous year (a long-standing conservation effort), as well as having participated in public hearings about water management and estuarine pollution, the latter being concerns that had not been on the group's agenda in earlier decades. The FFWC's influence also was felt in its representation in many of the bi-gender organizations and panels that arose during this period. The 1968 convention report noted that FFWC members were on the Governor's Natural Resource Committee, the Florida Resource-Use Education Committee, and the Florida Conservation Council, while others had participated in the Governor's Conference on Environmental Quality, a wilderness workshop on Everglades National Park, and the organizational meeting of Florida Citizens for Clean Air. At the same time the article celebrated the fact that Evelyn Waybright, of Jacksonville, the FFWC conservation department chair, was named "Outstanding Conservationist" for 1967 by the Florida Wildlife Federation and the Sears Roebuck Foundation for her work on various state boards. In a nod to modern times and rising female equality and power, women were integral members of these new boards, working with men to address important problems and receiving public recognition for their effectiveness. FFWC provided female representation on these panels, signaling its continuing importance and influence.[20]

In response to growing concerns about air and water quality, in 1957 the legislature created the Florida Air Pollution Control Commission, giving it power to hear and act on pollution complaints. Polluters first were given a chance to fix their problems; ultimately the commission could seek a court injunction against the offender. A decade later the legislature passed a bill creating the Florida Air and Water Pollution Control Board, which wielded greater authority over other state agencies. At its first meeting in 1967 the all-male appointed panel was tasked with implementing the seven-thousand-word legislation, which called for industry to comply with new rules, likely to cost "hundreds of millions of dollars." Women turned their attention to this new commission; in 1970 Board Chair Nathaniel Reed said he had received telephone calls from "women in tears" who lived near a polluting St. Petersburg trash incinerator. If tears worked, women were willing to use those, too.[21]

Into the fray of ecological issues came a new women's organization, the

League of Women Voters (LWV), a nonpartisan group created in 1920 to support women's new voting rights. The LWV had state and local chapters that followed the national group's lead in many areas. In 1971, after a year of study, the LWV decided to support federal air pollution controls on "industrial production, government installations, fuels and vehicles," opening the way for action at all levels, according to the LWV, which continues to support air pollution restrictions.[22]

At the behest of the national group, the South County League of Women Voters in Boca Raton conducted a six-month study of the effects of air pollution in Palm Beach County. The report, released in April 1971, named the sugarcane industry and transportation as the worst offenders, sending alarms through the league. "This area is beginning to get into the Los Angeles syndrome," said Jean Meddaugh, chair of the local league's environmental quality committee; she noted that one solution would be more effective public transportation. Another committee member, Judi Marsh, said there was no doubt that Florida was cleaner than other states but added her concern that "air pollution is being left behind in our concern with the water supply." As part of their participation in Earth Week—a modern creation born of the 1970 Earth Day celebrations raising international consciousness—the Boca Raton group created and distributed posters for air pollution awareness that put a new twist on children's nursery rhymes, titled "Polluted Mother Goose." A sample:

> Old Mother Hubbard
> Went to the window
> To give her poor dog some sun
> But when she got there
> What used to be air
> Was sulfur and hydrocarbon![23]

Nearby Miami was another hotspot of air pollution, but unlike in Jacksonville and Central Florida, its problems were the result of a growing population that brought with it smoky laundries, burning garbage dumps, city trash incinerators, electrical generators, and emissions from jets and automobiles, the latter of which had determined the city's development patterns. Agriculture also complicated the problem with seasonally fired sugarcane fields and nasty smoke from tires that were burned to warm fields and citrus groves during freezes. Without its steady offshore breezes for some pollution dispersal, the city might have suffered Los Angeles's smog problems as early as 1961, but it was not immune to the problem. Activists pointed to yellow-brown hazes during traffic rush hours (visible from offshore or from elevated highways) as evidence of Miami's fouled atmosphere. McCluney suggested that residents "stand near to U.S. 1 during a rush hour and notice the burning sensation in your eyes. This way you can actually *feel* the air pollution problem." The automobile's dominance in local transportation was "most confounding," wrote Miami journalist Juanita Greene. "The problems it creates are painfully apparent."[24]

Fears about the city's air quality arose in the early 1960s, when an oil refinery complex was proposed on Biscayne Bay in the Homestead area south of Miami. The Seadade Industries refinery would be joined at its site with related industry. It required cutting a deep-water port in the shallow aquamarine bay for tanker ships as well as a deep channel through the bay and an offshore reef for boat transportation. Refinery proponents promised to employ 18,540 employees in an industry that would process 50,000 barrels of oil daily. Although job creation had long been touted as positive for Florida, many concerned local citizens now looked past that, worried instead about the project's potential toll on natural resources as well as possible pollution of the nearby Everglades National Park and the John Pennekamp Coral Reef Preserve on Key Largo. The resultant furor, wrote Luther J. Carter, "contributed to the birth of a potent Dade County environmental movement."[25]

The Seadade project was approved with little opposition in 1962 by the Metro-Dade County Commission and supported by the Greater Miami Chamber of Commerce and two Miami newspapers—all notorious for their pro-development stances. Shortly after the Metro-Dade vote, however, a group of twelve dissenters formed the Safe Progress Association (SPA) to fight the project. Members included airline employee Lloyd Miller, SPA leader and president of the local Izaak Walton League; several University of Miami marine biologists; author Philip Wylie, whose writing years earlier had stopped the discharge of raw sewage into the bay; and three very important women: Belle Scheffel, treasurer of the local Nature Conservancy group and described by Carter as "a tiger on the garden club circuit"; Juanita Greene, a veteran *Miami Herald* reporter who wrote many pro-SPA articles; and Polly Redford, a Miami author described as the "intellectual center for environmental thinking in south Florida." Redford had published articles in national magazines and a year later would publish a book that questioned how "progress" was affecting the natural world. She was very active in the local Audubon Society and, having founded the local Izaak Walton League chapter with her husband James, understood the dynamics of male-female groups. In a 1971 essay Redford, recalling the SPA campaign, wrote that a single person might have little influence in such issues. However, she said, "the minute he joins with two or three others and calls himself an organization, his power increases a hundredfold." Ad hoc groups disappeared as new problems arose, Redford wrote, adding that those continuing to participate in the issues often joined national organizations such as the Nature Conservancy, Audubon Society, and Izaak Walton League, which offered a number of advantages such as publications, research, and "representation in Washington."[26]

These were strong, opinionated, vocal females experienced in working with men in environmental efforts and (in the cases of Greene and Redford) in the workplace, reflecting the new world of women. As a seasoned reporter, Greene took SPA's side in her articles, even though her newspaper's male-dominated editorial management endorsed the project. A veteran of the world of fact finding and a friend of activist-author Marjory Stoneman Douglas, Greene was willing and able to use her talents to publicize and participate in a number of South Florida issues. Redford, too, worked with men in publishing her books and in group activism.[27]

In many ways these powerful female personalities represented the new face of America's women in the 1960s, as women increasingly joined the workforce, helping their families rise in income and status. In 1950, 34 percent of women worked, a number that jumped to 38 percent in 1960 and 43 percent in 1970. Although women were getting more education and finding more employment opportunities, there remained great disparities in income, in women's ability to hold traditionally male jobs, and in their rising up through corporate ranks, impediments often described as the "glass ceiling." It was a new economic world in which women were firmly entrenched, and many expected equal opportunity and pay based on their merit and achievement. The reality, however, was that women's salaries and promotions lagged behind those for equally qualified men. Such disparities for women, as well as African Americans and other disfranchised members of society, led to great upheavals in the 1960s. The Civil Rights crusade and its protests, writes historian Sara Evans, "provided a new model for social change and a language about equality, rights, and community that transformed public discourse in a decade." When Kennedy was elected president in 1960 and called for public activism, it was a goal that women embraced. Professional women as well as radical feminists challenged the status quo, culminating in the Presidential Commission on the Status of Women, chaired by former first lady Eleanor Roosevelt. The committee's 1963 report detailed a number of problems women encountered in the workplace, including discrimination, unequal pay, legal inequality, and a lack of childcare. As a result Kennedy issued a presidential order requiring that civil service hiring eliminate sex considerations, and the Equal Pay Act of 1963 made it illegal to pay men and women different wages for the same work.[28]

Another milestone that year was the publication of *The Feminine Mystique* by Betty Friedan. The book questioned cultural assumptions and images that women could find complete fulfillment as wives, mothers, and homemakers. Friedan argued that the essential problem was that women needed "to grow to their full strength as human beings" before they could find love and fulfillment—and that it might be found outside the home. The book caused a tidal wave of media attention and debate about women's roles—a public conversation that had been fostered a year earlier with the publication of Carson's *Silent Spring*. Chemical companies vilified Carson, in part because of her sex, but her warnings could not be ignored and led to congressional hearings that supported her findings. Women's voices, including those of Carson and Friedan, gained volume, leading Americans to question cultural norms that had long made women second class citizens. These were rules largely dictated by a patriarchal society that dominated government and industry. Now women challenged this masculine authority, refashioning their roles in the world.[29]

In its "Statement of Purpose," the National Organization of Women, founded in 1966 to advocate for women's civil rights, declared that "women first and foremost are human beings, who, like all other people in our society, must have the chance to develop their fullest human potential. We believe that women can achieve such equality only by accepting to the full the challenges and responsibilities they share with all other people in our society, as part of the decision-making mainstream of American political, economic and social life." Greene and Redford were recognized professionals in their fields, gaining a certain amount of autonomy that allowed them to channel their passions in their work—much like Douglas. They were valuable members of advocacy groups, serving as an inspiration and example for other activists. Through their environmental work, these women also carved out important public personas that raised awareness of female capabilities and competence.[30]

SPA had little money but made up for this with talent and passion. It attacked on three fronts: that Biscayne Bay would be harmed by industrial pollution; that trade winds likely would blow air pollution from the refinery and petrochemical plants over the county; and that dirty industry was not compatible with the quality of life that Dade County residents desired. Despite the developer's assurances to the contrary, SPA argued that no refinery could be pollution-free. In response, Metro commissioners in 1963 adopted a pollution-control ordinance and touted it as the toughest in the United States. A federal air pollution control official, writes Dewey, found the new law "to contain 'all safeguards against evasion that can reasonably be written into law, in the present state of knowledge.'" In developing the ordinance, Metro caused a delay in issuing a building permit for the project. In addition, Seadade had trouble getting a dredging permit from Metro to dig a channel, giving opponents time to organize, grow, and rally before any bay destruction could begin.[31]

SPA members used all their contacts and talents to raise public awareness. Redford wrote that Scheffel constituted the SPA Women's Division, "and a heavy-armored one at that," because of her contacts with numerous environmental and garden groups that were coming to reflect the new ecological ethic and could still raise a ruckus with their large membership. Because "garden-club ladies are also women's-club ladies," Redford noted, "it wasn't too long before women's groups began passing anti-refinery resolutions, too." Male SPA members visited community groups with more male-based membership, including sports clubs, exchange clubs, chambers of commerce, and service clubs, helping to spread their position to every organization possible. The group, Redford estimated, reached 400,000 people in Dade and Monroe counties with their concerns. Redford also put her pen to work, writing about the project for *Harper's Magazine* in February 1964, stating that SPA was not against industry, just that which was "dirty."[32]

The science of ecology, now becoming part of the public conversation, and concerns about the impacts of environmental degradation on the economy figured greatly in the SPA campaign. The group gathered information about oil refineries and pollution. It also warned "that the project could damage tourism and make the area the 'Smogville of the south,'" writes historian Jack E. Davis. Slowly, public opinion shifted toward SPA, with support coming from the *Miami News*, the cities of Miami and Miami Beach, and more than three dozen civic groups. Seadade ran into new problems when it came into conflict with a proposed city of Islandia to be built on several outer islands in Biscayne Bay. The final blow for both projects, however, was the group's strategic decision to seek federal protection for much of the bay. Miller got the backing of Metro and met with Washington officials, including U.S. Representative Dante Fascell, who endorsed the concept. When federal researchers prepared a required report on the southern part of the bay, they determined that the coral reef and flora and fauna of the bay were of national significance, surprising even SPA members as regards biological richness. The new preservation scheme was the product of rising national ecological consciousness and new activist tactics. Six decades earlier, state Audubon societies had set aside land and hired wardens to protect bird habitat and nesting areas. However, it is unlikely they would ever have tried to stop a major business such as a refinery in favor of birds, because they simply did not understand (or had yet to experience) the impact of habitat degradation on avian populations. Preserving Biscayne Bay gained momentum with an election change in Metro members, who ultimately denied the Seadade building permit. In 1968 the Biscayne National Monument Act preserved 96,300 acres of seabed and islands, ending the Seadade and Islandia projects forever. Carter wrote that Redford attributed the victory to a "strong showing at public hearings, thousands of letters and telegrams from conservation club members, bumper strips, etcetera, etcetera—the whole paraphernalia of a modern political campaign." The result was an activated local force of environmentalists who would have much to dispute in coming years.[33]

Women from all walks of life and from across the state, from Jacksonville to Lakeland to Miami, used their voices and talents in the 1960s to combat dirty air that threatened the health of the state and themselves. To do so meant opposing not just industry but also the "business as usual" attitude that had allowed polluting industries to operate with little or no regulation in a time-honored national and state tradition of giving priority to jobs and revenue—not quality of life. By refusing to support the status quo, these activist females helped stir public discontent and helped force a change in government practices, culminating in the 1970 federal Clean Air Act amendments removing obstacles that had sheltered polluters in the past. In essence the air pollution skirmishes that Florida women encountered were a new incarnation of the issues that had activated female alarms at the dawn of the twentieth century. Simply put, men and male-dominated interests that revolved around income and profits were ruining the state's natural systems *then and now*. They had killed birds for the millinery industry, clear-cut forests for lumber products, and erected countless signs to promote business, uglifying the landscape. Women stood up to these practices, but by midcentury the dangers to the natural world were more insidious. Pollution, although "invisible" at times, was a clear threat. With the health of their communities and families at risk, evident in coughing children and damaged agriculture, Florida's women found new impetus to enter into environmental disputes, bringing with them honed organizational skills and professional talents. Disturbed that the clean, refreshing air they expected to find in the state was now threatened by car exhaust and industries, women energized the budding movement in new arenas, seeking to make the state a better, safer place for everyone.[34]

Figure 1. Canaveral National Seashore exists today largely because of the work of Doris Leeper. Photo by author.

Figure 2. Clara Dommerich in 1900 helped organize the Florida Audubon Society in her Maitland living room. Courtesy of the Maitland Historical Society.

Figure 3. One of the tragic fashions of the late 1800s and early 1900s was the display of bird feathers and bodies on hats, which endangered Florida's wading birds. Courtesy of the Sloane Collection.

Figure 4. Four women (Katherine Bell Tippetts is third from left) with two students in 1913 display a seventy-foot petition to save Florida's robins; their efforts inspired a state protective law. Courtesy of the Florida Audubon Society.

Figure 5. May Mann Jennings, of Jacksonville, was a clubwoman powerhouse whose efforts to improve state forestry practices gained her the reputation as the "Mother of Florida Forestry." Courtesy of the State Archives of Florida.

Figure 6. Logged-out Florida pine forests like this one in the early twentieth century inspired women to demand better treatment of the state's natural resources. Courtesy of the State Archives of Florida.

Figure 7. The internationally acclaimed and beloved Everglades owe their existence in large measure to the activism of the state's environmental women. Courtesy of Kim den Beste.

Figure 8. Clubwomen in 1918 at Royal Palm State Park, Florida's first state park that would become the nucleus of Everglades National Park. Courtesy of the State Archives of Florida.

Figure 9. Streets signs like these found on a Mt. Dora street in 1917 caused many women to demand controls on what they considered to be ugly, unsafe visual blight. Courtesy of the State Archives of Florida.

Figure 10. Elizabeth Virrick worked tirelessly for better housing and sanitary conditions for the poor living in Coconut Grove. Courtesy of HistoryMiami.

Figure 11. Marjorie Kinnan Rawlings, Pulitzer Prize winner for *The Yearling*, taught a nation to appreciate rural Florida but also was alarmed about state forestry practices. Courtesy of the State Archives of Florida.

Figure 12. Marjorie Harris Carr led successful efforts to stop the federally funded Cross Florida Barge Canal that threatened to destroy her beloved Ocklawaha River. Courtesy of the State Archives of Florida.

Figure 13. Marjory Stoneman Douglas was a noted author, activist, and patron saint of the Everglades. Courtesy of the State Archives of Florida.

Figure 14. Pollution, like this spewing from a Jacksonville plant in the 1950s, led to many demands for cleaner, healthier air. Courtesy of the State Archives of Florida.

Figure 15. Protestors demand action in a 1989 demonstration against toxic waste. Courtesy of the State Archives of Florida.

Figure 16. Mary Grizzle was a state legislator whose advocacy curbed harmful sewage discharge into Tampa Bay. Courtesy of the State Archives of Florida.

Figure 17. This Everglades dredge was part of the effort to drain the vast wetlands, creating damage that the state and nation are now spending billions of dollars to repair. Courtesy of the State Archives of Florida.

Figure 18. Newly hatched sea turtles head to the ocean from a Volusia County beach thanks in part to efforts by local women who sued the county to protect the creatures. Courtesy of the State Archives of Florida.

Figure 19. Doris Leeper was a noted New Smyrna Beach artist and primary mover in the 1975 creation of Canaveral National Seashore. Courtesy of the Atlantic Center for the Arts.

Figure 20. Dorothy Sample opposed dredge-and-fill efforts in St. Petersburg and then became a noted conservationist in the state legislature. Courtesy of the State Archives of Florida.

Figure 21. Ivy Stranahan in the early 1900s worked tirelessly to help Florida's Seminole Indians. Courtesy of the State Archives of Florida.

Figure 22. Joy Ezell holds a sample of water from the nearby Fenholloway River in Taylor County; she has worked for two decades to try to stop pulp mill pollution of it. Photo by author.

Figure 23. Jeannie Economos is a passionate activist seeking justice for Lake Apopka farmworkers who suffer health problems from decades of pesticide and chemical exposure. Photo by author.

Figure 24. Victoria Tschinkel, former secretary of the Florida Department of Environmental Regulation, remains involved in state conservation efforts. Courtesy of the State Archives of Florida.

Figure 25. Virginia Wetherell was a state legislator before heading environmental agencies, including the Florida Department of Environmental Protection. Courtesy of the State Archives of Florida.

Figure 26. Carol Browner, former administrator of the U.S. Environmental Protection Agency, often emphasized her role as a mother in promoting a healthier environment. Courtesy of the Center for American Progress.

7

Restoring Waters

It was a sore sight for eyes and a nauseating stench for anyone downwind: millions of gallons of untreated sewage bubbling up in a pinkish glow off Miami Beach's famed coast.

Called the Rose Bowl because of its color, the odiferous area featured "turds, condoms, paper, cigarette filters, and balls of clotted grease" that floated on the Atlantic Ocean's surface, only to be windborne farther along the Florida shore, an appalled Polly Redford complained in 1970. Under pressure from state regulators, the city of Miami Beach "graciously agreed" to extend the outfall of this sewage dumping an extra five thousand feet "to the edge of the Gulf Stream, which it is hoped, will soon whisk the objectionable matter out of the state entirely," perhaps to Georgia or the Carolinas, the journalist-environmental activist wrote. "But with luck, some of the condoms and cigarette filters may make it all the way to England, and do their bit to build up beaches there." It was all perfectly legal, "though a citizen would be arrested for emptying his chamber pot on his neighbor's doorstep."[1]

By midcentury, Florida's waters were a mess. Rapid population growth and urban development had turned rivers, lakes, bays, and coastal waters into cesspools, damaging important natural systems and the quality of life that many residents—and tourists—had come to expect. And the nation was taking notice. In a 1949 *Look* magazine article titled "Polluted Paradise," Miami writer Philip Wylie complained that many of the waters near the state's resort areas were degraded: "The clear blue bays that once characterized the peninsula have become an opaque gray-green wherever man has been in residence in numbers for any length of time. The rivers have been fouled for most of Florida's cities dump raw sewage and industrial waste into the nearest waters." As with air pollution, many industries and government agencies viewed water pollution as the cost of doing business, of catering to companies that employed residents. Activist women, however, refused to look the other way and demanded change, forcing the state along a new path.[2]

The "attitude toward treatment in most Florida communities has been primitive, to use the kindest word," wrote historian Raymond F. Dasmann in 1971, adding that Jacksonville dumped raw sewage into the St. Johns River; Tampa Bay "has been described as a potential disaster area" from pollution, phosphate mining discharge, and oil spills that killed the estuary's vital seagrass; and Collier County continued to approve construction without adequate treatment systems. Virtually every municipality dealt with sewage by dumping it into nearby waterways, leaving their freshwater and marine ecosystems destroyed or on the verge of collapse. The Amelia and Fenholloway rivers, with the blessing of the legislature, were filled with pulp mill poison; Lake Apopka, once a bass-fishing haven in Central Florida, was dying from its long-time use as a repository for a variety of wastes; suburban development threatened Lake Jackson near Tallahassee; agricultural and cattle runoff polluted the Kissimmee River and Lake Okeechobee; trash and weeds filled drainage ditches; and automobile traffic coated roads with greases and chemicals that rains washed into already fouled waterways. Many believed that the dilution of liquid waste into larger bodies of water would adequately dispose of it; others believed that the state's "intense sunshine" would purify land and water.[3]

The biggest threat to Florida's waters, including its vast underground supplies, was sewage from its swelling human population. In 1945 Richard Tait, president of the Florida chapter of the American Society of Sanitary Engineers, warned that 90 percent of municipal sewer systems emptied "onto beaches, or into bays, rivers and streams, contaminating the water." With such practices, Tait said, came greater threats of diseases that could "ruin this state, its land values, its business and its tourist trade." Cities could not keep up with growth needs, allowing homes to use cesspools or septic tanks that could pollute wells and underground aquifers. By 1960 the state had only one sewage treatment plant. Four years later, increased funding, particularly from the federal government, had improved the situation, but little more than half of the state's 6 million residents were served by sewage treatment operations.[4]

Disgusted female writers and activists of the period repeatedly pointed out the ills of untreated sewage, particularly in the Miami area, refusing to let the issue rest. When the city laid a sewer pipe that routed waste into the "sweet water" of the Miami River, there were complaints "and so the sewer was extended out into the channel," wrote Miami journalist Helen Muir in 1953, adding: "Out of sight, out of mind would be Miami's treatment of sewage through the years until the day would come when she had fouled up her clear, sweet river and her blue shining bay to such an extent that it was no longer out of sight and fish would die and sea gardens would disappear and the beautiful Biscayne Bay would lie, a pollution between man and God." It was too huge a problem to ignore. By 1971 eighty-nine sewage treatment facilities in Dade County daily discharged 35 million gallons into the county's canal system, 110 million gallons into the ocean, and 1.4 million gallons into drain fields; leaking septic tanks caused additional misery.[5]

This was not a Florida-specific problem; since the late nineteenth century, urban areas across the United States had been dealing with water issues and their attendant health problems. In Chicago the Chicago River was the depository of the city's sewage, livestock manure, and wastes from meat-packing plants, rendering an unmistakable odor that threatened health and comfort. By 1871 city engineers had reversed the flow of the river into the Illinois River and away from Lake Michigan, preserving drinking water supplied from a two-mile tunnel built under the bottom of the lake. That did not remove the pollution, which still caused trouble during spring runoff and heavy storms, but it pushed the trouble farther away from population areas based on the belief that dilution would solve the problem. Prior to 1938 untreated sewage and stormwater from Minneapolis was dumped directly into the Mississippi River, which would carry it down to "disappear" into the Gulf of Mexico. But the broad Mississippi was not big enough to absorb the noxious mass and not swift enough to make it unnoticeable. The results locally were permanent stench, diseases, fish kills, and reduced use of the river for recreational and commercial purposes. Residents in Newark, New Jersey, once swam, fished, and boated in the beautiful Passaic River; by 1882, with the city's sewers dumping directly into it, the river was described as "disgusting to taste and smell." In 1899 Congress took limited action in favor of waterways with the Rivers and Harbors Act, which made it illegal to throw garbage and refuse such as chemicals, oil, or acids into navigable waters; unfortunately, liquid sewage was exempt, so the practice continued. Some voices raised alarms about the need for better sanitation practices, including environmental chemist Ellen Swallow Richards, who argued for clean water and milk supplies as part of a healthy home and community. Still, cities were disinclined to fund necessary treatment improvements, often continuing to discharge lightly treated or raw sewage into local waterways. Not until the New Deal public-works programs in the 1930s did sewage treatment receive serious attention, but no real action occurred for another three decades, with the advent of large-scale federal funding.[6]

By the 1950s and into the next decade it was evident that the technologies of the past were not controlling water pollution. When foam and suds washed up on shorelines, "sometimes hundreds of miles from the nearest source of contamination," writes historian Robert Gottlieb, clearly there was a serious problem stemming from laundry detergents in regular use in American households. Detergents laden with phosphates—some of them from Florida's polluting mines—caused serious environmental problems by raising the nutrient level in water bodies, causing algae blooms, noxious weed growth, and eutrophication. For America's women, ironically, keeping a clean home and fresh laundry was complicated by the aftermath of the effect on water pollution. In the 1960s untreated municipal and industrial discharge caused lake eutrophication, fish kills, a blob of untreated sewage that formed off Staten Island, New York, and the dirtying of many saltwater bays that were declared unfit for humans. And then there was the previously unimaginable: a river caught fire. On June 22, 1969, the oil and debris-filled Cuyahoga River near Cleveland, Ohio, burst into flame, an ironic symbol of the country's polluted waters. An oil spill off the coast of Santa Barbara, California, earlier the same year brought the reality of pollution damage into every household through the evening news broadcasts.[7]

With these indelible images on the nightly news, Americans were forced to change. The extent of the problem made it unavoidable. While it had been acceptable in the 1920s, with a population of 968,470, to use Florida's rivers for waste disposal, four decades later with an increase in population to 4.95 million in 1960, such practices became unconscionable. Federal regulations passed in 1965, 1970, and 1972 were similar to air pollution laws, setting standards and implementation for industry and government. The 1972 act was innovative in its requirement of technology standards far more stringent than the air measures demanded.[8]

Florida was late to the problem, having escaped most urban issues until the post–World War II development boom that sent its population numbers skyrocketing to 6 million people by 1969. And with them came a lot of flushing toilets. By 1970 Governor Claude Kirk declared that Dade, Broward, and Palm Beach counties were committing "environmental suicide" by continuing to dump poorly treated sewage into their coastal waters. Women's and garden club members, whose attention was moving from birds and trees to issues of modern ecological concern, also voiced their concerns, passing a number of resolutions to capture the attention of state officials. In 1955 the 24,000-member Florida Federation of Garden Clubs (FFGC) passed a resolution at its annual convention declaring its opposition "to the wanton pollution and eventual destruction of all rivers, streams and lakes in this former paradise, by the dumping of sludge, sewage or any other noxious material detrimental and injurious to the purity of such waters which can render them unfit for the most suitable and useful purposes of man." The group urged the state to enact legislation to halt the pollution "before such evil practices do irreparable harm." Pollution was immoral and evil, and it needed to end. Framed as such, this was clearly women's work.[9]

A number of attacks on water pollution opened by the late 1960s as national, state, and local groups combined forces to press for improvements. A leader in water activism was the League of Women Voters (LWV), a national grassroots organization founded by suffragists in 1920 to teach political effectiveness to newly enfranchised women. The nonpartisan all-female group, which also admitted male members as of 1974, and its state and local chapters concentrated on issues deemed important to its supporters and the public. While the LWV never endorsed specific candidates or political parties, it encouraged members to exercise their voting rights to press for legislation and governmental action to preserve the environment. This was a new form of female activism—the powerful voter. Although it would be many years before Florida's legislature had any substantial female representation, female suffrage had created a shift in political power. In theory women no longer had to rely on the tactics of May Mann Jennings, Katherine Bell Tippetts, and Mary Barr Munroe: letter writing, the goodwill of elected officials, and activating the "old-girls network." Now they could participate in choosing government leaders and had the option of running for office themselves. Interestingly, while the LWV developed a large nationwide base for its efforts, the General Federation of Women's Clubs (GFWC), long a conservation stalwart, started losing membership and leadership—the victim of more specialization in community organizations. Such was the case in Florida, where the Florida Federation of Women's Clubs (FFWC) kept its focus on environmental issues and collaborated with other groups; by midcentury many of its members took their activism into local issue alliances that included both women and men.[10]

In 1956 the LWV decided to focus on water, deeming it an issue of major public concern and inspiring activism by its local chapters. Four years later, writes historian Adam Rome, the "league had become a major player in the debate about the federal responsibility for water quality, and league members continued to lobby for government action" through the decade. In 1969 the LWV showed its growing power by helping to organize the Citizens' Crusade for Clean Water, a coalition of three dozen groups, including the American Association of University Women and GFWC as well as bi-gender organizations such as the Izaak Walton League. Their objective: exerting political pressure on Congress to spend the full $1 billion appropriated for pollution efforts, including matching grants for sewage treatment facilities, instead of the $214 million then in the proposed federal budget. Through their influence, national leaders were forced to revise the budget, eventually agreeing to an $800 million appropriation. In a September 1969 address in St. Petersburg to the board of the League of Women Voters of Florida (LWVF), Ruth Clusen, LWV second vice president, emphasized the importance of the Citizens' Crusade and of local action and participation. She said many people steered clear of water and sewer issues because they lacked expertise, but "a person doesn't need scientific understanding. You only need to know that water has to be treated in order to insure there being enough water in the right place at the right time." In a blow to the male-dominated professional world, Clusen declared that a citizen did not need an engineering degree to express an opinion about the topic. "All a person needs to say is that the water in the area where he lives needs to be clean enough to swim in, to boat in, to fish in, and leave it to the scientists to make the technical decisions to bring this about."[11]

The St. Petersburg league was particularly focused on water issues. Even before the national group chose the topic, in 1951 the St. Petersburg group adopted a study of the city's sewage system; three years later members decided to support an improved system for the city. A decade later the group joined with the Clearwater league to speak at a public hearing in favor of creating aquatic reserves for the coastal Caladesi Island area and embattled Boca Ciega Bay. When an election was held in Manatee County to decide whether to adopt a pollution control code and create an air and water pollution board, the league there jumped into action, distributing four thousand flyers, a hundred posters, and sample ballots as well as appearing on a local television program and providing radio spot announcements in favor of both measures. The pollution code and board were approved by a nine-to-one margin. This was a group that made use of every available means of communication, an essential part of any successful activist effort. Florida's women already had used radio, newspapers, and internal club publications for alerts. Now they added television to their arsenal, acknowledging its dramatic effectiveness in disseminating images and information. To gain further public attention and political action, in 1959 the

LWVF co-sponsored a Florida Water Resource Conference with the University of Florida. It followed up with workshops in the next two decades, often teaming up with ecologically minded groups to make a difference. The LWVF's 1972 seminar on Environmental Quality was held "to inform the public of the necessity for environmental restrictions in this rapidly growing state." On the agenda: oil spills, solid waste disposal, air pollution, wetlands, and energy.[12]

League members were eager and competent participants in a variety of programs, testifying at a 1970 hearing by the state pollution control board that Tampa Bay needed improved sewage treatment and limits on dredging. A year earlier a league-sponsored Tampa seminar drew some six hundred people to hear about the ills facing the bay—namely eutrophication caused by an influx of nutrients such as phosphates (likely mined locally) and nitrates from many sources. Sewage and industrial pollution had contributed to the long-term degradation of Tampa Bay, once a vibrant estuary with celebrated fishing grounds. By the 1960s and 1970s the bay's bottom, once covered in lush seagrass, had become "lifeless muck," leading many to call for action, including Mary Grizzle of Belleair Shore in Pinellas County.[13]

Grizzle had eased into local politics, going from PTA president—a position that might be expected of a mother of six—to leading the Florida Federation of Republican Women. With legislative reapportionment in 1963, Grizzle, described as "quiet" and "rather bashful," won a seat in the Florida House of Representatives, becoming the first Republican woman in the legislature on votes delivered by both sexes. There she worked on a number of women's rights issues, including supporting the Equal Rights Amendment, requiring child care licensing, and passing the Married Women Property Rights Act, which allowed married women to buy property or start businesses without their husbands' permission. In 1978 Grizzle was elected to the state senate, where she served fourteen years, using her position to oil the mechanics of legislation, particularly in ecological issues that were close to her heart and home. Her finest achievement for the environment came in 1972 when she co-sponsored a bill that set tough new standards for sewage dumped into Tampa Bay and other area waters affected by seven counties. Grizzle argued that the bay, with its shallow bottom and slow tidal action, needed protection from nutrients and phosphates that had destroyed rivers and bays elsewhere. Her work, according to a local newspaper editorial, kept the bay from "turning into a sewage retention pond during the 1970s." It was estimated that in 1972 Tampa and St. Petersburg daily dumped twenty-eight tons of untreated sewage into the bay, but by 1980 Tampa had installed advanced wastewater treatment, and St. Petersburg not only became the first city in the state to give secondary treatment to all its sewage but was moving toward zero dumping in the bay—actions that helped bay recovery efforts and were forced by Grizzle's legislation. Fifteen years after her initial legislation, Grizzle helped enact a law requiring that treated wastewater be "almost clean enough to drink"—a victory for all Floridians. For her work on natural resource and women's issues, Grizzle was inducted in 2003 into the Florida Women's Hall of Fame, and a state office building in Largo was named for her.[14]

In many ways Grizzle had earlier women conservationists to thank for blazing the trail to her political success. Fifty years earlier Ruth Bryan Owen had forged new ground with her 1928 election to Congress and her subsequent championing of Everglades National Park. Owen firmly believed in the importance of women's political participation while also working within the socially acceptable image of women in the domestic sphere that was popular in the early part of the twentieth century. According to historian Sally Vickers, Owen "adroitly enlarged the domesticity to include politics" by arguing that "modern mothers have found that laws come into the home, that laws affect the lives of their children. It is a woman's duty to know the laws that touch her children." Women were not leaving home to enter into politics—it already was home as far as Owen was concerned. As Vickers notes, "this was bold rhetoric considering the general scorn for women and politics," but it did not stop Owen from becoming the state's first congresswoman—an accomplishment that required male and female votes.[15]

As a Republican, Grizzle likely was influenced by the recent spate of environmental advocacy by Republicans such as Governor Claude Kirk, environmental advisor Nathaniel Reed, and President Richard Nixon. As members of a rapidly growing minority party, these politicians embraced ecological causes, such as opposing the Cross Florida Barge Canal, to their political advantage, gaining a reputation as a "green" party—an image national Republicans would abandon hastily a decade later. For now, however, this was the party that harkened to Theodore Roosevelt, the country's greatest conservation president. Women such as Grizzle were continuing that tradition while also forging new legislative paths with their focus on natural resource issues. Grizzle's presence and agenda in Tallahassee signaled the end of long-held male views in which nature was sacrificed to the god of economics. Tampa Bay was a treasure to the entire public, deserving of care and governmental cleanup. The crisis was evident, the science was clear, and women were gaining political power and leadership to change environmental business as usual.

While Grizzle concentrated on cleaning up Tampa Bay, skirmishes over water quality raged in South Florida, involving large-scale projects proposed to cater to the growing populace. The first project was expansion at Turkey Point on southern Biscayne Bay of a power plant belonging to Florida Power and Light (FP&L). Ironically, FP&L proposed the site after it was denied expansion of another plant that officials feared would cause air pollution—a battle led by the Izaak Walton League and journalist Juanita Greene. Now opponents worried that the Turkey Point facility, with two oil-fired units and two proposed nuclear units, would affect the bay's water with its output of heated water from the plant cooling system. This wastewater, they warned, would damage or kill marine plants and animals in the shallow bay. With tempers running hot, Kirk asked the federal government for help, resulting in a February 1970 water pollution conference in Miami organized by the Water Pollution Control Administration (WCPA) of the U.S. Department of the Interior. The WCPA was familiar with Florida's water issues; the previous month, it had held a conference in Pensacola that resulted in several polluters being required to clean up discharge in the nearby Perdido River and Escambia Bay. The Interior Department filed suit to force FP&L to create a cooling system that avoided thermal discharges into the bay. In November 1970 another lawsuit was filed by an unexpected source—a female FP&L stockholder sued the company's top executives in an effort to stop the discharge. Abigail Starr Avery, of Lincoln, Massachusetts, contended that FP&L leaders violated state and federal laws in their attempt to dump heated discharge into Biscayne Bay and asked for $300 million in damages for their mismanagement. Avery, who described herself as a "small stockholder," assured the news media that her suit was "not a gesture." Emphasizing that she was a member of the Lincoln Board of Health and her husband was a member of the city's water commission, Avery said, "We're very much concerned, as almost everyone is now, about pollution problems." Ultimately the discharge issue was settled in 1971 in federal court, with all parties agreeing to FP&L's proposed closed-cycle cooling canal system. Today the power company touts the site as a wildlife boon that attracts sixty species of birds and animals, seventeen of which are endangered.[16]

Other environmental controversies erupted in South Florida during the same period, including the proposal to build a jetport in the Everglades and continuing water issues in the national park. Women—from teenagers to Marjory Stoneman Douglas, in her seventies—were integral to both efforts. Joe Browder, a television news reporter, was recruited onto the board of the Tropical Audubon Society in Miami by two of the area's strongest female environmentalists: Polly Redford and Alice Wainwright. They encouraged him to focus on the area's budding natural resource issues, and when the position came open, they endorsed his move to become a paid regional employee of National Audubon and primary organizer of the anti-jetport crusade. The outspoken Wainwright, the first woman elected to the city commission (in 1961) and later its vice mayor, had sponsored many city beautification ordinances and measures to ban dangerous pesticides. She had worked with Elizabeth Virrick on the Coconut Grove slum clearance campaign and had fought the Seadade project. Wainwright was inspired by an aesthetic sense to save her community, telling a group that "in the heart of each of us is a desire to create or preserve something of natural beauty for those who follow us."[17]

Browder also engaged younger workers in the cause. Charles Lee, now director of advocacy for the Florida Audubon Society, started working with Audubon as a teenager and found inspiration from its board, including Redford and Wainwright. Young women from the Everglades School for Girls also joined in, following in the footsteps of earlier women activists, particularly their role model, Douglas. Juliana Field, whose parents were good friends with Douglas, worked in the field with Lee, meeting with rural landowners, hunters, and local residents to find ways to engage the community. Joining them were two other Everglades School students, Lili Krech and December Duke, whose high school senior project was a study of the cooling-water discharge from the Turkey Point plant. Undertaking their research at the time the issue was being debated by authorities, the seniors found water temperatures in Biscayne Bay that were higher than set limits, and they documented dying turtle grass, an essential part of the estuary's biology. As part of her work, a school community service requirement, Duke used a survey to interview government officials about pollution problems in the area. She also followed up on concerns about sewage discharge with her own experiment—she flushed peanuts down a toilet at Miami City Hall and then watched with city officials as the peanuts appeared in the bay. Four years later the city and county created the Miami-Dade Water and Sewer Authority and later expanded a wastewater treatment facility by 50 percent. Duke and Krech inserted scientific facts into the controversy to bolster their views—an effective weapon in the arsenal of female environmental activism.[18]

To counter the jetport project, Duke and Krech, accompanied by another classmate, Mary Beth Norton, spent many weekends over a two-year period driving hundreds of people by jeep and minibus to the jetport site for a first-hand look at the project. They pointed out that the jetport was to be built on the sacred site of the Green Corn Dance, a ritual conducted by the Miccosukee Indians, which amounted to "an insult to the Indian culture." Duke, now December Duke McSherry, said it took them an hour to reach the spot—but once there, visitors were usually won over to their cause. She recalls: "We were neck-deep in alligator ponds." When Duke left for college in New York she carried on her activism there by demonstrating against Eastern Airlines, a jetport supporter, and gaining media attention to help build anti-jetport sentiment. Browder says the work of these teenagers, in combination with fishermen, working-class people, and members of some of the oldest families in the area— "every spectrum of Miami society"—added to the campaign's legitimacy.[19]

Two days after the inaugural Earth Day in 1970, an Associated Press article announced: "Florida Mounts Heavy Attack on Pollution." Author Ben Funk wrote that "as the 1970s arrived, Floridians woke up to the fact that the end of their cherished way of life could be near at hand." Funk documented recent environmental victories against FP&L at Turkey Point, the jetport, and the barge canal but added that the new state concern was pollution, highlighting degradation of bays in Tampa and Pensacola and health problems among Palm Beach residents exposed to water and air pollution. In response to these problems, a group of fifty-two people formed Conservation '70s, known as the C-70s, to lobby for environmental issues in Florida. Promoting a "get tough" policy, the group joined in what eventually became successful grassroots activism against the Everglades Jetport and the Cross Florida Barge Canal. The unique nature of the group was that half the members of its twenty-member board of trustees were elected officials and bureaucrats, giving C-70s savvy expertise in lawmaking. The downside was that some of its actions were neutralized by internal politics. Other members included the LWV, the FFWC, the Florida Audubon Society, and The Nature Conservancy. C-70s president Lyman Rogers described it as a "people's movement" with a unique structure that gave the state "a nonprofit Florida corporation conceived expressly for researching the need and developing a format for proper legislation and environmental protection funding." The banner period for the group was the 1970 legislative session, in which forty-one bills sponsored by the group were passed. Although most were minor, some bills had a big impact, including constitutional amendments that allowed sewer bonds to be issued; the banning of sales of submerged lands except in the public interest—a blow to dredge-and-fill efforts; the setting of coastal construction setback lines; and the creation of a Coastal Coordinating Council to create plans for coastal areas. Eventually C-70s "faded as a presence in Tallahassee" because of leadership problems, according to historian Luther

J. Carter, but "not before demonstrating that conservation could be a potent lobbying force."[20]

Florida's political embrace of environmentalism grew larger in 1971 with a new governor, Reubin Askew, who replaced the environmentally minded but quirky Kirk and ushered in a new era of serious concerns that sparked protective legislation. Noting the accomplishments of C-70s, Askew, in a May speech to the Izaak Walton League, said the state's top priority was to "reassess our existing governmental structure in the entire environmental field." The growth that made Florida the ninth largest state, with a population of 6.8 million people, also needed attention, Askew said, adding that "nothing short of ecological suicide would discourage people from settling in a state with the balmy climate and other natural assets which those of us already here take for granted." Two months later, speaking before an air and water conference in Miami, Askew talked about ecology, natural resource degradation, and restoration, noting that the conference was convened "to head off a catastrophe from which we may never recover." Askew continued: "We must do everything within our power to build a peace in South Florida, as well as in the rest of our great state—a peace between the people and their place, between the natural environment and the man-made settlement, between the creek and canal, between the air and the airplane—between the works and the life of mankind." The next year Askew included a sense of urgency in his address to the Florida legislature, noting that residents were consistently ahead of elected officials in efforts to protect the environment. He exhorted the state's political leaders to enact new protections, warning, "It is not melodramatic to say that Florida, like California, is in great danger of becoming a 'Paradise Lost.' It is not off-beat or alarmist to say that continued failure to control growth and development in this state will lead to economic as well as environmental disaster." Legislators heeded his advice, approving land and water management bills that attempted to put controls on state growth, mandating regional reviews of large projects, creation of water management districts, and the issuance of $200 million in state bonds to purchase "environmentally endangered lands" and $40 million for recreation lands. Voters overwhelmingly approved the bonds in November 1972.[21]

Askew's Florida Water Resources Act of 1972 opened the door to rethinking how to manage the state's water. The Florida Department of Natural Resources (DNR) was responsible for creating a statewide plan that would analyze water resources and then institute measures to protect their quality and quantity. The legislature created five water management districts to serve as regional bodies focused on regulating major state watersheds, particularly water basins, such as the Suwannee River, the St. Johns River, and the Everglades. It was a novel idea with a concept that followed nature's boundaries rather than those created by politicians. After four years of haggling, legislators finally set water district lines, and voters in 1976 approved a constitutional amendment granting the districts ad valorem tax powers. Now the districts, with appointed governing boards, were established and had funding for their projects. They became operational on January 1, 1977—and they provided new political opportunities for women.[22]

The water management boards were filled with political appointees, who included few female members—although any representation by women in state agencies was an improvement at this point. It was evidence that politicians (and voters) were recognizing the power of the female voice and vote and finding a place for it at the table. Although they were usually in the minority, women appointees to the water boards did create a break in the all-men's clubs that had long dominated state government. At the St. Johns River Water Management District (SJRWMD), only one woman served with fourteen men in the 1970s; a decade later two women served with fourteen men. In the 1990s there were six women board members with ten men. Though fewer in number, the women proved to be capable, important contributors to decisions about the state's water resources, often rising to top leadership positions that would have been unthinkable in earlier decades.[23]

Frances "Fran" Sharp Pignone was one of those early appointees, having ventured into environmentalism and politics through the League of Women Voters of Orange County (LWVOC). Having grown up in a rural, lakefront setting, Pignone never imagined the growth that would come to Central Florida during the 1970s in the wake of Walt Disney World and other theme park development. Her engagement in environmental issues evolved "sort of by chance," when a friend invited her to join the LWVOC in the 1960s. It was a "wonderful" group, she recalls, composed of educated women interested in everything from tax policy to textbooks. When visiting speakers came to address LWVOC functions, Pignone, who lived near the Orlando airport, would often be their driver. One was Bob Graham, a young legislator from Miami who was a leading proponent of the state's 1972 water laws. Pignone offered to help Graham if he ever ran for governor—and he did just that, winning election in 1978 with support from Pignone and her husband and friends. When he was looking for an appointee for the SJRWMD governing board, Graham sought Pignone's advice, eventually deciding that she was the right person for the job; she said she was chosen without any agenda from Graham.[24]

Pignone was one of two women appointed to the SJRWMD in late 1979; she served her term until 1987, chairing the group from 1981 to 1983. Pignone was in the minority, but she was a quick learner who steeped herself in facts to deal with the district's issues, which included pollution, water runoff, and limited water resources. One issue during Pignone's term was acquisition of major land tracts to protect and restore the natural landscape in order to sustain and protect water resources. The problem was that many projects involving riverine restoration were new, with no models to follow. To make land purchases, the district had to raise taxes—never a popular action and thus one that required political courage. She stated: "If it's important enough, you have to be willing to use the tools you have." One of her tools, perhaps better described as a talent, was Pignone's inclusiveness, her willingness to set up a process to inform and consult with everyone from legislators to scientists to staff to cattle ranchers in trying to achieve the board's land acquisition goals. She also stressed removing politics from the process, basing everything on "fair recompense" to landowners. Eventually the water management district acquired 200,000 acres that were crucial to restoration of the upper river, slowly gaining the public's support along the way, and Pignone developed a reputation as a "straight talker who isn't afraid to take a strong stand to protect our precious resources." Former *Orlando Sentinel* columnist Mike Thomas describes her as "very smart, a relentless digger and a strong public advocate. She understands the process. She doesn't work behind the scenes. She asks her questions for all to hear. She demands accountability." Pignone went on to serve on the Orange County Planning and Zoning Board, the Orange County Commission, and the East Central Florida Regional Planning Council, where she faced the increasing problems caused by Central Florida's rampant growth.[25]

Patricia Harden, a degreed biologist, brought lengthy environmental activism as well as her scientific knowledge to the SJRWMD, serving on the board from 1991 to 1999 and chairing it from 1993 to 1995. Having worked in environmental sciences for Walt Disney World, Harden understood state permitting processes, water quality issues, mitigation, and governmental lobbying. She also was active in trying to protect the spring-fed Wekiva River that flows through suburbanized Orange, Lake, and Seminole counties on its way to the St. Johns River. She came to the SJRWMD with a philosophy that worked for male and female sentiments: there was room for growth that did not destroy the state's natural resources.[26]

Harden was a charter member of Friends of the Wekiva River (FOWR), incorporated as a nonprofit in 1982 to seek protection for the fifteen-mile-long river. The group, composed partly of local Audubon members, was organized four years earlier out of concern about the river, the dumping ground for wastewater effluent from the city of Altamonte Springs. FOWR became a force with which to be reckoned when it came to development in the river's watershed and its tributaries. The group helped gather facts that led to the city of Altamonte Springs's Project APRICOT—A Prototype Realistic Innovative Community of Today—that took wastewater once discharged into the river system and instead recycled it for irrigation use.

FOWR also flexed its muscles by getting the Wekiva River designated as an Outstanding Florida Water (OFW) in 1983, gaining protection for land in the river basin, and pressing for planning and buffer rules in the area to protect the river. Harden, FOWR past president and board member, helped gather data for the nineteen-pound petition that led to the OFW designation, using her skills as an organizer as well as her technical knowledge to get other professionals involved. She helped assemble scientific support for the 1988 Wekiva River Protection Act, which set strict development guidelines in the river's watershed area. Facts, professionalism, teamwork, and pragmatism, she says, gave FOWR credibility and were key to its successes. "I think one of the important messages that we gave whenever we spoke in public was, 'We are not against growth. We understand the economy of growth. But we are for growth that protects the long-term quality of life. That there are ways to have growth that you don't have to destroy all the natural resources that we ultimately depend on.' And that was our message," she says.[27]

Florida women during the second half of the century also continued their drive for beautification, working largely through anti-litter campaigns. As historian Samuel P. Hays notes, the postwar era brought with it new consumer prosperity. An emphasis on "rapid product obsolescence" and a rise in packaging, Hays writes, made refuse disposal a growing problem. Women's groups that had long crusaded against abundant signs and roadside trash as part of the City Beautiful movement remained committed to the issue as the century aged. One of the leaders was Hilda Fox, who helped organize the Roadside Council of Pennsylvania in 1939 using the phrase "Don't Be A Litterbug," a slogan that quickly found its way into the public's conscience. In 1952, under Fox's leadership, the National Council of State Garden Clubs adopted the "Don't Be A Litterbug" campaign, which was enhanced by a drawing of a bug that had been used by the FFGC for a year. Sensing the rising public tide, companies that manufactured throwaway products "sought to place responsibility for action on the general public," Hays adds, and the result was Keep America Beautiful (KAB), a marketing program that urged Americans to put their trash in appropriate receptacles instead of along roadsides. The KAB was organized in 1953 and within a few years produced public service announcements to convince people to change their habits. The program got a huge boost in 1965 when Lady Bird Johnson, the wife of President Lyndon Johnson, joined in the effort and helped promote the Highway Beautification Act that same year. The Johnsons, who motored on many occasions between Texas and Washington, D.C., were dismayed by the junkyards and billboards that lined America's roads. Lady Bird Johnson wanted to end the visual blight and promoted replacing it with landscaping and wildflowers. In this effort she was joined by many groups, particularly garden clubs that embraced her message, and by her husband, who made it a legislative priority. The 1965 act, which attempted to regulate billboards and control visibility of junkyards, was considered by many to be a failure because of its compromises with the billboard industry. But Johnson considered it a victory for her beautification cause, and many women hailed her success.[28]

Although they often were overshadowed by other environmental groups during this era, garden clubs and women's groups in Florida were leaders in state efforts to control litter, creating anti-litter committees to conduct publicity campaigns about the issue. May Mann Jennings and another FFWC member served on the Florida State Chamber of Commerce Beautification Committee in 1955, promoting a program that placed trashcans at highway stops with the slogan "Don't Be A Litterbug." In 1972 the FFGC joined forces with the Florida Department of Transportation to combat litter—a problem that cost the state $1 million annually to address. They created Glenn Glitter, a flashy bug character that personified "Glitter Bug" to promote (and perhaps jazz up) the effort, entitled "Keep Florida Glitter Clean." Glenn's image was put on trash containers, and he was used for classroom education lessons. In a 1973 article in the *Camellia*, a publication for Pensacola area garden clubbers, Mary B. Williams emphasized that there was much work to be done to stop the visual blight caused by roadside trash. On a recent drive she had spotted beer cans, drink cans, whisky bottles, empty cartons, abandoned cars, and various abandoned appliances. "We Americans junk 48 billion cans every year, 18 billion bottles, 100 million tires and 20 million tons of papers," Williams wrote. "The physical mass—five or six pounds per person per day—amounts to enough blight [to cover] 1,700 square miles of land with a layer one foot deep." Williams said litter was costly to taxpayers and caused traffic accidents. "Think of litter as wasted resources and recycle it. Become a part of all recycle programs," she urged. "Litter control is suited to do-it-yourself action." Askew, who grew up in Pensacola, likely had seen the same ills. In a 1971 speech to a Keep Florida Beautiful group in Tallahassee, the governor said cleanup efforts were essential to attract tourism, and trash dumping could no longer be tolerated. "'Keep America Beautiful' no longer is the motherhood slogan it once might have been. It now says something very uncomfortable to those who've been willing to dirty the public's nest while feathering their own." Askew also promoted recycling, saying it was "not a corporate frill. . . . It is a public responsibility." In the coming decades various groups promoted recycling, among them women's clubs, garden clubs, and the LWV.[29]

No group personified the struggle against pollution in Florida better than ManaSota-88, led for three decades by the tenacious Gloria Cann Rains of Palmetto. Formed in 1966 as part of a two-year health study by federal and state health services, Florida State University, the University of Florida, and the Manatee and Sarasota county commissions, ManaSota-88 was one of fourteen projects around the country designed to assess problems associated with growth and address them before they overwhelmed local resources. From the study evolved the nonprofit of the same name, the goal of which was to preserve the health of the environment and welfare of local people—with a 1988 deadline for success. Members came from a variety of backgrounds. When 1988 arrived they decided they had not accomplished their goal, and they continued the organization, which still exists today. At the helm for the first thirty years was Rains, who came to Florida for a sunny, waterfront retirement and instead found a passionate calling that consumed the rest of her life.[30]

Rains and her husband John, who had retired from the U.S. Air Force, moved to a waterfront home on the southern end of Tampa Bay in 1969. For several years, Rains recalled, they "did all the traditional things that people do when they come to Florida," including boating, which gave them a deep love for the area. "And after three or four years of that, it's sort of like too many desserts— you have to do something productive," she said in a 1990 interview. "And then I think you have to have—and I think most people do—a commitment to sort of justify, to put something back into the life you had so much from." When an offshore oil off-loading platform was proposed near Port Manatee, seven miles from their home, the couple's interest was roused. It would be a multi-year conflict that involved a referendum and administrative hearings before a lack of profitability ended the proposal. John Rains used his talents as a leader in the Manatee County chapter of the Izaak Walton League; Gloria Rains got involved with ManaSota-88, becoming its chair in 1977 and leading efforts that reached into a number of pollution-related topics in the region. Even though she was unpaid, Rains put in twelve-hour days, writing lengthy monthly news-letters, loading file cabinets with reports and data, educating herself on some very technical issues, and recruiting others to the cause. By 1988 the group, like the Wekiva River protectors, obtained OFW designations to protect Sarasota, Lemon, and Terra Ceia bays; helped get part of the Myakka River designated as a Wild and Scenic River; worked to preserve wetlands; and forced the reloca-tion of an offshore site for dumping contaminated sediments. Most often, the group found itself in disputes of a David-versus-Goliath nature with the pow-erful phosphate industry and with electric utilities, arguing that their ongoing or proposed practices would pollute area air, water, and land. ManaSota-88 faced off against the U.S. Environmental Protection Agency (EPA) and the Florida Department of Environmental Regulation (DER) to press for tougher enforcement of existing laws and rules, often threatening to file lawsuits. The group made good on many of those threats in court, appealed to federal and state agencies, lobbied government bodies, and appeared in news media to get their science-backed positions heard. And while many members, male and female, participated in the fact gathering and protesting, Rains was their pas-sionate, fearless leader.[31]

In a 1988 fundraising letter, Rains said the 2,500-member group could not "afford to relent. In fact, the job of protecting the environment is even greater than it was 20 years ago." With a state population that increased by 800 people daily, Rains wrote, "comes the need for more support services and increased stress on our water supply, our wetlands, our fisheries, our air quality and out lands." She added: "ManaSota-88 efforts prove that a relative few people with limited resources, up against powerful and well-financed opposition, can still make a difference." Rains had little praise for large environmental groups or politicians—she thought they were too willing to amend their positions. "The way we look at this thing—when you go into an environmental issue you don't go in to compromise. You go in to fight for what you know is right because you know that the legislators or the department heads or whoever is going to compromise," she said. "You go in with the strongest position that you have with the best evidence you have and you stick to it, you don't compromise." Given this stance and despite her diminutive size, Rains was a huge figure in natural resource issues, often characterized as being extremist, with a "pit-bull quality" criticized by her opponents. That characterization might have been a compliment for a male activist; in later life, it would be one for Rains. An advocate of the philosophy that "any person can make a difference," Rains was lauded upon her death in 2000 as a person who did just that. "A lot of people will never know what a difference this woman made to their quality of life here through her efforts these past 30 years against the phosphate industry, water and air polluters and overdevelopment," wrote Bruce Pitzer, who served as ManaSota-88 treasurer for ten years. "She is truly irreplaceable."[32]

In Grizzle, Pignone, Harden, and Rains, Florida women had new models for environmental activism. No longer were women reliant on their club connections and spouses to get legislation approved for important issues. Gone was the sometimes solicitous, soft voice that many had employed in the past to keep from offending the male power structure. The days of "polite wording" in petitions were finished. Driven by deeply felt concerns about the health of their communities and families, women stepped to the forefront of clashes involving pollution. They eschewed the long-held (and masculine) voice of commerce that said pollution was simply the price of a strong economy, and in doing so they prodded government bodies and agencies to take action. From the legislature to bureaucratic boards to advocacy groups, they worked shoulder to shoulder with their male counterparts, using their talents in many ways, from writing to rallying the public to organizing symposiums and researching topics. And they more often took up the reins of organizations, guiding them into the future. In the final decades of the century, women increasingly became important leaders in Florida's environmental movement, not only heading organizations but also running new bureaucratic agencies and winning elected office in order to improve the state's natural resources. The men had made a real mess of things. Now it was up to women to make a difference.

8

Endangered Species and Lands

As the boat roared down the Ft. Lauderdale waterway, Judith Delaney Vallee felt her blood rise. How could boats be allowed to travel so recklessly when there were slow-moving, endangered manatees just below the water's surface? The marine mammals were "practically being mowed down by speeding boats" in an area that had no warning signs or speed limits to prevent deadly collisions, she recalled. Something had to be done.[1]

Like a good citizen, Vallee reported her observations to the Florida Marine Patrol, only to be told the agency was unable to respond. She "was just incensed" and determined to act. She visited neighbors, gathering signatures on a petition to the mayor that called for making a section of the Middle River a manatee sanctuary, which would mandate lower boat speeds. Like all effective female activists before her, she was persistent, contacting anyone who might help in hopes of gaining governmental cooperation. After all, the creatures had been protected for a decade by the 1973 federal Endangered Species Act (ESA), which mandated strict protections for plants and animals on the brink of extinction. The law embodied the realization that many American species, such as the Carolina parakeet (gone in 1918) and the Caribbean monk seal (last seen in 1952), both Florida denizens, could easily disappear without legal safeguards. ESA put the well-being of biota above the development and industry that often threatened it, mandating governmental cooperation and participation.[2]

But Vallee did not get help from city leaders, who rudely dismissed her pleas. At a marine council meeting one male member advised that she did not need a city ordinance. Instead, he suggested, the next time Vallee saw a fast-moving boat, she should throw a tomato at it. The insulting remark left Vallee "flabbergasted" and resolute. And that, in the long run, was a good thing for Florida's manatees.[3]

During the last decades of the twentieth century, as the state's population boomed beyond anyone's wildest predictions, Florida women such as Vallee were critical players in efforts to protect the state's endangered species and lands. Working alone, with advocacy groups, or with attorneys who pressed their causes in court, environmentally minded women helped slow boats in manatee zones, end traffic on sea turtle nesting beaches, stop large dredge-and-fill projects in estuaries, and preserve unique natural areas. They fought development in a pro-growth era in order to protect Florida's precious ecological assets, using tactics long employed by female activists in new and creative ways. Although many faced ridicule and sexism along the way, they never lost sight of their mission to save Florida. And the state is a better place today because of it.

Bright and resourceful, Vallee vented her frustration by volunteering with the Broward County Audubon Society, and in 1985 she went to work as administrator for the Save the Manatee Committee, an organization set up in Maitland under the umbrella of the Florida Audubon Society (FAS). Vallee had a degree in art history and had never run an association, but she quickly learned on the job, answering telephones, making public appearances, helping people "adopt" manatees through donations directed at specific animals, and aiding lobbying efforts in Tallahassee. One day FAS lobbyist Charles Lee suggested that Vallee ask the legislature to approve a special state automobile license tag for manatees that would help fund her cause. The resulting "Save the Manatee" license plate became a hit; in a move she would later rue, Vallee agreed to direct all proceeds not to her organization but to manatee research and education programs. From 1990 to 2007 license plates netted $34 million for manatees, placing them clearly among the state's most beloved creatures. Since then, a number of other troubled Florida species have been highlighted on license plates to gain revenues, including sea turtles and the critically endangered Florida panther.[4]

The Save the Manatee Club, which included male and female leaders, split from FAS in 1993, and Vallee became executive director of the nonprofit body; in 2006 she served as its development director. The group's marketing results were astounding—in 1982 some 75 percent of Americans did not know what a manatee was; by 1990 the club had more than 23,000 members from countries around the world, a number that grew to 40,000 by 2010. It made the manatee an icon for endangered species and gained the special attention and affection of everyone from governors to popular musician Jimmy Buffett, who helped found the organization and came up with the superb marketing ploy of having people "adopt" individual creatures through financial donations. However, the animals remained in trouble, mostly from human causes such as boating collisions—the very thing that first inspired Vallee's activism. Unquestionably, her leadership was integral in the vast makeover of the manatee's public persona and the development of a strong grassroots base. Her philosophy was to appeal not to an elite environmental audience but to the uninformed general public. "We have to reach the people who don't know. We have to tell the people who don't know so that they can change and help be the part of the solution." What propelled her through so many years? "It was sort of like a calling—you know, not by any religious entity or anything—but I can't imagine having done anything else. I think I was very lucky because I found something that absolutely just gripped me to the very core of my being and I don't think very many people have that in their lives."[5]

With a population of 15.9 million people by the year 2000, Florida's boom took a great toll on its resources. The state's varied climes and unique biota, some of it found nowhere else in the world, made it an Eden in many people's eyes, but the ongoing and seemingly inevitable collision with development put many of these natural wonders at risk. Florida ranked as one of the states with the most endangered species; its own list of endangered, threatened, and commercially exploited species exceeded five hundred plants and animals. Myriad pressures from habitat loss and degradation, over-collecting, and invasive nonnative plants and animals (think Australian pines, Brazilian pepper, pythons, and lionfish) imperiled a number of native species in the richly biodiverse peninsula.[6]

While Vallee worked to save manatees, other women devoted their energies to the protection of sea turtles that dwell throughout the Caribbean and Gulf of Mexico, many using Florida beaches for nesting areas. Although their exact numbers were difficult to determine, by the early 1960s it was clear that every variety of sea turtle was endangered from overharvesting of turtle meat, eggs, oil, and shells. Loggerhead turtles, which customarily lay eggs in thousands of nests on Florida's east coast beaches, were on the decline, in part from loss of nesting beaches and from being caught in fishing nets and on fishing lines. Other problems ensued when turtle hatchlings, reliant on moonlight to reach the ocean, died when they errantly traveled toward lights in beachfront developments and along roads—or into the paths of cars that drove on several beaches. Seeking a way to make a difference, Shirley Reynolds and Rita Alexander of New Smyrna Beach began marking turtle nests for protection and monitoring hatchings. They camped on the beach to keep cars from driving over nests and lobbied Volusia County for increased turtle protection. By 1995 they decided that the best solution was through the courts, and they sued the county, claiming that nighttime beach driving and lights from shoreline developments hurt the ESA-protected creatures. Many residents discounted the lawsuit until a federal judge ruled in the women's and the turtles' favor, forcing the county to enact protective measures.[7]

Depending on one's point of view and beach-going habits, Reynolds and Alexander were either heroes or villains. One person called Reynolds "the most-hated person in Volusia County." The women were accused of trying to end all beach driving, the best access most people had to the shore. It was, after all, one of the tourist selling points of Daytona Beach, and stopping it, some argued, would hurt the area's economy—a common business response to environmental issues. But these women believed turtles deserved higher consideration. By suing under the ESA, the women found a legal route to force governmental action, leaving sea turtles as well as other coastal creatures in that section of Florida safer from human encroachment. Reynolds told a local newspaper that turtle protection "has a domino effect on everything. The byproduct is endless. It's a wonderful, fabulous ecosystem if it's just allowed to function as such."[8]

Reynolds and Alexander had learned, as did Marjorie Harris Carr with the Cross Florida Barge Canal battle, that lawsuits could forge change. Women had found another path to changing business as usual, another step in the evolution of the environmental movement, which now included the creation of single-focus groups like Save the Manatee. Lawsuits also benefited women in other ways. As historian Margaret Rossiter documents, in the last three decades of the century, many women scientists and government workers used the legal system to seek equal employment treatment and opportunities, opening new paths for their gender.[9]

Nowhere were growth and its attendant problems more apparent than along the state's 2,000 miles of tidal shoreline, which includes 650 miles of coastal beaches and the perimeters of 4,500 islands. As historian Gary Mormino notes, the "most recurring image of Florida is that of a beach." Postcards, advertising, and media made this the most enduring American vision of the state—and the image of what new residents wanted to possess. Although no spot on the peninsula was more than sixty miles from the coast, the ultimate Florida dream was waterfront living; coastal counties added 10 million new residents between 1950 and 2000. As a result of beachfront and waterfront development, citizens began losing access to their favorite recreational sites, watching as pollution eroded and endangered the state's waters, with no end to growth in sight. Despite politics and hurricanes, Mormino notes, "Nothing, it seems, can keep the world from wanting to live and play on Florida's beaches." In loving their beaches, Floridians and the tourists they worked hard to lure also were destroying the beaches. Saving or preserving beaches, however, was not as easy a task as creating a city park and often meant conflict with prevailing economic interests that saw major profits in shoreline development. Once again, a Florida woman was willing to step into the fray.[10]

Doris Leeper fell in love with the southern Volusia County Atlantic coast during a 1958 summer fishing trip and bought a wooden two-story home located on a barrier island in the small community of Eldora. In 1960 she moved from Atlanta to the waterfront site, an inspirational setting that Leeper, an accomplished artist and sculptor, spent the next seventeen years fighting to save. She could do so because she was a successful career woman in a field that provided self-sufficiency and encouraged unfettered thinking. Leeper had long been concerned that island visitors were tearing up fragile dunes with their cars to gain access to the beach. Here she fought against tradition—cars had been driving, even racing, on Volusia County beaches since the beginning of the century. When Leeper asked for dune protections and legal enforcement, she butted heads with fishermen and the local male sheriff. In an unpublished autobiography coauthored with James J. Murphy, Leeper recalled, "My outspokenness stirred quite a bit of controversy" among those who claimed their only access was through the dunes. Although she began receiving hate calls, Leeper persevered, campaigning for a ban on cars on the beach and dunes and working to gain federal protections for the area. Leeper, known as "Doc" from her early medical education, formed Friends of the Canaveral National Seashore, a bi-gender citizens' group, to help guide the effort that in 1975 saw the establishment of the twenty-four-mile national seashore. Congressman Lou Frey recalled that Leeper convinced him of the need for the designation, adding that she "was a conservationist before it was the 'in' thing to be." Leeper quickly learned that a federal designation was not the end of the battle; a lack of enforcement of no-driving rules soon escalated her war with the sheriff, and she sparred with federal park officials about road projects on the property.[11]

Largely due to Leeper's determination, the Canaveral National Seashore became one of the jewels of Florida's east coast and has remained home to twenty federally protected endangered species—the ninth highest among the 394 properties owned by the U.S. National Park Service. Extensive media coverage notwithstanding, the seashore's own website history four decades later failed to mention Leeper, instead crediting congressmen, county commissioners, and local chambers of commerce. Clay Henderson, an environmental attorney who worked with Leeper and describes her as "a driving force behind establishment of the park," says her omission is the result of her detractors working to "rewrite history." Henderson remembers that the "local business community and political establishment saw her as an uncompromising zealot while a growing community of educators, artists, and environmentalists spoke of her with great pride." For the next two decades Leeper fought for protection of the seashore and other areas. She formed the Friends of Spruce Creek to lobby for state purchase and preservation of a fragile 2,500-acre Volusia County tract that was posthumously renamed in her honor. At the same time Leeper helped found the Atlantic Center for the Arts in New Smyrna Beach, was named Florida Ambassador for the Arts, and was included in the Florida Artists Hall of Fame. When she died in 2000 Leeper was remembered as talented, persuasive, and visionary. "She was a big thinker and attracted smart, well-educated people and attracted money to finance those big ideas," Henderson recalls. "As we say to this day, we didn't know whether it was really a good idea or not, we just knew it was impossible to say no to Doc!"[12]

Like Leeper, Diane Dunmire Barile did not like to be told "no," but unlike her, Barile ran into a series of barriers in her efforts to protect the Indian River Lagoon (IRL) on Florida's east coast. Barile never intended to become an environmental activist—like Leeper, her original life plan was to go to medical school. But that was a difficult major for a woman in the sexist 1950s, so Barile changed her major to biology at the University of Florida, where she took some of the earliest classes in ecology, still considered a "weird" topic in those days. A series of life events intervened in Barile's plans, and by the early 1970s she was a married mother of three, living in Palm Bay near the lagoon. It was a role familiar to previous generations of Florida women, except that Barile had too much education, curiosity, and opportunity afforded by rising female prospects to stay within the realm of the home. To "keep my mind," Barile took courses at the nearby Florida Institute of Technology (FIT).[13]

One day she heard an address by Dr. Howard Odum, the famed University of Florida ecosystems ecologist. Barile told him about a project that troubled her: a proposed lock and dam planned by the General Development Corporation (GDC) on nearby Turkey Creek. GDC claimed that building the dam and diverting fresh water from the St. Johns River watershed into the IRL would improve fishing in the lagoon. Barile, with her scientific training, did not think it made sense—and neither did Odum. They devised a plan whereby Barile would study the project, gather data about the area, and work with Odum to earn her master's degree at FIT. Unlike many women before her in the sciences,

Barile had a responsive, encouraging male mentor to guide her through a new approach to the natural world. And it paid off.[14]

After much painstaking research, Barile revealed in her 316-page master's thesis that the project was a boondoggle proposed by GDC on vast landholdings in order to justify digging an elaborate canal system. With lots fronting on canals, GDC could claim that they were "waterfront" property, despite the fact that it would take boaters hours to reach navigable ocean waters. There would not be more fish but instead damage to the IRL estuary, along with a sprawling housing development and potential damage to the water supply. GDC—which may have discounted Barile initially because she was young, attractive, and female—was not happy. The corporation attacked Barile's findings, threatened to sue her, and tried to get her fired from her job with the city. Instead, GDC found itself facing opposition from various agencies and was forced to modify its plans, giving some of the land in one of Barile's beloved places to the local Audubon society for a park. "It's my favorite spot," she said. "I always thought that everybody is put here for a purpose and that that park was my purpose. And once I got that done I could just live a life but it just didn't work that way." Life had bigger plans for Barile.[15]

Just as biological studies had informed Carr, Barile's training taught her the importance of the 140-mile-long IRL and made her keenly aware of the impact of nearby development and drainage. In 1985, while teaching at FIT, she became executive director of the nonprofit Marine Resources Council (MRC), created by a group of concerned scientists, environmentalists, fishermen, and leaders in government and business. One of the group's greatest accomplishments was the 1989 designation of the IRL as an Estuary of National Significance, a federal act that provided millions of dollars in funding for research and protection of the waterway. Through the MRC and Barile's leadership, local government reduced sewage dumping and runoff pollution, and local residents and political leaders learned to love the IRL, once thought of, she said, as "something you crossed on the way to the beach." Still, troubles at the IRL were great: 1989 studies showed a 30 percent loss in seagrass beds and an 80 percent loss of mangrove swamps that act as filters for the area. Ironically, one of the areas threatened by nearby development in the IRL was the Pelican Island National Wildlife Refuge, the nation's first wildlife refuge. Perhaps channeling Frances Latham, who taught scientists about the pelicans and their roosting areas, Barile warned about the importance of the refuge and the potential damage incurred by developments such as golf courses, polo grounds, and resorts that were proposed over the years. Although she preferred to be thought of as a scientist, she was aware that she would be pegged forever as an environmental activist. Her work went beyond the academic, beyond writing a paper and putting it on a shelf, because she could not simply stand by when faced with the facts she gathered: "I wanted to see something happen."[16]

Like others of her generation, Barile located her activism within a local group with male and female members and focused on a specific region and problem. Many other women in this time period did the same, often as founders of groups that worked to save imperiled landscapes. Dagny Johnson helped organize the Upper Keys Citizens Association in the 1970s to monitor growth in the northern Florida Keys, particularly in Key Largo. The group supported preservation of land and wildlife and opposed a massive development project called Port Bougainville, which was halted after news media exposed a scandal at the site. Instead, the property was preserved in 1982 as the Dagny Johnson Key Largo Hammock Botanical State Park in recognition of her work to protect land that was home to a variety of endangered species, including the American crocodile, the Schaus swallowtail butterfly, and the Key Largo woodrat. Farther south in the Keys, DeeVon Quirolo helped found the grassroots Reef Relief organization in 1987 to support research and educate the public about the area's fragile and arguably endangered coral reefs. Quirolo, a lawyer, worked with her husband, Craig, in establishing the group, which focused on reef damage caused by grounded boats, overfishing, and phosphate pollution.[17]

Mary Barley came to love the Florida Keys and the adjacent Everglades during holidays spent there with her husband, George. After massive algae blooms hit Florida Bay in the 1980s and 1990s, leaving the watery expanse behind their vacation home looking like pea soup, the wealthy couple investigated the causes and came to the realization that the health of their aquatic backyard reflected that of the entire Everglades ecosystem. It could not be resolved in a piecemeal fashion, and it needed comprehensive solutions that reached all the way from the Kissimmee River system in the north through Lake Okeechobee to the national park. George decided to devote all his energy to the Everglades, turning over the daily operations of the couple's Orlando development company to his wife. Then, in an unexpected tragedy, he died in a 1995 airplane crash. After gathering with a group of friends and Everglades proponents, Barley took up her husband's cause, chairing the Everglades Foundation that he founded and leading political campaigns aimed at cleaning up the system. It was a tribute to her beloved husband but also the culmination of her talent and skills. She approached her full-time cause using facts, hard-earned political savvy, and indefatigable fervor. Her sustenance: "The Everglades. It's a place worth saving."[18]

Barley became equally comfortable describing the biodiversity of the Everglades, the political ups and downs of her work, and her distaste for the sugar industry, which she believed profited in multiple ways from its pollution and abuse of the state's ecological and political systems. "I have as much animosity towards them as I [have passion] about saving the Everglades," she says. "Sometimes if I get really tired I say, 'You know what, they're not going to win. I'm not going to allow them to win.'" She was a worthy opponent, and one her foes could not ignore. Barley hated politics "with a passion." But she knew that the Everglades and its restoration relied heavily on state and federal political maneuvering, so she stayed involved, supporting the related Everglades Trust that placed lobbyists in Tallahassee and Washington, D.C. She also found comfort in knowing that for every dollar Everglades supporters spent, opponents had to spend "ten to one hundred times more. . . . Because we are in the right and they are in the wrong. And so to convince somebody you have to spend a lot of money to take right to wrong." Although she used science in her crusade for the Everglades, Barley also used her business expertise, employing projections showing how the wetland system provided jobs and supported commercial business. "You have to play in the political field that you are given and right now it's an economic field." Barley may have been an unintentional environmental activist, but like many women before her, once she engaged in an issue, she used facts and dogged determination to oppose business, lobbyists, and governments—all male bastions.[19]

Like Barley, Helen Digges Spivey became an activist after witnessing troubles in her very backyard. In 1970 she and her husband retired to a home that fronted on a creek leading into spring-fed Crystal River, a major winter refuge for endangered manatees. She tracked and reported manatee sightings, but soon her attention was drawn to issues related to the health of the river, particularly herbicides that were sprayed to control plant species, and nutrient overload from sewage effluent. Believing that "you just can't let something as beautiful as Crystal River die," Spivey channeled her anger over poor environmental practices into learning about how to stop them. She talked to experts, learned to evaluate technical documents, and collected information about the issues, using her findings to raise public awareness and force governmental action. While serving two terms in the 1980s on the Crystal River City Council, Spivey fought to stop the city sewer plant from dumping treated nutrient-rich effluent into her canal, from which it entered the river and caused heavy algae growth. She made the issue visible by displaying a gallon jar filled with dirty, dark green river algae and assorted bugs at her council desk during meetings.[20]

Some audience members "couldn't keep their eyes off of it and the scary critters wandering around [in it]. It was like the elephant in the room," she recalls. Later the city began spraying the discharge on an inland field. Spivey also carried the jar to a Tallahassee meeting of the governor and cabinet to support her request to stop a city from dumping sewage effluent into an adjacent spring run. "That's where I met now [U.S.] Senator Bill Nelson, who was a Cabinet member. We've been friends since then. He said I was unforgettable with my jar."[21]

Spivey was often labeled a "radical environmentalist"—a tagline with which she disagrees: "Just loving nature shouldn't make you a radical." After she was defeated in 1996 in her reelection bid for the legislature, Spivey rechanneled her activism to advocate for manatee protection (with Save the Manatee Club), for animal abuse prevention, and against riverfront development; in 2010 she helped get the fragile Three Sisters Springs property, a critical manatee habitat, included in the Crystal River National Wildlife Refuge, resulting in a number of awards and citations. In May 2011 U.S. Representative Debbie Wasserman Schultz, who served with Spivey in the legislature, announced that Spivey, dubbed the "Manatee Lady," had received the U.S. Fish and Wildlife Service's 2010 Regional Director's Conservation Award. She described Spivey as "an iconic leader in the protection of Florida's special ecosystems."[22]

Florida's environmental women were aided in their campaigns by a rising and changing tide of public opinion in the latter part of the century. Many had come to see natural resource destruction and degradation as a central issue and now used ecology as a household world. A sign of this new awareness was the nation's first Earth Day celebration, held on April 22, 1970. What was initially expected to be an education-based event grew into a grassroots celebration involving 20 million people—and one that continued to be annually celebrated. Florida found its own way to celebrate Earth Day, notably in the Dead Orange Parade in Miami that mimicked the annual King Orange Parade, a popular event that annually preceded the city's Orange Bowl, a college football event and tourist mecca. A number of floats illustrated poor environmental conditions, but perhaps the most telling participants were the stroller-pushing mothers who led the parade, "declaring the pollution of adults to be the debt of children." An eleven-year-old girl held a sign asking: "Biscayne Bay: When we grow up will it be a sea of fun or a sea of filth?" The maternalistic and symbolic message of community and personal health offered by the protesting mothers was clear, a continuation of the long female struggle to clean up the ecological mess of men in favor of their children's future. The women's demonstration at the public event also portended a future in which leaders would be well aware of the toll of business and industry on the natural world.[23]

Earth Day, writes historian Adam Rome, offered many "well-educated housewives" a "chance to break out of their routine. Though they were not ready to seek jobs outside the home, they had skills that they didn't use raising kids and doing laundry, and Earth Day offered especially satisfying volunteer work." Although environmental work was "exciting and challenging," he writes, women "could justify their commitment in traditional terms: They did not want their children to inherit a polluted world."[24]

In response to a growing public demand spurred in part by environmental crises, Congress had implemented groundbreaking laws and policies, many of them based on ecological principles. The Clean Air Act (1963) and Water Quality Control Act (1965) addressed pollution issues, while the Wilderness Act (1964) and the Wild and Scenic Rivers Act (1968) attempted to preserve wild lands and free-flowing rivers. Ecology literally became the law of the land with the National Environmental Policy Act (NEPA), which was passed in 1969. It required that federal agencies consider the environmental impact of any proposed actions. To enforce the new laws, the act created the federal Environmental Protection Agency (EPA), which consolidated various pollution-related programs. Next came the Clean Air Act of 1970, which named 189 pollutants and set standards to regulate their emission into the atmosphere. The Clean Water Act of 1972 also regulated pollutants, this time those going into waterways, while mandating rules for restoration with the ultimate goal of no discharge of pollutants. A series of other laws followed, addressing topics such as pesticides, hazardous wastes, and ocean dumping, leading many to dub the 1970s the Green Decade.[25]

Although the complexion of this movement was changing, some of the Florida's stalwart women's groups, including the Florida Federation of Women's Clubs (FFWC) and Florida Federation of Garden Clubs (FFGC), continued advocating for the cause and leading education efforts associated with it. These traditional women's groups and their national associations had to adjust their attitudes and projects to adapt to new scientific knowledge and ecological thinking that were permeating the country. The National Council of State Garden Clubs, which had promoted the concept of "conservation as love of nature and support for vitally important projects for protection of local or area endangered resources," now emphasized "environmentalism and ecology," according to historian Eleanor R. Crosby. This new consciousness arose from garden clubbers' recognition of the natural resource depletion caused by "two world wars, population increase, spreading urbanization and earlier western migrations." At the same time the nature of environmental groups was evolving to its more modern manifestation, albeit too slowly for some groups that organized quickly to address specific problems found in their members' backyards. Liberated by gaining the vote and with rising demands for equality—developed in part from their labor in World War II efforts—many women refused to be relegated to separate spheres and took their talents and energies, once expended in garden and women's clubs, into other organizations that included both men and women. The FFWC and the FFGC still asked members to fund efforts and write letters, but the real power moved to single-issue grassroots organizational efforts in which members regularly attended governmental hearings, demanded action from elected officials, and, if ignored, pursued relief in the courts.[26]

One all-female organization, the Junior League, often regarded as an exclusive social group in many communities, flexed its environmental muscles in several Florida communities during this period, taking on the male establishment. In 1970 the Junior League of Miami (JLM) developed the Miami River Restoration Project to help improve a once beautiful waterway that had become "grossly polluted and used as the graveyard of numerous derelict hulks." Janice Pryor, chair of the group's Community Arts Committee, recalled that when the Junior League presented the concept to different community and civic leaders, "their attitude toward us was very cavalier . . . they thought of it as a pipe dream." That disregard increased the group's determination. Members surveyed the river, climbed embankments, worked around debris (and local homeless people), and compiled information about property owners, zoning, river conditions, and ordinances affecting the river. League member Susan Revello writes that two league members "attended a course in pollution control at Miami Dade Junior College" in preparation for the project. She noted that "before environmentalism was a widely embraced 'cause' the JLM vigorously pursued efforts to reclaim the Miami River from the jaws of its polluters." The group generated publicity about the river and monitored government agencies, winning an award for inspiring revitalization of the city's waterfront. Members became leaders in river efforts, giving the organization a new persona in the community.[27]

The Junior League of Sarasota (JLS) also jumped into environmental issues in the 1990s with an effort to ban pesticide use on athletic fields and playgrounds in the county in order to protect children from cancer-causing chemicals. The JLS joined forces with the Manatee-Sarasota Sierra Club and the Pesticide Education Center in San Francisco, California, to create the Coalition to Stop Children's Exposure to Pesticides, gathering more than a thousand signatures on a petition to the county. In 1989 the JLS supported state legislation that required notification of chemical spraying in an effort to protect the public health. Once again a women's social group was moved to action when it came to protecting natural resources that affected family and community health.[28]

Florida women were also at the forefront of a ground shift in thought about and treatment of wetlands and estuaries, some of the state's most maligned and ignored landscapes. Since statehood, leaders had dreamed of ridding the state of its vast swamps through drainage schemes aimed at creating arable land, an "improvement" for human use under the old conservation model. Government agencies also had endorsed creating new, expensive, and taxable waterfront properties through dredge-and-fill operations that aimed to turn bay bottoms into housing subdivisions. This attitude was common across the United States; through the nation's history it had been standard practice, indeed good commerce, to fill in what were considered to be wastelands. But by the 1950s Americans were rethinking such practices and coming to place great value on coastal lands and estuary systems. Historian Joseph V. Siry observes that in "place of Progressive definitions of conservation, in the postwar period, at both grass-roots and bureaucratic levels, an ecocentric understanding evolved, which viewed wise use (conservation) and protection (preservation) as mutually supportive." Preservationists and conservationists now forged a "new conservation" with innovative federal legislation. As demand for more coastal development increased—an estimated 53 percent of the U.S. population is on the coastline—new conflicts arose about the proper use of these areas.[29]

In 1959 debates erupted in the San Francisco area after the U.S. Army Corps of Engineers produced a pamphlet that promoted filling 248 of the 435 square miles of wetlands in the Bay Area by the year 2000. In place of wetlands, newly created land would be used for housing, industry, and transportation. At the same time a nuclear power plant was proposed on the coastline fifty miles to the north. "While these proposals appeared necessary for the future growth and prosperity of the greater bay region," Siry writes, "subsequent events, the callous disregard of public sentiments by a few corporate officials, and an alliance of local preservationist groups upset the plans." Several grassroots alliances formed to contest the projects, and they were joined by national organizations, including the Sierra Club and the League of Women Voters. Save the San Francisco Bay Association, led by faculty wives from the University of

California, was one of the strongest citizen groups. It stressed aesthetic values of the landscape and swelled in membership by 1965 to nearly nine thousand people. The groups demanded legislation, dredge moratoriums, and oversight committees to address the issues.[30]

Controversies also flared up in New York, particularly the Long Island area, where growth, wetland destruction, and the use of the pesticide DDT to control mosquitoes aroused public attention. Citizens who had escaped the environmental mistakes of New York City, where thirty-four square miles of tidal marshlands had been destroyed, did not want the same mistakes repeated. By 1967 Long Island had lost 29 percent of its coastal wetlands in a ten-year period, with 88 percent of the remainder "vulnerable to destruction," wrote Polly Redford, a Miami Audubon leader, activist, and journalist of the period. She criticized attitudes and actions throughout the nation that were killing tidelands: "We Americans go right on treating our tidelands as sewers and garbage dumps," she wrote. "Whenever possible we drain them, dredge them, and fill them with rubble and rubbish which we then call improvements and enter on our tax rolls." Problems in Long Island, she added, were "just as true of Boston, Norfolk, Miami, Tampa, Mobile, Houston, or San Francisco," where dredge-and-fill projects "not only destroyed the marshes but dropped the bay bottom thirty feet in places, too low for light to reach marine plants."[31]

When disputes arose, women were often at the forefront of ecological thinking and action, working in concert with men and often with traditional female groups. In 1962 Dr. Walter Boardman, executive director of The Nature Conservancy, lauded the environmental activism of female garden club members, citing their support for efforts to save lands once thought to be undesirable:

When it is proposed for instance that a swamp should be drained, it is the garden club people who best understand the importance of what is to many "waste land." They see the future significance if another vital resource is lost forever. The vital complex of life to be found there is understood. Not only are the flora that may be unique to the swamp appreciated, but the relationship of the host of higher and lower forms of life to be found there to the surrounding countryside is recognized. Since they stand to make no personal gain from the preservation of the swamp, their appeal carries more weight than though moved by selfish interests. Furthermore, if it becomes necessary to raise money for the purchase of the acres in question, garden clubbers are sure to be found active on the project committee.[32]

In Florida a major battlefield in the fight over treatment of wetlands and estuaries was Boca Ciega Bay, located in the upper Tampa Bay area of St. Petersburg. Between 1950 and 1970 the rich estuary, one of the state's most pro-
lific fish nurseries, was "laid to waste" by bay filling, writes historian R. Bruce
Stephenson. Its "demise was a product of neither ignorance nor an apathetic
public; Florida's first ecologists and grassroots activists combined to fight and
articulate the costs of dredging and filling the estuary. Rather, Boca Ciega fell
victim 'to that gleam,' as one St. Petersburg resident put it, that 'just never
died in the Progress Boys' eyes.'" As early as 1956 marine biologists argued that
dredge-and-fill projects would destroy the bay's ecology—a "radical concept"
at the time in the state, Stephenson adds. The future of Boca Ciega Bay became
a noisy dispute as grassroots opponents stood up to development interests and
to county commissioners who had never opposed a fill permit that promised
more taxable lands. Women were energetic, effective leaders in the anti-fill effort, working on equal footing with male fellow environmentalists.[33]

Much controversy swirled around a Boca Ciega Bay project proposed by
developer Albert Furen. In 1953 he bought the rights to fill 504 acres of bay
bottom that abutted six shoreline acres already in his possession. He applied to
the Trustees of the Internal Improvement Fund (IFF), a commission composed
of the governor and cabinet members, for a permit to turn the bay bottom into
residential lots, eventually selling the project to a different developer, who proceeded with the fill plans. The major opponent was the Alliance for Conservation of Natural Resources (ACNR), a group formed in 1954 by Mary Bigelow,
Ann Davis, and Floyd Brown to oppose bay fill. Bigelow, who had fallen in love
with the area in the 1940s, moved there in 1951. "Three years later, she awoke
one morning to the dull roar of a dredge," writes Stephenson. "Incensed that
her waterfront vista was being transformed into a subdivision, she organized
the ACNR by gathering members from eight civic organizations" and traveled
to Tallahassee many times between 1954 and 1958 to testify on behalf of the
group.[34]

Davis was president of the Garden Club of St. Petersburg and an ACNR officer who understood the power of numbers and wielded it. At an April 1957
hearing before the Pinellas County Commission, Davis warned: "If you want
us to bring 1,100 members up here to protest this fill, we'll do it. We are defi-
nitely against it and will continue the fights." She could make good on that
threat: since the city of St. Petersburg had agreed to the project, the group
already had sent two thousand protest letters. It is important to note that although she helped found an environmental group and was willing to stand up

to the county commission, Davis was still a woman of her era, identified in the media as Mrs. Robert Davis. As with many women of her generation and most of those in prior centuries, Davis was publicly identified as someone's wife, not as a liberated individual with a separate identity. That type of recognition was not provided on a regular basis until the final decades of the century.[35]

Ecology figured large in the arguments against bay dredge-and-fill projects. As part of their decision-making process, Pinellas County commissioners heard the testimony of marine biologist Robert Hutton, author of *The Ecology of Boca Ciega Bay*, a 1956 analysis that warned of enormous estuarine damage that the infill would cause. The report, a precursor to the environmental impact statements eventually required by federal law, was a first for an environmental conflict. County leaders approved the project anyway, ignoring Hutton, his report, and the ACNR. The ACNR fought the project in court, ending with a loss in the state's highest court.[36]

Women found a number of ways to oppose dredging—often trying to *prevent* another natural resource mess in the state. In 1956 Barbara Falk, described as the "self-styled 'Lady Hermit' of lower Boca Ciega Bay," made a plea for $1 per person donations to save the bay from what she characterized as "land pirates." Falk owned God's Island, an isle that would have been "virtually" surrounded by proposed bay fill projects. She and her husband pledged $1,000 to the campaign, hoping that the money would be sent to Governor LeRoy Collins for a public purchase of the submerged lands in the lower part of the bay. The irony of the need for the public to buy what were already deemed public lands illustrates the inverted thinking and actions of governmental figures who readily allowed developers to buy submerged lands to "create" property. In a newspaper interview, Falk stated that she was not against progress, but if it "were not for men and women like our conservation club members and nature lovers" and other threatened property owners, "we would not have any natural resources. This area would be a pumped in desert of sand."[37]

A decade later civic groups combined forces to confront new Boca Ciega dredging projects. In 1965 they formed the Committee to Save Our Bays and distributed forty thousand handbills urging people to protest to their county commissioners. Vice chair of the group was Mary Louise Mills, who succeeded Katherine Bell Tippetts in 1941 as president of the St. Petersburg Audubon Society. The group was a merger of ACNR and another group, Save Our Bays; membership of the new organization was estimated at fifteen thousand people. The Committee to Save Our Bays launched successful opposition that year to a proposed $4.7 million project by the Southwest Florida Water Management

District to create a seventeen-square-mile freshwater lake by impounding the upper portion of Tampa Bay.[38]

Although the loss of large portions of Boca Ciega Bay was a tragedy, it signaled a change in the state. Dredge-and-fill projects, once deemed good for tax rolls, suddenly came under scrutiny with the growing opposition of citizens' groups. And sometimes those groups were heard. A proposal for a twelve-acre fill by developer Alfred Zabel in 1958 encountered "fierce opposition" from homeowners' groups and went to the Florida Supreme Court before Zabel obtained a permit in 1965. The project still needed review by the Army Corps of Engineers, which received a tide of protest. In 1967 the Corps refused the permit; it was the first time the federal agency had denied such a request for environmental reasons. Project opponents revived Hutton's earlier ecological findings, arguing that previous dredging and filling of the bay had damaged seabed grasses, leading to $1.4 million in annual fishing losses. The decision was appealed to the federal courts, and in 1970 an appellate court set a national precedent when it denied the project, finding that science now proved the extensive damage caused by dredging on marine systems. Boca Ciega Bay had set a new national standard.[39]

The campaign to save the bay also helped put a woman into elected office. At a 1966 hearing for which two hundred people gathered at the Garden Club of St. Petersburg, Dorothy Eaton Sample, vice president of the Pasadena Property Owners Association, updated the group on the Zabel project and urged members to ask their congressional representatives to "use their authority for the people's rights" in the battle. After the meeting Sample stood at the door and collected money for opposition efforts. By 1971 she was president of the St. Petersburg–based Save Our Bays, and she had spent several years opposing fill projects and offshore drilling in the Gulf of Mexico. Three years later Sample ran for the state House of Representatives, describing herself as a "conservationist and substitute teacher." She lost that election but won the post in 1976 and served twelve years, earning accolades for her environmental sensitivity. In 1984 she observed in an unquestionably gendered way that the "whole Bay has been raped." Sample died in 2002, remembered as "a great leader for Pinellas County."[40] Not only had women proved to be competent environmental soldiers, as Sample demonstrated, but they were able to use the cause to come out of the house and enter the House, proving their aptitude to take on important confrontations and lead the charge to benefit the entire community.

The political winds were shifting for male leaders as well. Late in life LeRoy Collins, who was governor from 1955 to 1961, called the Boca Ciega damage a "monstrous desecration"—another first in a state where many previous governors were elected on their promises to fill in the state's wetlands, particularly the Everglades. Hutton's report helped frame the "Bulkhead Law" that the State Land Use and Control Committee used to regulate dredge-and-fill operations. In 1967 Claude Kirk appointed as his environmental advisor Nathaniel Reed, who "immediately set out to limit dredge-and-fill operations," writes Stephenson. That year they supported passage of the Randell Act, which required environmental studies from developers who wanted fill permits. Permits dropped from some two thousand a year to two hundred in 1970. In 1969 Florida enacted an Aquatic Preserve bill to protect its estuaries; Boca Ciega Bay became the first area so designated. Although it was too late to save much of the shallow lagoon's rich habitat of nursery grasses, the designation heralded a seismic change in opinion and practice wrought of damage, experience, and citizen opposition.[41]

Federal efforts were simultaneously initiated to protect coastal areas, culminating in the 1968 National Estuary Protection Act, which encouraged local governments to safeguard vital marine habitat through planning. It also required federal agencies to consider ecological impacts of development projects in these areas. Ironically enough, in 1970 the federal act was used (and ultimately upheld in appellate court) to deny a dredge-and-fill permit for a project in Boca Ciega Bay. The courts now relied on scientific reports of the ills of dredge-and-fill on marine systems to refuse the practice, setting a new standard for the bay and the nation. Ecology was starting to win.[42]

Swamps, estuaries, sea turtles, manatees, and a host of endangered species and fragile lands had many women to thank for their very existence by the late twentieth century. Funneling their zeal and anger while encountering sexism and antiquated thinking, Florida's environmentally minded women conducted factual studies, launched campaigns, prodded government officials, and went to court in order to protect the state's nature and natural resources. It became a path to election to office for some and an unexpected detour to a more meaningful life for others. Their legacy continues today.

Part III

Women Take the Lead

9

Seeking Environmental Justice

They are native people uprooted from their traditional homes, first by war and then by land development schemes, their hunting grounds damaged by agricultural runoff. They are African American families whose yards and homes were contaminated first by chemicals from nearby companies and then by federal cleanup efforts. They are rural residents whose leaders were so eager for jobs that they sacrificed a river's well-being—and consequently their own—to attract polluting industry. And they are poor farmworkers sprayed by chemicals as they toiled to put food on others' tables, never suspecting that their backbreaking work could lead to long-term health problems.

These are the faces of environmental injustice in Florida, the people who have suffered worst from a century of pollution, land manipulation, and questionable public policy. They often did not know about menacing environmental hazards or have the ability to escape from them. Often the true toll of their exposure became evident only decades later. Because many were impoverished or belonged to minority groups, they were viewed as economically and politically powerless, and as a result their concerns received scant attention from government and corporate entities that may have exposed them to harm. That is, until a variety of Florida women began advocating for justice—a mission that included forcing greater regulation and restoration of the state's natural resources. Building on the successes of previous generations, these women increasingly took on public leadership roles in areas that often required them to oppose the male business-as-usual community.

"It was no coincidence that the age of ecology was also an age of environmental inequality," writes historian Andrew Hurley. The less fortunate, typically African Americans and poor whites, "found themselves at a severe disadvantage, consistently bearing the brunt of industrial pollution in virtually all its forms: dirty air, foul water, and toxic solid wastes." It was far cheaper and more politically expedient to locate chemical dumps and polluting industries in poor, minority-dominated communities that might welcome (or at least not object to) any project in the hopes of more jobs and income while remaining unaware of the long-term health issues the project posed.[1]

The awakening to these issues in the 1970s and 1980s came to be called the environmental justice movement. No longer was it possible to look only at damage to natural resources and beauty; now the accompanying face of human suffering was apparent, rousing activists of all ages and ethnicities and both genders—and particularly women, who viewed their role as that of protecting the environment. This was true of women around the globe; they became key activists who spurred much-needed improvements, observes Cesar Chelala, an international medical consultant and author. As employees, homemakers, and mothers, women "are susceptible to health problems and hazards in several situations," particularly in the reproductive process, when toxic substances can affect pregnancies and cause birth defects, he writes. This is supported by a United Nations survey showing "women, when compared with men" prefer a lower standard of living "with fewer health risks rather than a higher standard of living with more health risks."[2]

A half-century before this movement was recognized, however, many Florida women were already working to improve living conditions for the state's native people, whose fates were tied to the watery Everglades. At first female activists were concerned with setting aside land for Indian reservations at the same time that parks, farms, and developments were being carved out of the newly drained wilderness. As the century progressed, the Seminole and Miccosukee people were confronted by the degradation of the landscape and the disappearance of wildlife upon which they depended for survival.

Florida's aboriginal inhabitants disappeared in the early eighteenth century, the victims of disease, slavery, and warfare. They were replaced by Indians who migrated from Alabama and Georgia, eventually developing their own cultural identities as Seminoles and, later, some as Miccosukees. Initially the Seminoles lived in the prime agricultural areas of north Florida, but after three wars with the federal government between 1817 and 1858, the Seminole population dropped from about 5,000 to an estimated 200 to 300 people. Many left the state for a reservation in Oklahoma, but those who remained, never having surrendered to federal authorities, were left living in the marginal lands of the Big Cypress Swamp and the Everglades. As author Michael Grunwald notes, "few of the Americans who had chased them there had a problem with that"—

they understood that it was a watery, insect-filled expanse largely considered a wasteland.[3]

That attitude, however, changed in the early twentieth century as speculators, government leaders, and business interests began the long drive toward draining the Everglades to create an agricultural paradise. Caught in the middle of these schemes—and eventually the development of Everglades National Park—were the Seminole people. Ivy Cromartie Stranahan of Ft. Lauderdale was one of the leaders in the efforts to help Florida's Seminoles, spending much of her adult life using her "old-girl network" connections to improve their living circumstances. A schoolteacher, Stranahan grew up on the Florida frontier and married a man who ran a trading post on the New River. They did regular business with Seminoles, who paddled to the trading post, often bringing their families and camping nearby. The childless Stranahan later recalled that "my young married life might have been a little lonely had it not been for the Indians coming to my husband's trading post." She invited the children into her home, where they explored rooms and tried on her clothes, sparking Stranahan to take action to relieve their needs. "All this time I looked upon them with great pity and regret because they were so unfriendly to our government, rejected our education and scorned Christianity." With a missionary's fervor but calm practicality, Stranahan began teaching the children in informal outdoor settings, using posters and pictures of Christian figures. When the trading post closed in 1911, she drove to Seminole camps to offer lessons, continuing to do so for more than twenty-five years. At the Florida Federation of Women's Clubs (FFWC), Stranahan rallied support for Indian education and lobbied for creation of a permanent reservation for the tribe. She served many years as chair of the FFWC's Indian Welfare Committee, striving to obtain rights and property for the Seminoles while at the same time trying to "civilize" them and spread Christianity among their ranks.[4]

Stranahan engaged federal agents, politicians, schools, and women's groups in her work. She founded Friends of the Seminoles (FOS) to provide additional support while keeping close ties with tribe members, trying to gain their confidence in government programs and education. Several scholarships for education at government schools and colleges were offered through FFWC, the Florida Daughters of the American Revolution, and other groups to Seminole youths to further their self-sufficiency. "A Seminole youth of this generation knows that we are not trying to make a white man of him and that we want him to be proud of his race, and remain an Indian as God created him," she wrote in an unpublished autobiography. "We want him to be capable of enjoying some of the conveniences and advantages of the present civilization and still be able to protect himself from the evils civilization brings." Stranahan and her sisters-in-arms were advocating Christianity above native religious practices and saw white-controlled but segregated educational institutions as the best course to ensuring the Seminoles' futures. A few students took advantage of the scholarships and attended schools out of state; no local white or black schools would accept Seminole students until the late 1940s.[5]

Another ardent Seminole advocate was Minnie Moore-Willson of Kissimmee, a writer and FOS activist, whose strident manner often gained her enemies. Moore-Willson wanted to give the Seminoles "cultural uplift," writes historian Jack E. Davis, but she also "thought Indian culture superior to Western in one regard. A steady opponent of drainage and commercial hunting, she maintained that Indians lived more wisely with the natural world, with Seminoles standing as the only true 'custodians' of the Everglades." The childless Moore-Willson and her husband, James Willson, made it their mission to help the Seminoles, their adopted children. And although Moore-Willson was an invalid much of her life and suffered from migraine headaches, she was a force with which to be reckoned. In the eighth (1928) edition of her book *The Seminoles of Florida*, Moore-Willson described the Seminoles, with a population then estimated at six hundred, as a "beggared and spectral type of a once powerful race." She said they had been forced into "the most desolate lands of Florida," and stated that Americans, in the push toward Manifest Destiny, were now "taking our time at finishing the extermination of the original Indian." The book offered Moore-Willson's plea for their aid and hope for their future, in much the same "civilizing" maternalistic vein used by Stranahan: "Let us then deal kindly with the tribes we have dispossessed, whose removal to the swamps has made room for our own enlargement. In the person of these descendants of a now disinherited race, who with shy, frightened faces still hide in the wilderness, we may yet atone in part for the tragedies of the past by making Florida a free, safe and Christian home for this patient and long-persecuted remnant of a once-powerful Indian nation."[6]

Moore-Willson recognized that Everglades drainage schemes might push the Seminoles out of their lands and reasoned, "There is at this time plenty of land for both interests." She said it was the federal government's duty to set aside land for Seminoles—and then spent the next few decades trying to ensure that it happened. It was a battle against male-dominated bureaucracy and, sometimes, against fellow clubwomen: in 1915 and 1916, during FFWC efforts to establish Royal Palm State Park, Moore-Willson argued that creating a Seminole reservation was more important than gaining acreage and funding for a state park. In 1917 the state approved 100,000 acres in the lower Everglades for the Seminoles, with Moore-Willson participating in the effort. In a pamphlet that year, Moore-Willson argued that the same justice and freedom that the United States was fighting for overseas in World War I should be extended to the Seminoles—"patriots that we know would spend their last drop of blood freely and gladly in defense of their native land and sacred soil they have loved so long." Mary Barr Munroe, of FFWC and Audubon, sent a letter praising Moore-Willson's fervent work on behalf of the reservation: "Congratulations dear woman on the splendid work God gave you to do and you have done it well."[7]

The Seminoles now had a large reservation, but as Davis notes, it was "woefully unsuitable for farming and grazing," the agricultural practices that had been the tribe's lifeblood. Moore-Willson recognized this but "regarded the acquisition of any land as a victory for Seminole welfare and the state of establishing additional holdings." When it became evident that Everglades National Park was about to be created, Moore-Willson started a new crusade, arguing that an additional 100,000-acre reservation should be provided on higher land adjacent to the park and that Seminoles should have full access to the park. Moore-Willson died in 1937, a decade before the park was dedicated. With the park's formation, however, Davis notes, the state created a new reservation, and three more were sited by the federal government, "encompassing less but more suitable land than that in the lower Everglades." Following a precedent set in other national parks, park agencies refused to extend Indian rights to hunt and fish within the park. The Seminoles were not forced onto the new reservations, but most eventually moved there. The state and federal governments had made provisions for the Seminoles, but without the constant prodding by Stranahan, Moore-Willson, and the FFWC, the Seminoles might have found themselves in tougher circumstances.[8]

It is important to note that many of these decisions were made without consulting the Seminoles, writes historian James W. Covington: "Nowhere during the entire proceeding had the Seminoles been consulted as to the value or use of the proposed reservation. White friends thought they could help by providing a reservation, but local opposition caused it to be placed in an area thought to have little value to the white man, and no money was provided for improvements. Had either the federal government or the state of Florida been willing to purchase good agricultural land for a reservation, a site with such assets would have been more suitable. The white friends of the Seminoles had accepted land that was good only for hunting and fishing, and the Seminoles refused to live there."[9] No wonder that the native people remained largely aloof and suspicious of aid extended from those outside their tribes. As for their environmental involvement, the Seminole people were simply trying to exist in their circumstances, not worried about the larger picture of natural resource degradation until later in the century.

Harriet Mary Bedell, an Episcopal Church deaconess and missionary, dedicated much of her life to working on behalf of the Seminoles. Bedell, who led by action rather than fervent religiosity, was a missionary in Oklahoma and Alaska before she was asked to recruit missionaries in Florida. In 1933 she visited the Seminole Indian Village tourist spot in Miami, which inspired her to see the real thing. After witnessing the difficult conditions of the Seminole people, she opened the Glade Cross Mission in southwest Florida's Collier County. From there, Bedell, who was given the name "Inkoshopie," meaning "woman who prays," acted to help sell native crafts to support the Seminole and Miccosukee people and to preserve their culture. Using her contacts around the United States, Bedell, described as "a small steam engine in dark-blue petticoats," traveled to help sell dolls, baskets, clothing, and carvings, with all the profits returned to the native people; she even traveled to Washington, D.C., to prevent Japanese imitations from being sold in America. Bedell taught sewing classes, made sick calls, helped young men find work, and conducted religious services. In recognition of her advocacy supporting Seminole sustainability in their homelands, Bedell was invited to give the invocation at the dedication of Everglades National Park. She died in January 1969 at age ninety-three; forty years later she was officially sainted by the Episcopal Church, and she is remembered with a feast day every January 8.[10]

The rights of the Seminole and Miccosukee people (the tribes split into separate entities in 1962) played a role in the Everglades through the remainder of the century. Part of the controversy that swirled around the proposed Everglades jetport in the 1960s was that it was located on the site of the Miccosukees' Green Corn Dance, a sacred tribal ground. This fact was cited by jetport opponents trying to expose the enormity of the jetport's desecration of the environment. Having initially supported the jetport because of the promise of jobs, the tribe eventually opposed the project in favor of saving the landscape, which was withering from drainage projects. The Miccosukees, numbering around three hundred people, lived along Tamiami Trail near the jetport site and witnessed the decline of the ecosystem upon which they relied heavily for food. "It happens to Indians year after year: progress wasting the hunting grounds," Miccosukee Chief Buffalo Tiger told the *New York Times* in 1969. "Indians used to have a good life here; clean air, clean water, plenty of food." Tiger said the once abundant wildlife was disappearing: "Now even the snakes are scarce. The fish and turtles are going. It's hard to make a living in the glades." It was evident that Indian interests were inextricably tangled in the fate of the Everglades—what happened with water quality and levels, and therefore the health of the ecosystem, directly affected their lives.[11]

Nowhere was this more apparent than in the Miccosukee opposition to a 1993 settlement between the State of Florida and the federal government involving pollution levels—particularly of phosphorus—in the Everglades. The tribe lived in the southern part of the national park and had hunting rights in one of the conservation areas, notes Grunwald. But they did "not trust the government that nearly wiped out their ancestors," and to improve the water situation they hired Dexter Lehtinen, a former U.S. attorney who had filed suit in 1988 on behalf of the park. As a result the tribe became "the defender of Everglades water quality, litigating to force Florida to live up to its obligations." Accusing the state of using their land as a toilet, the Miccosukees also raised the stakes when they set acceptable phosphorus standards far stricter than those agreed to by the state; the tribe then supported a proposed constitutional amendment to impose a tax on sugar to pay for Everglades cleanup programs. The ballot proposal failed, but the Miccosukees took their place firmly and aggressively in Everglades initiatives. By the start of the twenty-first century the Miccosukees faced a threat from mercury contamination of the fish in their homeland. Released into the air from natural and industrial sources, the toxin was detected at unacceptable levels in the food chain that led to the native people's tables, prompting state health investigations. It was clearly a case of environmental justice—the lives and livelihoods of the Miccosukee people depended on the health of this vast ecosystem.[12]

Other groups of American Indians also dealt with toxic pollution, caused, ironically, by uranium mining on their own lands. From 1944 to 1986 mining corporations, responding to the demands of the postwar nuclear age, removed at least four million tons of uranium ore from property owned by the Navajo Nation in the American Southwest. Many of the miners were Navajo men who needed jobs when employment was scarce and were subjected to poor working conditions that exposed them to radioactivity. The uranium extraction, writes historian Ted Steinberg, caused "serious problems with both water and soil contamination," raising cancer rates and health concerns. In 1979 a dam at a New Mexico uranium mine burst, sending radioactive wastes into the Rio Puerco River, where radiation levels remain high. Mining during the past century also left the Navajo Nation with 520 abandoned mines, four inactive milling sites, a former dump, contaminated groundwater, and buildings with elevated radiation levels. Concerned about cancer deaths and illnesses, miners' widows began demanding a federal response, culminating in the 1990 federal Radiation Exposure Compensation Act (RECA), which gave financial compensation to mine workers. Although the Navajo Nation banned uranium mining in 2005, it continues to battle with the federal government, which approved licenses for uranium extraction on Navajo property. In South Dakota the grassroots native group Women of All Red Nations (WARN) raised alarms in 1977 about health problems caused by high radiation levels from uranium tailings washed into a nearby river. WARN members, worried about high rates of birth defects, cancer deaths, and sterilization among women on Indian reservations, were female voices seeking justice.[13]

Women also were central players and leaders in the fight over Love Canal, one of the preeminent American environmental conflicts of the 1970s, pitting blue-collar residents against local, state, and federal governments. As their concerns grew about public health, particularly the sickness of their children, Love Canal residents discovered that their housing development and local school in Niagara Falls, New York, was built atop a former chemical dump. The area's working-class men "found it difficult to accept the fact that they were unable to protect or provide adequately for their families," writes historian Carolyn Merchant, leaving it to women to bring the issue to the public. Housewives with no prior political or environmental experience united in their anxiety about their children's well-being. Lois Gibbs, who had a sick child, helped mobilize the Love Canal Homeowners' Association (LCHA) to exert political power and get answers. As historian Temma Kaplan notes, most of the women who were active in the group "would be happy to find themselves back in a Love Canal that no longer exists, baking cookies and taking their kids to dance lessons." Instead, they were compelled into civic action that disrupted their lives and forever changed the way Americans view their surroundings and their government As a result of homeowner activism, in 1978 the area was declared the first federal disaster area not caused by a natural disaster; the federal government, through a New York agency, eventually agreed to buy homes so that residents could relocate.[14]

Love Canal had a lasting impact, writes Steinberg, galvanizing "women around the issue of environmental justice," leading to the organization of many other women's groups concerned with health and ecology. Rather than asking how to achieve a legislative victory, as mainstream groups do, Gibbs and other groups sought "what is morally correct," often eschewing litigation in favor of public protests. As a result, Steinberg notes, many were branded as "overemotional" women; one Maine woman who told her doctor she was worried that her well water was contaminated found her fears downplayed, and she was "prescribed a tranquilizer."[15]

Race was another central factor in environmental justice. In 1982 a predominantly African American community of low-income residents in Warren County, North Carolina, fought against a toxic waste dump planned nearby, worried it would foul their water supply, hurt the economy, and damage human health. They lost the battle, but by using nonviolent protest tactics of the Civil Rights era, they raised the issue of environmental racism to a national level. Racism also was central to a dispute involving a major hazardous waste site in Pensacola, Florida, that came to be known as "Mount Dioxin": efforts to clean up businesses had contaminated a nearby African American neighborhood by creating a mound of 255,000 cubic yards of chemical-laced soil. And it was women who challenged this chemical dump, taking on the bureaucracy and Big Brother–like behavior of the Environmental Protection Agency (EPA) in an effort to resolve chronic health issues in the neighborhood.[16]

In the Jim Crow segregationist era in the 1950s and 1960s, African Americans living in Pensacola had few areas where they could buy homes. One possible site was bordered by railroad tracks, the Agrico Chemical Company (a chemical fertilizer plant), and the Escambia Wood Trading Company (ETC), where utility poles, railroad ties, and foundation pilings were treated with creosote. This was the friendly, tree-lined childhood neighborhood of Margaret Williams, whose father worked at Agrico and whose home often was coated with residue pumped into the air by the two plants. Her family kept the windows closed to keep out fumes; while walking to school she often had to cover her eyes and nose. During rainy periods, runoff from ETC sometimes pooled in neighborhood yards, prompting company employees to pump out the creosote and put sand in contaminated areas. Wastes went into an unlined landfill, an unlined containment pond, and unlabeled drums. As a result residents, with no knowledge of any contamination, suffered the fumes from the evaporation, and those using shallow wells had to clear an oily substance from their tap water. Eventually, the Agrico and ETC sites were declared federal Superfund hazardous waste sites; the land around Williams's home was discovered to be contaminated with dioxin, arsenic, polyaromatic hydrocarbons, and the banned pesticide dieldrin. In 1991 ETC was abandoned through bankruptcy, leaving the government and taxpayers to foot the bill for any cleanup work.[17]

That same year the EPA discovered elevated pentachlorophenol (PCP) in ETC soil up to fourteen feet deep. As part of the cleanup efforts, some 54,000 cubic yards of soil and sludge were piled up sixty feet high on the site, hence its moniker, "Mount Dioxin." By 1993 it had grown to 255,000 cubic yards, and a year later ETC became one of the EPA's 1,300 Superfund sites. Williams, a retired teacher, became alarmed at the EPA cleanup in 1992 when airborne dust from the excavation sparked a series of health issues among residents, including skin and eye irritations, nosebleeds, headaches, nausea, and breathing difficulties—all symptoms associated with dioxin. It propelled her into activism, she said: "As with most people, environmental issues had never crossed my mind." Frances Dunham recalls that residents began seeking answers from the EPA, which was mishandling the site contaminants and "minimizing the health threats from the plant and their actions and proposing to site an incinerator to burn the waste." Dunham, who was active with Planet Well, a now-defunct nonprofit that helped grassroots groups, said she was "surprised to find such a critical situation virtually in our backyard, but it was just the sort of cause we had formed to tackle." ETC neighbors met with Dunham, and from that arose Citizens Against Toxic Exposure (CATE), a nonprofit group that consolidated concerned citizens in order to improve their political power. As CATE president, Williams, described as a "very dignified and determined presence," led the organization for many years. Initially she thought it would be easy to obtain the help of local elected officials to stop the EPA work. "I was surprised and amazed that we got no help at that time," she later recalled, adding that the EPA claimed it was doing all it could but instead was making things worse. "We thought they were coming in to help us," Williams said. "This recklessness would not have occurred in non-minority or wealthy neighborhoods."[18]

Unable to halt the EPA cleanup, CATE, following the example of Love Canal homemakers and in contact with Gibbs, began to press the federal government for relocation. Eventually the EPA agreed to move 358 African American families. To achieve this, Williams and CATE members used a number of strategies. Working with other activists and groups, they sought and received media attention. A month before the 1996 presidential election, the Pensacola problem was featured in a full-page advertisement in USA Today's Florida edition, with photographs of children opposite a quote from the campaigning President Bill Clinton: "No child should ever have to live near a hazardous waste site." It was public relations genius, and within two days EPA agreed to the relocations, making this one of the first African American communities moved under the Superfund program.[19]

Dunham, who is white, lived more than twenty miles from the Superfund site but was one of CATE's active members. She helped by penning articles, newsletters, and reports; testifying at hearings; creating T-shirts, banners, brochures, and presentations; and doing anything else that put the topic in front of the public's eyes and the government's attention. In an article for an area publication she wrote that cases like hers provided a means for all demographic groups to unite, since Americans were learning that toxic chemicals can affect anyone. Some men were involved in CATE, but the majority of members were women. "I'm not sure why," Dunham states, "but this has been the case with nearly every environmental group I know." Women, perhaps because of their childbearing and caring, "may have a special inclination to protection," according to Dunham. "Also, women, being generally excluded from the old boys' clubs, may be less apt to conform to the pressures of business interests when it means abandoning their values (environmental & otherwise). People of color are frequently victimized by environmental and occupational abuse in a way that is hard to ignore." Although Williams died in August 2011, CATE endures under the guidance of her daughter, Francine Ishmael. The group monitors the ongoing site cleanup, offers health seminars, and works with the Escambia County Health Department to provide health screenings and tracking for some six thousand former area residents who may suffer long-term effects from the chemical exposure.[20]

The reality is that African Americans and Hispanics are more likely than whites to live near Florida Superfund sites. A 1998 analysis showed that race and ethnicity were "the most salient factors in predicting the location of hazardous waste sites," write sociologists Paul Stretesky and Michael J. Hogan, adding that "this form of injustice may be increasing." Florida census information showed that the percentage of blacks and Hispanics living near Superfund sites increased from 1970 to 1990.[21]

Robert Bullard, a leading scholar of environmental justice, confirms these studies, finding that half of the 9 million people living within two miles of hazardous waste facilities in the United States are minorities. Residents living in close proximity to these sites are subject to elevated rates of asthma, cancer, diabetes, and kidney failure. "Just because you're poor, just because you live physically on the wrong 'side of the track' doesn't mean that you should be dumped on," he writes. It is also no coincidence that many polluting industries and projects are located in low-income areas, especially in the impoverished South, which has courted industry to diversify its agriculture-dependent economy. "The South, in general, was attractive to the worst types of industries. Florida was associated with the blighted South," writes historian Gary Mormino. "Florida may have been better off not getting them." For many communities, the allure of jobs and tax revenue was the dominating factor in welcoming companies, without any consideration for the long-term effects that might be imposed on the local landscape and population.[22]

That was the case in Taylor County in 1947, when government officials hailed the proposed construction of a large pulp and paper mill. The sacrifice for this business was the health of the slow-moving, tannic Fenholloway River, once the site of water bottling and recreation ventures. In post–World War II Florida the county was losing population: in 1940 Taylor County had 11,565 residents, a number that dropped to 10,416 ten years later. Officials in Perry, the county seat, joined with the Procter and Gamble Company (P&G) in asking the state legislature to designate the Fenholloway for industrial usage, meaning that any pollutant or chemical sewage could be discharged into the river. It was easy for the all-male legislature, which met an hour away in Tallahassee, to give unanimous consent, since this meant jobs, industry, and tax revenues in a rural, low-income area. Local pine forestry could supply trees for the plant's cellulose products, and the river could supply the plant's water needs and carry away its polluted discharge along a twenty-six-mile meander to the Gulf of Mexico. By 1966 the P&G Buckeye Cellulose plant employed 840 residents with an annual payroll of $6 million; the company paid another $3 million annually to buy timber from local landowners. This significant economic impact was just what the area's business leaders expected.[23]

The agreement, writes historian Gloria G. Horning, "is a classic example of 'environmental blackmail.' That is, if a state or community will allow an organization to build an environmentally unfriendly plant or dump, and pollute the air, water and land as it pleases, the organization will provide jobs." It was a disaster in the making, initiated through a collaboration of industry and government. A precedent had been set six years earlier, when the legislature declared Nassau County in northeastern Florida an "industrial county," allowing sewage and industrial discharges into its waterways. It was a designation in the "public interest," wrote historian Luther J. Carter, and the subsequent "defilement of the Amelia River and destruction of shrimp nursery beds by pulp mills" were, "by legislative fiat, defined as acts of corporate citizenship instead of crimes against nature." By 1954 Buckeye Cellulose was producing cellulose and paper products and emitting a distinctive odor many likened to rotting cabbage or eggs; to local business leaders, it was the sweet smell of success from the county's largest employer. Initially few questioned the value of the plant, even though it employed a variety of chemicals, used up to 85 percent of the river's flow, and daily discharged 50 million gallons of treated effluent carrying a distinct chemical odor. By 1992, however, this economic boon began to be viewed as an ecological disaster, largely because of the passion and persistence of a hometown woman who refused to see a compromised river as anything other than a tragedy.[24]

Joy Towles Ezell's family reached back five generations in Taylor County, raising cattle and growing timber. Her grandfather, Martin Towles, was among the few who opposed the Buckeye plant in 1947, warning that it would ruin local water supplies. In 1954 she and her father and grandfather witnessed a massive fish kill on the Fenholloway River caused by the paper plant. "I think that was probably my first experience with realizing how destructive a company can be to the environment." Ezell, who holds two agriculture-related degrees, had been working in Alabama selling farm chemicals when she returned home in 1981 to care for her aging grandmother. After being told that the family's household water, which came from a well, smelled "like it's got Buckeye in it," Ezell started investigating. To her shock she discovered that the Fenholloway and many area wells were contaminated with dioxin, a dangerous carcinogen that closed Love Canal and has been implicated in three-quarters of the nation's Superfund hazardous waste sites. And it was coming from the P&G plant, a byproduct of the mill's processes to make cellulose products such as disposable diapers and sanitary napkins—ironically, items geared toward a female market. Here was a company stripping the land of timber, and then processing it with chemicals that left polluted air and water, in order to create products that one day would end up in landfills, another abusive use of the land.[25]

Once Ezell smelled the chemicals in the tap water, she and the rest of the family switched to bottled water. She started gathering data and asking questions, often feeling as if she was the only person who understood the hazardous compounds released into the water and air by the plant. Ezell's work with regulated agriculture poisons had qualified her to understand the dangers of the Fenholloway. She continued to work for chemical companies, trying to develop methods to apply pesticides carefully and with minimum human contact, but eventually made the "conscious decision" to quit the industry in 1986. "Ever since then I've been a very adamant pesticide activist," says Ezell, who in 1982 helped create the Pesticide Action Network, a national group that presses for alternatives to chemicals. She switched to a career in agricultural marketing and started work in earnest on the river.[26]

In 1989 Ezell and thirty other people formed Help Our Polluted Environment (HOPE) because, she said, "basically all we had was hope." She ran a newspaper advertisement seeking residents who might want to join in a class action suit against the mill concerning water quality. Two days later the *Tallahassee Democrat* began publishing a scathing series about the condition of the river—just the kind of media attention Ezell had been trying to inspire. For the next two weeks Ezell received hundreds of telephone calls from local people who shared her concerns, including mill employees, parents, fishermen, and many people who had been told by the local health department that their well water was contaminated and undrinkable. The class action suit did not succeed for technical reasons, but HOPE had been born, and Ezell had found an unexpected new role as an environmental activist and leader of a group of 500 loosely affiliated members, a considerable number, but still less than the 1,200 people the plant employed at the height of its production—a number that dropped to 650 by 2002. As Ezell's son Trey used to point out, she was the right person for the job: she was locally born and from a heritage family, she knew people in the community, and she was educated about chemicals. Every time she drove him across the Fenholloway on the way to school, Trey goaded her, saying, "You need to do it for me." He died in a car accident in 1991; Ezell says, "So, I still do this for him."[27]

By then, concerns about the river were gaining momentum. In 1990 the EPA warned residents not to eat fish from the river, and state health officials warned them not to drink water from their wells. In the spring of 1991 HOPE members attended a meeting of the state Environmental Regulatory Commission (ERC), offering two fish dinners to an ERC commissioner and a P&G executive—one fish from the nearby pristine Steinhatchee River, the other from the Fenholloway. When they refused to identify the source of each fish, the meal was declined. However, the ERC did vote to tighten standards for dioxin in Florida rivers.[28]

Through the years Ezell received her share of hate mail and threatening telephone calls, to which she would respond that she was armed and ready for the callers to visit. A local newspaper called her an "armed radical environmental terrorist," although she says the only person she has terrorized is the P&G public relations representative. Some HOPE members also were targeted, including two female P&G employees who owned a fish camp that was vandalized; one of the women was raped and her throat was slashed—

sexualized violence that may have been meant to send a message to HOPE's many female members. The sheriff's department showed little interest in the incidents; eventually the camp was burned and the women left the area. The Fenholloway also began to appear on the national media map, featured in many outlets, including *National Geographic* and *Sixty Minutes*. With continuing pressure and data that indicated health problems among local residents and in marine life, mill managers agreed to supply bottled water to local residents and to drill six hundred new wells. In a major victory in 1998, the state redesignated the Fenholloway from a Class V industrial river to a Class III, requiring more stringent water quality guidelines to make it officially fishable and swimmable. But then the state gave the mill, which changed hands in the early 1990s and now is known as Buckeye Technologies, a variance that allowed it to continue business as usual until it could find a solution. In one cleanup scheme the mill offered to build a pipe to deliver its outflow directly into the Gulf of Mexico; the river certainly would be cleaner, but the Gulf already had a seventeen-square-mile ecological dead zone at the mouth of the river, and its important estuaries would be affected. In 2001 the EPA declared that the mill's wastewater contained two hundred times more dioxin than is safe, disputing the company's long-term claims that its dioxin wastes were "non-detectable."[29]

In the early twenty-first century, the third decade of her campaign, Ezell charged along, armed with facts, humor, and patience. Using the same tactics employed by other female activists, Ezell emphasized being a woman and a mother, telling local residents that her work was for them and for the health of the entire community. The key to the Fenholloway battle, she says, is the grassroots involvement of women. Most men look at it as an issue of jobs and the economy; women's focus is on the health of their children, and when that is threatened, women can become an unstoppable force, unconcerned with any arguments that have allowed the river to be polluted for so long: "You mess with a mama bear and you've got trouble on your hands. I think that's pretty much what it is." Women Ezell has met in similar conflicts around the country, including Gibbs at Love Canal, she says, share a keen interest in health, particularly when it involves their families and children, and presenting an environmental message in those terms brings feminine energy to an issue. "Women are fierce about protecting their children and so they are going to stand up and do the right thing. No matter how scary it might be or how intimidated they might feel in their community, women eventually get the gumption and the strength to stand up and say what needs to be said."[30]

Ezell's comments reflect the domination of the grassroots movement by women, who made up 80 to 85 percent of local activists in the 1980s and 1990s. Merchant sees this movement for environmental equity as "an eco-feminist issue. The body, home, and community are sites of women's local experience and local contestation. Women experience the results of toxic dumping on their own bodies (sites of reproduction of the species), in their own homes (sites of the reproduction of daily life), and in their communities and schools (sites of social reproduction). Women's leadership and organizing skills gained in grassroots struggles empower them to change society and themselves."[31]

While local residents in Pensacola and Taylor County learned to raise their voices to confront ecological ills, scant attention was given to Florida's farmworkers, who historically were among the most oppressed and overlooked victims of environmental injustice. Their grueling lives of poverty were documented repeatedly, with lesser attention given to the health problems they incurred from contact with toxic chemicals used in agricultural fertilizers and pesticides. Female activists spoke up on behalf of this almost invisible group, using a multitude of strategies to raise public awareness and to demand funding and protective governance.

The plight of the nation's farmworkers came to national attention with the 1960 broadcast of *Harvest of Shame*, a CBS television documentary that detailed the difficult lives of the agricultural workers who had put the food on many Thanksgiving tables a day earlier. Renowned journalist Edward R. Murrow called the 2 to 3 million migrant laborers "the forgotten people; the under-educated; the under-fed." The documentary showed workers who traveled from the bean and sugarcane fields of Florida's muck lands to the apple orchards of New York. A worker could afford only dilapidated housing on an annual income of $900 and barely had enough funds to buy food. Murrow intoned: "They are the migrants, workers in the sweat shops of the soil—the harvest of shame." In 2010 CBS revisited the documentary and the issue, reporting that many factors have changed: migrants had changed from poor whites and blacks to poor Hispanics, with most coming from Mexico; annual income was $10,000 to $12,500, which was an improvement, even in 1960 dollars; yet workers had no health, overtime, or sick pay benefits. Advocates had secured agreements with some companies to improve wages and working conditions. The changing demographics of Florida's farmworkers, whose numbers had reached as high as 435,373, including family members, also changed many of their concerns, which included legal status, immigration, and language. *Harvest of*

Shame preceded Rachel Carson's *Silent Spring* by two years, but the effects of fertilizers and pesticides on agricultural worker health remains a concern in the twenty-first century.[32]

In the Central Florida agricultural community of Apopka, farmworkers had to contend with all these issues while also living in one of the state's most polluted environments. Once upon a time the city of Apopka and its environs had seemed a natural Eden. Nearby Lake Apopka, once the second largest lake in the state, was a recreational haven, drawing fishing enthusiasts from across the country to its bass-rich waters. Bird watchers came to its marshy shores to see the abundance of migratory species that made it their winter home or way station. Local farmers grew citrus, ornamental plants, and vegetable row crops, aided by the region's rich soil. But unknown or unacknowledged by many people, Lake Apopka, like many of Florida's waterways, also served as the waste depository for area industry and residents; in 1920 the city of Winter Garden started dumping raw sewage into it, and citrus processing plants did the same with their wastewater. During World War II, as Americans worried about a food shortage, the Army Corps of Engineers built a levee along the lake's north shore, turning 20,000 acres of filtering marsh into farmlands. The rich muck soil produced three crops a year, with the help of pesticides and fertilizers—a system that continued for the next fifty years, with runoff carrying phosphorus and chemicals into the lake. These practices began in an era when faith in technology soared and there was little concern about the effects of these chemicals on the environment. And why should there be? The crops were flourishing in what had previously been deemed a wasteland. The ecology of the lake was not widely understood, and the language of business spoke loudest.[33]

In 1980 Tower Chemical Company, a pesticide production and packaging company, spilled a toxic chemical into the lake, killing 90 percent of its alligators. By the end of the century anyone could see that the lake was dying, as algae blooms became the norm and the water turned a murky green, resembling pea soup. Since sunlight could not penetrate to the lake's bottom, aquatic plants died, and native fish lost their habitats. Non-native plants took over and fish kills were common. Many alligators, a species that has roamed the earth for millions of years, died or began to suffer from reproductive problems. The lake was an ecological nightmare. As historian Nano Riley noted in 2005, "Now Lake Apopka stands as lifeless testimony to what can happen to a pristine body of water when humans tamper with nature."[34]

Scientists eventually discovered that the lake was a cesspool of poisons caused by chemicals spills, wastewater, and pollution from farm runoff. The state bought out the farms to end the chemical contamination and began earnest efforts to clean up the lake; by 2000 the state had paid more than $200 million for 90 percent of the farms. The muck lands were reflooded in 1998 to restore natural habitat for wildlife, and after a few weeks more than 41,000 birds were seen feeding at one time, which many heralded as a sign of success. But several months later, an ecological tragedy occurred when an estimated 676 birds, mostly wading and migratory species, died on the lake's shore from overdoses of a variety of lethal agricultural chemicals, including dieldrin and DDT, both banned for more than twenty years. The compounds had bioaccumulated in the lake's fish, eventually poisoning the hungry birds. By the time the investigation was over, scientists believed that up to 1,000 birds might have died, many after flying out of the area. Outrage among bird lovers, environmentalists, news media, and taxpayers spurred further cleanup of the farmlands. At the same time the St. Johns River Water Management District conducted other restoration projects at the lake, including an elaborate marsh flow-way that circulates lake water in a kidney-like system to remove phosphorus; harvesting of gizzard shad, a fish that carries a large amount of phosphorus in its body; restoration of aquatic vegetation; and removal of invasive non-native species such as hydrilla. With so much attention devoted to the lake's fish, birds, and water quality—and a budget in the millions of dollars—it was worrisome to many people that so little attention and funding went to the human element of the picture.[35]

Many of these problems confronted Ann Kendrick and Cathy Gorman upon their 1971 arrival in the Apopka area. Answering a call by the bishop of the Catholic Diocese of Orlando, the two young nuns in their twenties, members of the Sisters of Notre Dame de Namur, came to the area after working with United Farm Workers of America (UFW) union activist Cesar Chavez in California. The young nuns were shocked at the conditions they found among the poor and largely African American laborers in Apopka. The workers, who came to include many Haitians and Hispanics, were often illiterate, living in shacks and lacking medical care and transportation. Soon two more nuns joined Kendrick and Gorman, developing a ministry focused on improving the health of the farmworkers in the community who toiled at area citrus groves, nurseries, and farms. The women, known locally as the "Apopka nuns," opened the Office for Farmworker Ministry in Apopka, from which they created eight separate nonprofit organizations offering health care, tutoring, naturalization and immigration advice, education, housing assistance, and family and legal services. Community leaders led six of the groups: the nuns believed local people had to learn for themselves to get what they needed. "In a lot of ways they've been the conscience for the community," said Bishop Thomas Wenski of Orlando. "They've inspired us to look at poor people in a new light and respond with generosity. Not paternalistically, but in a way that empowers them and allows them to find their own dignity." For their work the sisters were recognized repeatedly with awards, ceremonies, and even honorary doctoral degrees. But their focus remained on the people they served. "We're swimming upstream," Kendrick told a local newspaper. "People who care about social justice, about the environment, about the human environment and making this world a more human place, we're losing ground."[36]

A companion organization to the Apopka nuns' work was the Farmworker Association of Florida (FWAF). Incorporated in 1986, it grew by 2011 to include more than eight thousand member families, with five offices in Central and South Florida. Many men participated in and led the group, but when it came to Lake Apopka, the go-to person was Jeannie Economos, who grew up in nearby Orlando. As the pesticide safety and environmental health coordinator for the FWAF Lake Apopka project, Economos spent many years raising awareness of the health problems of the area's farmworkers. She notes that the state spent more than $100 million to buy farmlands in 1998 to restore Lake Apopka but only $200,000 to retrain the displaced farmworkers, many of whom had no other job skills and suffered from lingering health problems. Thousands of people who made a living planting, picking, and packing vegetables came into contact—some for several decades—with the same chemicals once sprayed on crops that killed and damaged lake wildlife and bedeviled cleanup efforts. Economos says little attention was paid to farmworker health, adding that FWAF, which operated five offices around Florida on an annual budget of less than $1 million, could not address it: "We do not have the resources to conduct any kind of specific study to determine the number of cases and how that compares to national standards."[37]

Florida has a long history of farmworker labor in agriculture. As historian Cindy Hahamovitch notes, Everglades drainage through the 1920s "exposed hundreds of thousands of acres of land" that could be planted in food crops "while northern fields were still under snow." By the mid-1930s, "South Florida agriculture was big business," attracting migrant farmworkers from along the Atlantic coast. As a consequence of this and the Great Depression that left many people out of work, Hahamovitch writes, it became "both possible and necessary for thousands of black southerners to migrate year-round in search of harvest work." Many worked in Florida in the winter and headed back north for other crops in the summer. By 1940 an estimated 40,000 to 60,000 migrant workers came to the state annually, working the vegetable crops that sprouted from Everglades muck. Growers and crew leaders who wanted to keep wages low exploited poor male and female migrants who were "stateless" since "they paid no taxes and did not vote." As a result local and state governments had little interest in their "health, housing, and working conditions," deemed to be the responsibility of the federal government. When the federal government did intervene, it was on behalf of growers, which undermined farmworkers' bargaining power. By 1973 UFW represented 40,000 jobs—10 percent of seasonal farm work—in California. In Florida the UFW in 1999 got a contract for mushroom workers in Quincy, making them the only unionized farmworkers in the state. However, because Florida is a right-to-work state, writes Riley, unionizing was difficult, and when established, unions "wield little power to increase employees' wages," leaving many to live in "squalid, crowded housing with poor sanitation." Union activity also was stunted in Florida because of the rising number of undocumented farmworkers from Mexico who were unwilling to protest against their employers. By the end of the twentieth century Florida had an estimated 200,000 to 350,000 farmworkers—an uncertain number compounded by the number of undocumented laborers.[38]

In many ways Economos's concerns reflected those of Minnie Moore-Willson in the early part of the century. Moore-Willson worried that native people and their needs were overshadowed by Everglades drainage and park plans, just as Economos saw Lake Apopka restoration ignoring nearby farmworkers. Neither woman had the political or financial power to resolve the problems alone. Instead, they relied on organizations to publicize issues and gain clout for the reparations they believed were owed to the oppressed people with whom they worked. However, Economos and FWAF were confronting an issue that Moore-Willson could not have imagined—the damage that postwar technology in the form of fertilizers and pesticides caused to the environment and the health of those who labored in the fields. It was an issue being raised by UFW in California at the same time.[39]

The FWAF surveyed 148 former farmworkers in 2006 and found that 92 percent had been exposed at work to pesticides, with 79 percent believing that the chemicals were key to their health problems, including arthritis, rheumatism, diabetes, allergies, and breathing and skin problems. Some 13 percent reported children with birth defects; 26 percent had children with learning disabilities; and 11 percent had a family member with lupus. Former farmworker Margie Lee Pitter, who suffered four miscarriages and never bore children, said she had no idea that her work in the fields might have caused her infertility. She realized later that aerial pesticide spraying made her sick: "When I started working in the 1960s, the boss just told us to go over to the side of the field when the plane came over with the spray so we wouldn't get sprayed on, but we all felt the mist in our faces 'cause it blew around. Sometimes we all had headaches, blurry vision and felt sick, but nobody told us it might be the chemicals."[40]

A 2011 study by the National Institute of Environmental Health Sciences linked pesticide exposure to autoimmune diseases such as lupus and rheumatoid arthritis, confirming the fears of many former Lake Apopka farmworkers that went unrecognized by government leaders. As local reporter Christopher Balogh notes, "No one disputes that it's in the air and water. But proving that it's in the people is a whole other matter." Economos acknowledges that it is a complex and controversial issue: "The farmworkers were exposed to many different pesticides, which vastly complicates the issue. It is not as black and white as 'cigarette smoke causes lung cancer.'" The problems of the Lake Apopka farmworkers were not unique, as evidenced by a number of national studies showing that chronic exposure to agricultural chemicals damages health. These issues were compounded by the fact that many workers migrated to work with different crops, did not speak English, and were illegal aliens, making them less likely to seek medical help. In 1994 Florida passed a "Right to Know" law requiring growers to notify workers of dangers from the pesticides they handled. Despite this, farmworkers frequently were injured in accidental poisonings, some of which resulted in court cases and financial rewards to injured workers.[41]

A half-century after *Harvest of Shame*, Economos says, "farmworkers are still invisible," and that status benefits agricultural interests; the labor force has no rights to organize and no federal labor safety oversight. Economos finds it ironic that consumers worry about agricultural chemicals only in terms of their own health, with little or no regard for the effects of the same chemicals on the human harvesters. This disconnect, Economos says, is due in part to racism, particularly the fact that most of the early Lake Apopka farmworkers were African American. Racism always made it culturally easier to ignore minorities, she says, firmly placing the Lake Apopka situation in the arena of environmental justice: "The consciousness that allows us to exploit people is the same consciousness that allows us to exploit the environment." The underpinning of modern agriculture, she says, was slavery: "We need a cheap, exploitable labor force to harvest our crops—we think we need it—in this country and so we have used that as a way to exploit people."[42]

Economos's concerns were shared by many other activists in the farmworker community. Friends of the Earth, an environmental group, worked with the FWAF, Farmworkers Self-Help, Florida Consumer Action Network, and the Legal Environmental Assistance Foundation to issue a 1998 report that detailed the deleterious effects on farmworkers (and on the Earth's ozone layer) of methyl bromide, a fumigant used in tomato and strawberry production. Riley writes that the EPA issued a directive to stop use of the chemical by 2001, "but many growers requested extensions." The federal government and pesticide producers were reluctant to acknowledge a link between chemicals and human health, Economos says, because that "would open up a whole can of worms. It wouldn't just be the Lake Apopka farmworkers. It would open up issues for farmworkers all over the country," and the possibility of financial liability being assessed against both groups. In the late twentieth century, lawsuits against various companies and government entities, including the EPA, were filed on behalf of farmworkers who believed their health was damaged by chemicals.[43]

In the agricultural world, as with sectors depicted in this chapter, women once again were the sparks that ignited activism. The core group of farmworkers who worked with Economos was female. Men tend to shy away from these issues, possibly out of a masculine need to deny any health problems or simply because they fear for their jobs and safety, she says, adding that women "are more courageous in many ways than men," perhaps because of their instincts for nurturing and protecting family members.[44]

For the past century, justice is what Florida women sought for the state's forgotten, ignored, and disadvantaged—the victims of politics and economics that determined the "best use" of Florida's natural resources. Draining the Everglades meant development, with little regard for the Seminole and Miccosukee people who took refuge there. A filthy, dioxin-contaminated river was the price to be paid for jobs in a rural community. Chemicals seeping into residential yards from industry were just hazards of the job, as were the poverty, decrepit housing, and chemical contamination visited upon farmworkers and their families. These were the "necessary" costs to be paid for progress in a state that was rapidly booming from 2.7 million people in 1950 to 12.9 million in 1990. Many Florida women, however, came to believe that such excesses and exceptions were unconscionable. The damage affected and sickened families, adding incalculable human and environmental costs to the price of Florida's "progress." Rising up in anger and with the solidarity of many others—from clubwomen to nuns to local activists—women once again were energized by their passion to clean up an environmental mess and help others. They took up the mantle for the dispossessed, some earning great success and others finding a lifelong mission that by the early decades of the twenty-first century had no end in sight.[45]

10

Women Leaders

When Muriel Wright Wagner was elected Escambia County's first female county commissioner in 1983, a campaign worker made her a large pink button. It proclaimed: "Don't call me honey, baby, lady, or girl. Call me commissioner." It was a sign of the times, of a growing women's equality movement in the late twentieth century that offered a bright new world for Florida's environmentally minded women. With the rising tide of female rights and opportunities, women integrated a love of and concern for their natural surroundings into professional and elected positions. In unprecedented numbers, women established and led organizations, served on political boards, and ran state and national bureaucracies. At the same time many were elected to local and state offices, carrying with them voter mandates to deal with Florida's unbridled growth.

But the road to public office was anything but easy. Women had to deal with an overwhelmingly male government structure and rampant sexism on every level as they pressed their agendas for change. Their stories and experiences demonstrate the shifting political tides of the era and reveal how these Florida women gained unprecedented influence, with one of them running the world's most powerful environmental agency.

Wagner moved to the Pensacola area in 1967, after her husband accepted a college administration job. Her activism was ignited when a local woman, Judy Coe, asked Wagner to look into a proposal that would create a pass through the nearby Navarre Beach coastal community. The project would have created a watery cut through a barrier island "supposedly to flush the bay out"—a pollution dispersal idea she says "is still not smart." Wagner and Coe visited local ecofriendly groups such as the Audubon Society and the Sierra Club and convinced them that the project "was not a very smart thing to do environmentally." They also sought support from the League of Women Voters of the Pensacola Bay Area (LWVPBA) to oppose the proposal. It was stopped, but the scheme periodically continued to "surface like a manatee and pop its head up so you always have to be on the alert." While an LWVPBA member, Wagner monitored the Escambia County Commission's work, and finally "I kept saying to myself, 'You know, I can do that.'" When a federal judge ruled that commissioners should be elected by district, Wagner quickly filed to run for office; her husband heard about it after the fact.[1]

This was not a woman who needed or waited for male approval—this was a strong individual who acted on her own instincts when the timing was right, the epitome of the feminist movement. Wagner did not win in her first attempt, but she persisted, becoming Escambia County's first elected female commissioner in 1983; she was often the commission's lone environmental vote.

Wagner ran on a platform of change and reform and conducted an extensive door-to-door electioneering effort. At a political rally prior to the election, she declared that "voters are tired of county government 'run by the good old boys,' and offered herself as a candidate with no strings to private interests," wrote local newspaper reporter Michael Burke, adding that Wagner "blamed the county for not enforcing laws and plans that will protect valuable resources such as the county's beaches, which she said are beginning to look like Miami Beach." Here was the new Florida political woman, calling out the "good old boys'" network, anchored for decades in the state's Panhandle, that had wreaked much of the destruction of the area's once exquisite coast, estuaries, and wetlands. Well-informed confrontation mixed with strong organization and plain speaking delivered the vote for Wagner, who touted her service as vice president of the local Audubon Society and as past president of the LWVPBA. Even though Pensacola was a bastion of conservatism, Wagner's election demonstrated that voters had seen sufficient problems to support her platform and candidacy. Perhaps they were truly afraid of becoming another overdeveloped beach community like those found in southeastern Florida.[2]

The expanding feminist movement and a reaction to abuse of power by male politicians, particularly in the Watergate era that saw the disgrace and resignation of President Richard M. Nixon, propelled many women into statewide office in the 1970s, observed Helen Gordon Davis of Tampa, who served in both chambers of the state legislature from 1974 to 1992. The public, she said, "turned to women as the panacea to all their ills. Those women who were elected at that time were older, mostly in their forties, more issue-oriented—coming from their studies with the League of Women Voters and the PTAs—and for the most part their purpose was to make the world a better place for their children and grandchildren to live." However, they were naïve about "power politics and unprepared for the condescension and derision that greeted every issue relating to women," including alimony awards, sex education, and displaced homemaker awards. Despite this, Davis said, women, "with a few great men," became the "conscience of the Legislature—the gadflies that opened new avenues of consideration for the social issues of the day—the farm workers, child abuse, mental health, day care, substandard salaries, etc." As Florida became politically more conservative, so did its female legislators, she said, declaring sexism to be "alive and well in Florida government," although less overt. When Senator Pat Collier Frank of Tampa spoke in 1990 to a Senate committee considering eliminating the Florida's Commission on the Status of Women, she encountered similar treatment, writes Allen Morris, historian of the state House of Representatives. When an "amused committeeman" suggested that there should be a similar group on the status of men, Frank replied that there was such a committee: the Florida Senate. "The abashed committee voted to continue the Commission."[3]

Like Wagner, Helen Digges Spivey of Crystal River was elected to state office on an environmental and ethics platform. It was a minor political miracle when Spivey was elected in 1994 to the state House of Representatives, becoming the only Democrat in the country that year elected to a traditionally Republican seat. Spivey did it without big money or yard signs, opting instead to chat with anyone who was interested in her views. Her own party warned her not to run for the office because she was female and too old—"the wrong thing to say." As a result, she immediately filed to run for election, which she won based on her record as an advocate for manatees and for protecting the river. She also refused to take large campaign contributions. When her opponent accepted big funds from Everglades sugar interests, Spivey responded with a flyer that read "How Sweet It Is."[4]

Wagner, Spivey, Frank, and Davis were part of the surge of feminism, civil rights, and environmentalism that swept through the United States in the 1960s, 1970s, and 1980s. Society and government were forced to respond to increasing demands for action in these movements, resulting in landmark state and federal laws. One of the era's highlights was the 1964 Civil Rights Act, the culmination of many years of grassroots organizing and protests by females of all ages and races. Title VII of the 1964 act included a prohibition against employment discrimination based on race, creed, national origin, and sex, making it "the strongest legal tool yet available to women," writes historian Sara Evans. Women demanded and expected equal pay, although it did not materialize. However, the growing women's equality movement, born in the civil rights struggle, had forever changed women's public participation. As Evans notes, women dared "to test the old assumptions and myths about female nature against their own experience and discovered that something was drastically wrong. And they dared because within these movements they had learned to respect themselves and to know their own strength." Ironically, many women around the nation had been stuck into subservient roles within the civil rights movement as secretaries and housekeepers, but most had seen a widening tunnel of opportunity and were heading for the light at the end of it.[5]

Like their civil rights sisters across the country, Florida women were important organizers in the movement; both white and black women held leadership roles. Ruth Willis Perry was a white, middle-class Miami resident who became incensed by the 1951 bombings that killed Harry T. and Harriette Moore at their home in Mims, Florida. The Moores were involved in the National Association for the Advancement of Colored People (NAACP). As historian Judith G. Poucher notes, Perry, who became an NAACP state and local officer, "repeatedly risked her life, reputation, career, and even a jail sentence to defy the racist agenda of the Florida legislature" in her work as a journalist and in testimony before the legislature's racist Johns Committee. Matilda "Bobbi" Graff and Shirley M. Zoloth, both white Jewish Americans, were active in Miami civil rights as well, Graff working with the Miami Civil Rights Congress until 1951, and Zoloth with the Miami chapter of the Congress of Racial Equality (CORE). African American women, including Mary McLeod Bethune, Blanche Armwood, and Eartha White, came from clubwomen backgrounds and were members of the National Association of Colored Women. As historian Maxine D. Jones writes, these women "launched a direct attack on poverty," implementing long-range strategies to improve education, voting rights, and economics, and to end lynching in Florida. Bethune, of Daytona Beach, earned the respect of many whites and has been characterized as one of the nation's most important civil rights leaders.[6]

During the same era, women assumed leadership roles in the gender equality movement, challenging the status quo that tried to put females in prescribed domestic roles. In 1966 a group of women, including feminist author and activist Betty Friedan, created the National Organization for Women (NOW) to focus specifically on the issues of women's rights and equality. As its name implies, the group had lost patience with national and state commissions and processes that seemed to stagnate, slowing any real change. These women wanted immediate results. NOW's purpose was: "To take action to bring women into full participation in the mainstream of American society now, assuming all the privileges and responsibilities thereof in truly equal partnership with men." In a sense, Evans notes, NOW was a "modernized version" of the nineteenth-century suffrage crusade, but the group suffered from a lack of organizational skills, which slowed its growth into a national movement. Still, it was a signal that times were changing for women, whose lives no longer resembled those of their mothers and grandmothers. By the late 1960s women's roles had changed dramatically, no longer mimicking the 1950s model of the happy housewife. The concept of women's liberation, or "women's lib," also arose by 1970, forcing Americans to rethink and debate women's roles.[7]

In many ways women seeking greater public acceptance and participation repeated successful strategies from the past. Seven decades earlier they bonded together in clubs, social circles, and garden groups to share common interests and concerns. From there they engaged in activism, finding support and bonds among members of the same sex, and honing their political skills to address issues created by male-dominated society. By the last decades of the twentieth century women once again looked to each other for backing. One of the biggest battles was that of the Equal Rights Amendment (ERA), first proposed in 1923 to mandate equal rights for both sexes. It failed, but was revived forty-nine years later, after "Congress suddenly recognized the political power of women," Evans notes, and "rushed to appease a constituency that potentially represented more than half of the voting public, making it possible to gain hearings, votes, and legislative victories with breathtaking speed." Congress approved the ERA in March 1972, and it was ratified by twenty-two states by year's end. However, the ERA never acquired the necessary thirty-eight states to be enacted, and it expired in 1982; Florida was one of the states that rejected the amendment. It was a disappointing result for feminists but a signal that the male-dominated Congress and other elected bodies were becoming more responsive to female constituents and their concerns.[8]

It was a time of opportunity for women who were proven organizers and leaders within ecology organizations. They carved out important niches in activism, sometimes with traditional groups, which often led to greater recognition and wider prospects in public service as appointed and elected officials. In "Creating a Different Pattern: Florida's Women Legislators, 1928–1986," law professor Mary Carolyn Ellis and historian Joanne V. Hawks offer a detailed examination of the background of the state's female elected leaders. Of the forty-nine women who served in the legislature, eight had been president of state or local League of Women Voters (LWV) groups; another eleven were LWV members. Many others were members of different business, professional, and same-sex groups. "The woman who spends a significant amount of time and energy on civic matters is usually able to gain valuable insight about society and political needs," they observe. "Participation in clubs has often been a factor in women's decisions to run for office." After the 1970s, they note, the LWV's increased lobbying activity on behalf of ERA "provided a training ground for women who believed that the best way to effect change was by getting elected rather than through lobbying efforts." Adds historian Adam Rome: "Study groups of the League of Women Voters were particularly good jumping-off places for careers in politics."[9]

As with Wagner, a number of environmental advocates arrived at the cause through the LWV and its local chapters. During her student days at the New College of the University of South Florida (later renamed New College of Florida) in Sarasota, Julie Morris met four local league members who asked for her help analyzing proposals that would convert a cattle ranch into a large residential development. Morris, daughter of a LWV member, was "predisposed to fit well" with the group and used her training to help assess the ranch's native land cover. Morris describes one of the women, Mary Kumpe, as "an extraordinary networker" who "encouraged and supported" Morris's involvement in community groups. Morris spent the next few decades of her life working on environmental issues. Kumpe, a public affairs consultant, later served for five years on the Southwest Florida Water Management District and was involved in many civic groups.[10]

Appointed boards also provided an important door for women to enter the state's environmental power structure. In the early part of the century some Florida women served on boards that addressed forestry, parks, and planning, giving a female sensibility to these efforts. Many decades later Florida women served on newly created governmental bodies that addressed concerns ranging from wildlife to water resources. During the 1980s and into the next decade, as different panels were formed around the state, Morris was appointed to a variety of boards, including those considering coastal management and state wildlife; she served as chair of the Florida Game and Freshwater Fish Commission in 1995—having been the first ecofriendly member of a body largely formed of avid hunters and fishers—and, four years later, served as chair of the Florida Fish and Wildlife Conservation Commission, a merger of the first group with marine fisheries management. She was often the only woman (and the only environmentalist) on these panels, a lonely role. It forced her to "hone my skills in terms of speaking up and being assertive," she says, and to rely on facts, working with staff, and using her ability to respect others and find resolutions.[11]

By the 1980s growth management was a major issue in Florida politics, arising from public concerns about the state's population explosion that brought with it a demand for more infrastructure, schools, housing, and commercial construction. The state had boomed to 9.7 million residents in 1980 and rose to 12.9 million in 1990. Development pressed into more and more natural areas where land was cheaper and easily accessed by the automobile, made ubiquitous by rising American wealth. Voters increasingly pressed their leaders for solutions, resulting in the 1972 State Comprehensive Planning Act. This legislative act, an attempt to encourage long-range planning, created a Division of State Planning to guide the initiative. However it was largely a failure as local governments ignored its guidelines. A decade later the legislature, with the strong endorsement of Governor Bob Graham, adopted the Local Government Comprehensive Planning and Land Development Act of 1985, which mandated that all local governments adopt long-term plans and submit them for state review. Leaders hoped that placing controls on local governments would stem suburban sprawl; but without the cooperation of local governments and state funding to enable concurrency of infrastructure, the legislation failed to manage rampant growth.[12]

Growth management drew a number of women into action. As a county commissioner Wagner helped Escambia County adopt a mandatory comprehensive growth plan, a central LWVPBA issue. "That was part of my goal, was to plan what we did in terms of how our county looks," she says, adding, "everyone thought I was stupid. Even the newspaper thought I was pretty dull." In a 1988 guest editorial in the *Pensacola News Journal*, Wagner linked the issue to quality of life and problems such as flooding and traffic gridlock. It is difficult to convince elected officials that those are the result of "haphazard growth," she wrote, warning that solutions "are not cheap nor easy. They require time, expertise, and money; they are the products of a process which means compromise." Wagner lost a reelection bid after one term, but stayed engaged in environmental work, serving on the state Environmental Regulation Commission, the county board of adjustment, the Audubon Society, and the LWVPBA, where she continued to monitor the Escambia comprehensive plan. She received awards from the Florida Audubon Society, the Florida Wildlife Federation, and from the *Pro Earth Times*, the latter declaring her to be a "standard bearer" for aspiring activists, noting her tenure of service "both publicly and behind the scenes, as an articulate voice for sound environmental politics on the local and state level."[13]

Across the state in Martin County, Margaret "Maggy" Reno Hurchalla was for many years the only elected woman on an environmentally and politically split county commission. Yet during two decades of elected office she achieved a number of protections that made the county a model of growth management.

Growing up in a rural homestead outside Miami, surrounded by pines, palmettos, and cow pasture, Hurchalla and her three siblings (her sister is former U.S. attorney general Janet Reno) were schooled in the outdoors by her newspaper-reporter parents. All have been described as "tall and rangy, independent, liberal, outspoken and a little quirky." After college and marriage, Hurchalla moved to coastal Jupiter in the mid-1960s, when her husband got a job with an aerospace firm. Although she describes herself as having been "barefoot and pregnant" while raising her four children, Hurchalla became interested in a number of ecological issues, in particular a plan to develop six hundred acres of coastal Stuart. She started a movement to have the beach bought by the state and enlisted the cooperation of the local Audubon Society. She pulled strings, contacted news media, and found friends to support the cause. The land was developed—but not at the concentration first proposed— and in response other like-minded residents and organizations, including the Martin County Conservation Alliance, pushed through a four-story height limit and a fifteen-unit-per-acre density cap on county construction in 1972. After chairing a county water board, in 1974 Hurchalla ran for county commissioner, touting growth management regulations; a Republican opponent advertised that she was "When You Buy a Swamp What You Own Is a Swamp Hurchalla" as a means to alert property-rights proponents to her long-standing environmental leanings.[14]

"Martin County has never had an election since then that was not fought about environmental issues," says Hurchalla, noting that anyone running for office must claim to be ecologically minded and to support the county's comprehensive growth management plan in order to be elected. Hurchalla became the first woman elected to the county commission, gaining a reputation as a no-nonsense, straight-talking representative who fought well into the twenty-first century for restoring the Everglades, preserving water resources, curbing urban sprawl, and saving wetlands. She continues to rankle; a news columnist described her in 2013 as "the spiritual leader of the no-growth, anti-business, anti-agriculture, and anti-private property rights faction in

Martin County. Actually, she has been for the best part of four decades. And, boy, does she love it."[15]

The greatest indication of feminine influence on Florida environmental efforts was the number of women in the 1980s and 1990s who held high-level roles in state bureaucracies overseeing natural resources and enforcement. Females from a variety of backgrounds, including science, law, and politics, became important leaders of these agencies, forging a new path for the status of women and for natural resource protection in the state. Elsewhere in the country, however, it was a difficult time as conservative political influences in the 1980s, heralded by the presidency of Ronald Reagan, tried to dim feminist and ecological gains. In one of his first presidential acts, Reagan removed solar panels that had been installed at the White House by his predecessor, President Jimmy Carter, and he eliminated Carter's tax credits for alternative energy sources. It was a highly symbolic act, indicating that conservative agendas were not friendly to environmental causes. Instead, historian Benjamin Kline writes, Reagan and his supporters set out to repeal ecofriendly legislation and to install "notoriously antienvironmentalist individuals" to head important agencies that dealt with those issues. Everglades activist Marjory Stoneman Douglas publicly criticized Reagan, declaring, "I don't think he gives a damn about the environment." By the 1990s Florida experienced a similar conservative climate as a surge in Republican pro-business power brokers tried to dismantle a number of environmental regulations, including growth management laws perceived as detrimental to the state's economic health.[16]

The conservatism of the Reagan era also lessened the influence of the women's movement; indeed, the Republican Party even withdrew its long-standing support of the ERA. Reagan's nomination for the presidency, writes Catherine E. Rymph, "marked a clear defeat for Republican feminism" and the end of liberalism within the party; it also profoundly affected the entire women's movement. Although some characterized the period as a "backlash" against women's rights, perhaps in view of a declining patriarchy, too much had changed to reverse all the gains that women had won. Many women continued to work outside the home, becoming increasingly visible in public ways. And the decade produced a number of female "firsts": a Supreme Court justice, an astronaut, an Episcopal Church bishop, a vice-presidential nominee, and a network news anchor. The women's movement evolved in many ways, producing such strands as ecofeminism, in which feminists emphasized the image of the Earth as feminine and engaged in activities such as opposing nuclear power plants, toxic waste, and acid rain—the damaging results of male-run industry and institutions. Many Florida women engaged in similar efforts.[17]

Florida women also were in the front line of "firsts," leading large environmental agencies that had morphed to deal with rising growth and ecological realities. In the earliest days of statehood, the Internal Improvement Board was the first agency to handle management of Florida's resources, but its main goal was to raise money and oversee swamp and overflowed lands—or see them "improved" through development, drainage, agriculture, and railroad projects. In 1885 it was replaced with the Board of Trustees of the Internal Improvement Fund (IIF), composed of the governor and seven elected cabinet members. It was this board that encouraged Everglades drainage and the Boca Ciega Bay dredge-and-fill project. Other agencies arose to deal with different conservation issues, and in 1969 the state created the Department of Natural Resources (DNR) to combine them; in 1975 the IIF was consolidated into the DNR, making the latter responsible for oversight of all state natural resources. That same year the state created the Department of Environmental Regulation (DER) to guide enforcement of and compliance with state laws. In 1993 the legislature merged both agencies, creating the Department of Environmental Protection (DEP), which at century's end remained the state's major natural resource regulator. The agencies were often confused with one another, and many staff members worked in one, two, or all of the agencies during the decades they were growing in order to provide necessary protection for resources under threat from development.[18]

The changing shape of the state's bureaucracies afforded opportunities for many women, who increasingly were able to negotiate their way and fashion science-based careers despite some vestigial sexual bias. Victoria Jean Nierenberg Tschinkel, who held a degree in zoology, landed a job in 1974 as a field inspector with IIF, which was expanding its wetlands permitting programs—this time to protect the fragile areas rather than to give them away. During her job interview she was asked questions about her marital status, her husband's future career path, and whether she was planning to have children—questions that later would be banned because of their sexual discrimination implications. When Pamela Prim McVety interviewed that same year to be an IIF wetlands field inspector, she was told by her eventual boss, Joel Kuperberg, a land management expert, that she was "too petite" and "wasn't tough enough to go in the field and stand up to construction workers and developers if [she] had to stop a development or bulldozers on site." Those were fighting words for McVety, who held a master's degree in zoology and had protested in graduate school when, because of her sex, she was given demeaning assignments, such as washing test tubes. McVety complained to the IIF personnel head, who confronted Kuperberg; he then hired McVety, later becoming one of her best friends and "a big fan."[19]

During the Reubin Askew and Graham administrations in the 1970s and 1980s, there was a wave of hiring scientists in environmental bureaucracies, opening doors for females such as Tschinkel and McVety, who went on to hold high leadership roles at DER. Agency leaders such as Kuperberg, Jay Landers, who headed DER, and Ken Woodburn, environmental advisor to both governors, brought a number of smart, talented women into these agencies because "they wanted professionals and people who were good at their jobs," says McVety. It was a sure indicator, as well, of society's increased openness to career women. McVety said it was an exciting time to be in the agency: "For me it was absolutely wonderful. I was surrounded by extremely bright, caring people who wanted to make a difference." Agency employees were well educated; Askew and Graham were governors (and role models, she says) who cared about the environment and pressed that agenda; and federal laws such as the Clean Air Act and the Endangered Species Act made it a stimulating place and time.[20]

It was a new era, but women still had to negotiate their way within a largely male bureaucracy and state government. The young, hard-working Tschinkel—a number of people used the word "brilliant" to describe her—rose rapidly in the bureaucratic ranks; at age thirty-three, she became DER secretary, a title she held from 1981 to 1987 during Graham's administration, a time of new environmental laws and stricter enforcement of them. Along the way Tschinkel dealt with many men that some women might find daunting; as the daughter of a "very intimidating" father, however, she could deal with them, pushing back when necessary, keeping her sense of humor, staying true to herself, and viewing obstacles as challenges to overcome. At the time a number of the state's numerous agencies were competing, trying to "out-environmental each other" in this new field, she says. Tschinkel worked on new wetland regulations, eventually becoming assistant to DER's Landers, in part because of her understanding of politics outside and within the agency as well as her strong record of working with different players. If she was not well liked, Tschinkel says, she was a "well-respected and certainly very well-tolerated" figure among most people within DER—except a few men who had a hard time accepting her authority and "personality."[21]

McVety says Woodburn "adopted many of us as his women. . . . [It] sounds sexist but it was paternal. I think he liked working with us and he made a point to stay connected." Woodburn, she says, regularly called different women in the field: "He was always interested in what we thought about an issue and we used him to convey information to the Governor."[22]

Estus Whitfield, chief environmental advisor to Graham and the two governors who succeeded him, says Graham viewed women as equals with men and chose the best qualified people for boards and agencies regardless of their sex. Women, he said, often offered new insights to environmental groups. "I found and still find that women add a different perspective to things, a little bit different mindset," he says:

> By and large women, I thought, still do, were a little more sensitive to situations, looked at situations a little differently without the macho mask and macho clout interfering with their thoughts, comments, and decisions. I don't know to what degree this might play into it but the women seemed a little less prone to be politically influenced by the next person who came along talking to them. They seemed to be a little more independent in their thinking and decision-making. I don't know the reason for that. Perhaps because they weren't impeded by the same things that men were, which is being men and the so-called stronger sex and so forth. Women were a gentler, and in many cases, a more thoughtful force than men.

He notes that there were exceptions to this among both sexes but says the presence of women in state government and on boards provided a different consciousness.[23]

In 1977, during Askew's tenure, Tschinkel became DER assistant secretary, the highest-ranking environmental woman in state government. In dealing with the heavily male political and bureaucratic powerbase, it helped that Tschinkel was not part of the "old boy political network"—and that she was tough but also "sociable, attractive, and reachable," she says. "They were intimidated maybe by my power a little bit but they knew that they could see me and talk to me." Raised and educated in California, Tschinkel was an outsider, but she got along with the "good old boys," many of whom were savvy and smart, she says: "They were foreign to me and I was foreign to them and I think that was an advantage to us all. We had to come to some kind of terms."[24]

When Landers moved to DNR to help that agency recover from a scandal, Tschinkel interviewed for the secretary position, but it went to Jake Varn, whom she succeeded in 1981. There Tschinkel managed a $114 million budget and a staff of 1,136 people responsible for programs related to air and water quality and quantity, solid and hazardous wastes, wetlands protection, and coastal management as well as programs for flood control and sewage treatment plants. It was an enormous responsibility at a time when the state was seriously considering the future of its water resources. She helped draft a bill to raise a documentary stamp tax in 1981 to fund the purchase of environmentally sensitive lands as part of the Save Our Rivers program and then helped expand it in 1985. Under her leadership a new groundwater protection rule was established, one of the first and most advanced in the country. She was particularly proud of wetlands regulations and hazardous waste programs created during her tenure, but emphasized that none of the legislation could have been accomplished without the cooperation of Graham and a willing legislature. Like many other female activists, Tschinkel says her strengths are in her ability to multitask and to act as an integrator of information—qualities she labels as feminine. She avoided emotional arguments, concentrating instead on scientific data and technical arguments, made easier by her own science background. After she left DER Tschinkel went into consulting work with Landers and was the first female state director of the Florida Chapter of The Nature Conservancy as well as chair of 1000 Friends of Florida, a nonprofit organization that promotes managed growth.[25]

McVety worked for thirty years in state environmental agencies before her retirement in 2003, participating in almost every major issue that faced the state during that period. In 1977 McVety replaced Tschinkel as assistant to the DER secretary; Tschinkel had been promoted to DER assistant secretary, and the two often combined efforts. McVety addressed issues that ranged from restoring the Everglades to stopping phosphate mining in the Osceola National Forest and using a variety of groundbreaking approaches to protect the Apalachicola River. "It was during that period with Vicki [Tschinkel] and the governor [Graham] that you could do those kinds of things. You just very carefully and professionally took each one and you just did it." McVety used her science background to inform her work and often wished decision makers were as well informed: "I've always thought, I still think, and if somebody made me in charge, I would make elected officials take a literacy test about the state of Florida so they knew the history, they knew the science, they knew the environment, they knew the culture, and only then would I think they should run for public office. Because you expect these people to be knowledgeable to make the best decisions possible for the public. But it doesn't happen."[26]

McVety later served four years as director of the DNR's Division of Marine

Resources, with a strong focus on saving manatees and other species. During her tenure DNR created a manatee protection plan for thirteen counties that required local governments to draw up blueprints for coastal development to lessen impacts on the marine mammals, and that enacted speed zones and other measures—actions that infuriated a number of waterfront developers and local politicians. McVety says she was removed from that post because her agency was too successful in a politically heated arena. She encountered this again in her role as DEP executive coordinator for ecosystem management from 1994 to 1999. Florida politics in the 1990s became increasingly conservative and pro-business; as a result environmental concerns about plants and animals that might hinder development were becoming suspect in political circles. But McVety would not give up the facts and the science for political expediency. With ecosystem management at the newly formed DEP, McVety worked to create a new approach to land protection, developing a comprehensive, integrated methodology that involved the public, business, governments, and environmental interests. The program, developed from recommendations gathered from meetings around the state, encouraged local citizens to determine their long-term goals to protect natural resources. It also promised to streamline regulations and the permitting process—something that appealed to many developers and industries. However, the ecosystem management program (and McVety's job) ended when Governor Jeb Bush, a Republican developer, took office in 1999. McVety finished her state career at the Division of Recreation and Parks and later worked for climate-change initiatives.[27]

Like McVety, Virginia "Ginger" Bass Wetherell began her career as a high school teacher but forged a path to environmental leadership that in many ways represented the huge shift in women's roles. In 1982, while working with a Pensacola drug abuse program, Wetherell says she was "literally" talked into running for the legislature. She ran as a conservative Democrat against the same-party incumbent (she later switched to the Republican Party) and won, largely through a door-to-door campaign that refused contributions larger than $100. Some men slammed the door in her face, saying they would never vote for a woman; nevertheless, she became the first female elected to the state House of Representatives from the very conservative western Panhandle. In Tallahassee the House freshman class contained a number of women, she says, and they met veteran female legislators who were focused on "a women's agenda"—issues involving women and children. Wetherell, however, opted not to join any women's caucus, but instead to be a "person representing Pensacola" with a broad agenda, a decision that garnered criticism from some women who wanted her to follow their lead, as well as from others who thought she should be at home taking care of her children.[28]

In setting this course Wetherell found acceptance among male House members, who were willing to mentor her and help her join committees. "There was nobody coddling you or holding your hand or treating you differently." Wetherell served on the Natural Resources Committee, which appealed to her science background. Those were "fun" years, she says, because during the Graham administration Florida was responding to federal environmental mandates and trying to be progressive on issues that included growth management, wetlands, and clean water. Wetherell also became involved in agriculture, trade, transportation, appropriations, and education committees, rising to deputy majority leader along the way.[29]

Florida's political tides shifted to conservatism with the 1986 election of Republican Governor Bob Martinez. Wetherell, with her proven legislative ability and environmental interest, became Martinez's deputy director of DNR in 1988; three years later she became the agency's executive director. In January 1993 Governor Lawton Chiles, a pro-environment Democrat, asked Wetherell to head DER and to work on his initiative to merge DNR and DER to create DEP, a process that required legislative approval and that generated controversy among ecologically minded activists, who worried that it would diminish regulations. Wetherell, the perceptive politician who could engage both political parties, helped get a unanimous vote in both chambers to do so. She then headed the newly created 4,300-employee DEP, with a budget of $1.6 billion, until 1998, an experience she says was "overwhelming" because the cultures of the two agencies were very different. DNR was about science, conservation, loving the land, and developing parks; DER was focused on enforcement and regulations. Wetherell's political background helped pass her legislative agenda in her first two years, but it also worked against her in the ecological community, where she was viewed more as a politician willing to compromise than as a staunch environmentalist. As a result she recognized that she might be regarded by activists as one of the agency's most unpopular secretaries; one coalition of environmental groups, unhappy with DEP's handling of wetlands and other issues, once asked Chiles to fire her.[30]

Although Wetherell had butted heads with McVety over manatee regulations, at DEP they worked together on reorganization and ecosystem management. Their partnership demonstrated a combination of skills that Wetherell says was needed by agencies and environmental groups to be successful in today's world. Wetherell was most proud of the state's land-buying program that purchased 1 million acres during her tenure. "It'll outlive everything else we do because so many other laws that we passed or programs that we developed will be changed and modified or abandoned or whatever over time. There'll be new programs but obviously the land is there, you know, forever."[31]

Tschinkel, McVety, and Wetherell demonstrated the value of female governance in the state's natural resource bureaucracies. Using their talents and expertise, these women demanded and earned respect from Florida's political establishment. McVety says it also was a reflection of the "quality of leadership in the state," particularly of Askew, Graham, Chiles, and Chiles's lieutenant governor, Kenneth R. "Buddy" MacKay Jr., who worked closely with environmental agencies. "I have not experienced the kind of forward, creative, progressive, inclusive caring leadership that Askew, Graham and later Chiles/MacKay provided from other Governors," she states. "If we dig deep enough, each of the state leaders that was good at this—Joel (Kuperberg), Ken (Woodburn) and MacKay probably had great mothers and all felt comfortable working with strong women. I never cared what sex someone was, nor did they. I think we all were more interested in intelligence and willingness to work hard for Florida's environment."[32]

When Wetherell took over DER, she followed Carol Martha Browner, who went on to become the most powerful environmental chief in the United States and, arguably, the globe. Appointed by President Bill Clinton, Browner was administrator of the U.S. Environmental Protection Agency (EPA) from 1993 to 2001, the longest tenure of any person in that position. Browner had a wealth of experience in grassroots and political fields gained in a variety of national and state roles. She used it in negotiations that included restoring Florida's Everglades, reauthorization of the Safe Drinking Water Act, strengthening air pollution controls, and cleaning up more than six hundred hazardous waste sites—many of the same issues she had dealt with as Florida DER secretary from 1991 to 1993 as well as previously, as a legislative staffer for the Florida House of Representatives and later for U.S. Senators Albert Gore of Tennessee and Lawton Chiles of Florida. During her political rise Browner developed a strong philosophy about the environment: "It's where we live our lives and how we live our lives. It's not just a pretty place to visit on vacation." When she came to DER in 1991 after the Martinez administration, which was not perceived as pro-environment, Browner was surprised by a standing ovation at an Everglades Coalition annual meeting following her announcement: "I'm an environmentalist"—a word that she says was not even recognized by the spell check function on her computer. Politically, however, times changed: "I can't imagine getting a standing ovation for saying I'm an environmentalist today," she said in a 2011 interview.[33]

As a woman and mother, roles she embraced in her private and public life, Browner recognized in her EPA work the importance not only of saving the country's beautiful places but also of fighting pollution and protecting health. She often referred to her son and used maternal language that many women had used earlier in the century to expand their spheres of influence. "What made it easy for me to be passionate was I always thought that in both instances there was a sense of justice. That these were common goods—our air, our land, our water—and that we had an opportunity and an obligation to really protect them for future generations and to protect them in ways that were focused on the most at risk," such as children, pregnant women, and subsistence fishermen. Health and environmental issues, she believed, were the same—good air quality protects children with asthma. When EPA was under attack by Congress, Browner emphasized the agency's focus on "healthy" air and water, a message that could reach a "far broader population and go beyond those people who traditionally consider themselves environmentalists." This tactic, she says, successfully reframed the debate publicly and politically about the need for the EPA and stronger pollution standards. Opponents, who snickered at her frequent maternal references, discovered that "having a mother out there talking about these issues was very compelling" and made it "harder for them to sustain the attacks." Browner says being a woman and coming extremely prepared for any testimony worked to her advantage and won public support. For her efforts, the National Mother's Day Committee named Browner "Mother of the Year" in 1997 for providing "children with a safer, healthier world."[34]

As a "tough and aggressive" politician, Browner gained her share of critics, who pointed to an expansion of EPA's powers, size, and areas of regulation, many of which were touted as bad for business. However, in 2008 Browner was appointed by President Barack Obama to serve as his administration's energy coordinator, a title often referred to by news media as "climate czar" for its emphasis on dealing with issues of global climate change. She served in that post for three years. Browner's legacies, she says, are protection of lands by the state, ongoing Everglades restoration efforts, wetlands protections, strengthening of EPA's mission, and tougher pollution standards. In these national roles Browner joined the growing conversation about the new concept of sustainability, helping set the foundation for a view that became central to twenty-first century efforts that promoted healthy economics, energy, and ecology to address environmental ills and improve quality of life. At a 1996 meeting of the

Governor's Commission for a Sustainable Florida, held in West Palm Beach, Browner noted that citizens had an interest in protecting "the health of the people of South Florida, the economy and the environment," which included protection and restoration of the Everglades and Florida Bay. The common goal: "To achieve a sustainable South Florida."[35]

In assuming the nation's highest environmental power, Browner was the beneficiary of the legacy of a century of Florida women and their efforts to save and repair the state's natural resources. They were trailblazers, using their energies, training, and grasp of facts to gain hard-won respect and power in a male-dominated and often sexist morass of business, government, and community leaders who had abused the natural world in favor of economic interests. Browner, Tschinkel, McVety, and Wetherell were inheritors, the fruit of a conservation and ecological ethic planted and nurtured by their predecessors. By century's end they had become some of the most powerful environmental leaders in the state and nation, the full blooming of a century of female efforts to save Florida's natural resources.

Epilogue

The Legacy of Florida's Environmental Women

Near the end of her life, Everglades activist and author Marjory Stoneman Douglas took the occasion of yet another public honor to reflect upon Florida's changing environmental ethic. A state that once promoted draining its vast wetlands was honoring Douglas, aged ninety-one, for her feisty, tenacious campaign to save and restore the South Florida system, signifying a vast shift in attitudes during the twentieth century. By 1981 Douglas was the icon of Florida environmentalism, and now her name would grace the new copper-colored building for the Florida Department of Natural Resources, a bureaucratic agency that arose in 1969 to address the state's ecological ills.[1]

"Actually the whole environmental movement is a thing that is completely new," she said, adding that environmental protections that once left many people skeptical currently held widespread support. She urged her audience of three hundred, which included the governor and cabinet, news media, and employees of different state agencies, to continue protecting the natural world. She closed her remarks using a line often penned by one of her regular correspondents: "Yours always for our beautiful and beloved Florida."[2]

Those sentiments might have come from any number of Florida women whose talents, energy, and organizing skills were vital to saving the state's environment in the twentieth century. Their work led to greater public awareness, political action, and fundamental change in addressing the ecological ills that plagued Florida—from disappearing wildlife to polluted air to damaged waterways. In effect, they were cleaning up the mess that male-dominated industry, development, and government had created, and doing it with great passion and determination. To create such change, Florida women developed a variety of public and personal strategies to operate and succeed within the changing social and political expectations of the twentieth century, expanding their roles and power from grassroots workers operating in women's groups to joining and leading mainstream advocacy organizations and running state and national bureaucracies. Along the way, women expanded their influence, forging new identities and gaining public respect for their talents. Douglas was a prime example; once booed and chastised as a "bleeding heart" and an "old lady in tennis shoes," she was now a force to be reckoned with, commanding the respect of governors, presidents, and political hopefuls.[3]

Douglas was the most famous natural resource advocate in a state that became "ground zero" for some of the defining ecological conflicts of the century, with threats to its unique ecosystems often bringing it into the national spotlight. Other noted female activists include May Mann Jennings, a former governor's wife who was active in forestry, beautification, and suffrage efforts in addition to her extensive women's club work, and Carol Browner, who began as an environmental activist and eventually led the U.S. Environmental Protection Agency. Many never saw the fruits of their efforts: Clara Dommerich helped found the Florida Audubon Society in her living room but died during its first year; Marjorie Harris Carr went to her grave fighting to restore the Ocklawaha River, an unfulfilled goal; and Margaret Williams passed before the final cleanup of the "Mt. Dioxin" hazardous waste site in Pensacola.

Whatever their experiences, expectations, and results, these Florida women held many things in common. Their primary goal was not to put their names before the public. Instead, they worked out of a sheer love of the state and the beauty they found in its wildlife and landscapes. In summertime thunderheads, they saw the mountains that enthralled western visitors. In delicate orchids, they found wealth beyond measuring. In disappearing birds, they felt personal losses. Roadside garbage, free-roaming swine, and proliferating signs were abominations of their personal Edens.

As scientific discoveries, ecological principles, and health concerns came to the forefront, women came to view industry and development with skeptical eyes. Whatever the chamber of commerce claimed, it was clear that smoke was not the perfume of success—it was filth and meant sick, coughing residents. Raw sewage bubbling into the ocean and bays was a smelly, germ-filled menace that threatened families and destroyed sea grass nurseries. Industrial hazardous wastes could silently contaminate entire neighborhoods that had housed generations. With these realizations, environmentally minded women discarded economic rationalizations in favor of protecting their families. And because most of them were members of the upper and middle classes and not employed outside the home or by big corporate entities, they were not fettered by financial concerns. They developed and spread a message about the effects of environmental degradation on public health that appealed to and expressed their feminine and, often maternal, instincts and packed a powerful punch when used in community meetings, corporate gatherings, and congressional hearings. Taylor County activist Joy Ezell warns that it is dangerous to mess with a "mama bear," especially the human incarnation, once riled up by threats to her offspring.[4]

These female activists often found form and power in grassroots organizing. Even before they could vote, state women lobbied for and achieved legislation to protect wildlife and create Florida's first state park. As women's roles and rights increased in society, so did their visibility and participation. And as job opportunities opened up in scientific and ecological fields, women became important leaders in state bureaucracies charged with protecting and regulating natural resources. At no point in the century were women ever in charge, since the state remained firmly male-dominated in government and business. And many men cared just as passionately about the natural world, helping to pass laws, lead organizations, and raise awareness. But the feminine voice had reached new ears and, aided by federal laws, court cases, and evident crises, it helped force a change in the way the state's biological treasures were viewed and treated.

At the dawn of the twenty-first century it was clear that Florida women were proven environmental leaders. In 2001 Fran Mainella became the first female director of the National Park Service, having previously been the director of the Florida Park Service. Renowned oceanographer Dr. Sylvia Earle developed a love of Florida beaches while growing up in Clearwater; she became the first female chief scientist at the U.S. National Oceanic and Atmospheric Administration, *Time* magazine's first Hero of the Planet, and an Explorer in Residence for the National Geographic Society.[5]

These are the early leaders of the new century—professionally trained women who, like so many before them, found inspiration in Florida's beauty and then turned their sights to saving it for future generations. They continue the work of the clubwomen, garden clubbers, county commission protestors, angry mothers, and grassroots organizers whose actions and words were precursors to the idea of sustainability that swept the planet as the twenty-first century dawned. We are the beneficiaries of their gritty determination. How we treat the Florida environment in the current century will determine whether we are worthy to be their heirs.

Notes

Primary, secondary, and online sources are all given shortened citations in these notes; all appear in full in the bibliography.

Introduction

1. Davis, *An Everglades Providence*, 227–28.
2. Works that address Florida women's environmentalism include Vance, *May Mann Jennings*; Davis, *An Everglades Providence*; Davis and Frederickson, *Making Waves*; Davis and Arsenault, *Paradise Lost*; Macdonald, *Marjorie Harris Carr*; and Derr, *Some Kind of Paradise*.
3. Davis, *An Everglades Providence*, 218–19; Bubil, "A Century Ago, Bertha Palmer"; Black, "Mounted on a Pedestal."
4. Hughes, *What Is Environmental History?* 4.
5. For more information on "municipal housekeeping," see Blair, *The Clubwoman as Feminist*; Scott, *Natural Allies*.
6. Kaplan, *Crazy for Democracy*, 1–2.
7. Blum, "Women, Environmental Rationales," 79–80, 83–84.

Chapter 1. For the Birds

1. Blackman, *The Florida Audubon Society*, 1.
2. Poole and Maitland Historical Society, *Maitland*, 50–53.
3. Florida Audubon Society Minutes 1900–1910, (hereafter cited as FAS Minutes); Whipple, *Bird-Lore* 2, 97; Blackman, *The Florida Audubon Society*, 1–4.
4. "Obituary 1," *New York Times*, November 10, 1900; FAS Minutes; *Bird-Lore* 2, 203.
5. Byrd, Unmarked newspaper clipping.
6. Whipple, *Bird-Lore* 2, 97.
7. Doughty, *Feather Fashions*, 1–2, 12.
8. Ibid., 16.

9. Ibid., vii, 23; Merchant, "Women of the Progressive Conservation Movement," 69.

10. Derr, *Some Kind of Paradise*, 140; Weidensaul, *Of a Feather*, 151.

11. Derr, *Some Kind of Paradise*, 136–37.

12. Graham, *The Audubon Ark*, 3–13; Philippon, *Conserving Words*, 55–73.

13. Ponting, *A Green History of the World*, 167–70; Dorsey, *The Dawn of Conservation Diplomacy*, 13.

14. Hays, *Beauty, Health, and Permanence*, 19; Graham, *The Audubon Ark*, 14–23; Breton, *Women Pioneers for the Environment*, 255–57.

15. Philippon, *Conserving Words*, 73–95.

16. Scott, *Natural Allies*, 141.

17. Rome, "'Political Hermaphrodites,'" 442.

18. Merchant, "Women of the Progressive Conservation Movement," 57, 69–73.

19. Hays, *Beauty, Health, and Permanence*, 13.

20. Dorsey, *The Dawn of Conservation Diplomacy*, 168; Wilson, *The Future of Life*, 18, 134–43. Wilson has much to say about human affiliation with habitats as well as certain species. Certainly the non-threatening songbirds lauded by Audubon Societies would fit this category.

21. Vanderpool, Whipple, and Dommerich Files, Maitland Historical Society; Campen, *Winter Park Portrait*, 36–37; Blackman, *The Florida Audubon Society*, 1.

22. Brake, *Man in the Middle*, vii.

23. Blackman, *The Florida Audubon Society*, 1–6; FAS Minutes; "Kingsmill Marrs Photographs."

24. Derr, *Some Kind of Paradise*, 137; Graham, *The Audubon Ark*, 22–23; Blackman, *The Florida Audubon Society*, 7–8.

25. "Memorialized by Audubon Society."

26. FAS Minutes; Vanderpool files; Marrs, "Florida Audubon Society," 220; Blackman, *History of Orange County Florida*, 200.

27. Vanderpool, "Florida Society!" 183.

28. "Memorialized by Audubon Society"; FAS minutes; "Kingsmill Marrs Photographs."

29. FAS minutes; Marrs, "Florida Audubon Society," 220; Graham, *The Audubon Ark*, 46; Blackman, *The Florida Audubon Society*, 8–13; Philippon, *Conserving Words*, 95.

30. FAS minutes; Graham, *The Audubon Ark*, 48–59; Poole, "The Florida Story Begins with Audubon Wardens," 6–8; Blackman, *The Florida Audubon Society*, 17–18; McIver, *Death in the Everglades*, 110–11; Marrs, "State Reports—Florida," 316.

31. McIver, *Death in the Everglades*, 163.

32. Marrs, "Florida Audubon Society," 220; FAS Minutes; Dorsey, *The Dawn of Conservation Diplomacy*, 181; Dutcher, "Report of the Committee on Bird Protection," 133.

33. Blackman, *The Florida Audubon Society*, 15.

34. Downing, "Oak Lodge 1881–1910," 12, 14; Brinkley, *The Wilderness Warrior*, 488–89; Cleveland, ed., "History of Pelican Island National Wildlife Refuge."

35. Kline, *First Along the River*, 51–55; Gottlieb, *Forcing the Spring*, 20–25.

36. Merchant, "Women of the Progressive Conservation Movement," 57–58; Evans, "Women's History and Political Theory," 120–28.

37. Rome, "'Political Hermaphrodites,'" 442–43, 454; Unger, *Beyond Nature's Housekeepers*, 76–77.

38. Merchant, "Women of the Progressive Conservation Movement," 72; Price, "Hats Off to Audubon."

39. Blackman, *The Florida Audubon Society*, 20–21.

40. Munroe, "Two Plume-bearing Birds"; Davis, *An Everglades Providence*, 212–14, 225.

41. Blackman, *The Florida Audubon Society*, 20.

42. Meyer; *Leading the Way*, xii, 45–58.

43. Vance, *May Mann Jennings*, 56, 100.

44. Weatherford, *Real Women of Tampa* and *Hillsborough County*, 170; Blair, *The Clubwoman as Feminist*, 119; Wood, *The History of the General Federation of Women's Clubs*, 247–70.

45. Blackman, *The Women of Florida*, 2:145; Blackman, *The Women of Florida*, 1:x; Blackman, *History of Orange County Florida*, 186; Blackman, *The Florida Audubon Society*, 25, 42; Marrs, "State Audubon Reports—Florida," 448; "Audubon Society Notes"; Dieterich, "Birds of a Feather," 3–27.

46. Poole, "Katherine Bell Tippetts," 61–63; Blackman, *The Women of Florida*, 2:70; Blackman, *The Florida Audubon Society*, 25, 42; "Presidents of the St. Petersburg Audubon Society."

47. Poole, "Katherine Bell Tippetts," 63.

48. Ibid.

49. Tippetts, "Notes on the founding and current status of St. Petersburg Audubon Society, Inc.," FAS; Eastman, "'Bird Woman' Took Wing"; Poole, "Katherine Bell Tippetts," 64.

50. "The Pelican: His Enemies Take a Swing at Him."

51. "The Pelican: John Jones and Audubon Society Aid"; Poole, "Katherine Bell Tippetts," 66.

52. "Nature Program Is Presented at Florida Art School Session," 10.

53. Blackman, *The Florida Audubon Society*, 31–33.

54. Poole, "Katherine Bell Tippetts," 70–73; Hartzell, "Everything She Did Was Her Way of Being Good"; Blackman, *The Women of Florida*, 2:70.

55. Poole, "Katherine Bell Tippetts," 67.

56. Davis, *An Everglades Providence*, 215.

57. Orr, *Saving American Birds*, 3; Blackman, *The Florida Audubon Society*, 26–30; Marrs, "State Audubon Reports—Florida," 367.

58. Blackman, *The Florida Audubon Society*, 21, 30–31, 44; Derr, *Some Kind of Paradise*, 138–39; Davis, *An Everglades Providence*, 193.

Chapter 2. Conservation and Forests

1. Earley, *Looking for Longleaf*, 1, 8, 14–16.

2. Ibid., 1; Udall speech, "The Conservation Challenge of the Sixties."

3. "Mrs. F. L. Ezell Pleads for Protection of Virgin Lands," 5.

4. Ponting, *A Green History of the World*, 256; Cronon, *Nature's Metropolis*, 151–54, 202–3.

5. Earley, *Looking for Longleaf*, 2.

6. Ibid., 3, 175.

7. Ibid., 86–87; University of Florida School of Forest Resources and Conservation, "The History of the School"; *Program* for presentation of seat and plaque; "Bronze Plaque Marks Coquina Garden Seat"; Tracy L'Engle Anglas Papers.

8. University of Florida School of Forest Resources and Conservation, "The History of the School"; Cowdrey, *This Land, This South*, 111–14.

9. Hays, *Beauty, Health, and Permanence*, 13–17.

10. Marsh, "Human Responsibility for the Land," 41, 44; Miller, *Gifford Pinchot and the Making of Modern Environmentalism*, 55–56.

11. Nash, ed., *American Environmentalism*, 73; Pinchot, "The Birth of 'Conservation,'" 75.

12. Brinkley, *The Wilderness Warrior*, 237–38; Hays, *Conservation and the Gospel of Efficiency*, 2, 47, 127.

13. Hays, *Conservation and the Gospel of Efficiency*, 142, 144.

14. Merchant, *Earthcare*, 110–16; Binkley, "Saving Redwoods: Clubwomen and Conservation," 171, n.21, n.22.

15. Jarvis, "How Did the General Federation of Women's Clubs Shape Women's Involvement?"

16. Binkley, "'No Better Heritage than Living Trees,'" 182–88, 189, 196–200, 202.

17. Adams-Williams, "Conservation—Woman's Work," 350–51.

18. Rome, "'Political Hermaphrodites,'" 450–51; Rimby, "'Better Housekeeping Out of Doors,'" 3.

19. Meyer, *Leading the Way*, 35.

20. Vance, *May Mann Jennings*, 1–8, 18–19, 79, 121.

21. Ibid., 1, 7, 118–20.

22. Ibid., 121.

23. Smith, "Clubwomen Should First Be Home Makers."

24. "Citation for Outstanding Contributions to Forestry," Jennings Papers.

25. Whitman, "Report of Committee on Conservation," 6–7.

26. Ibid., 7.

27. Whitley, "Forestry and Wild Life Refuges"; Blackman, *The Women of Florida*, 2:134.

28. Jeffreys, "Forests, Their Use and Beauty," 13, 24.

29. Ibid.; Earley, *Looking for Longleaf*, 20–25.

30. King et al., eds., *Fifty Year History of Florida Federation of Garden Clubs*, 14–17; Florida Federation of Garden Clubs, 1932 (hereafter cited as FFGC, with year), *Board Reports, March 21, 1929–March 20, 1935*, 7; FFGC, 1932, "Florida Federation of Garden Clubs Board Meeting, March 14, 1932."

31. FFGC, 1935, "Florida Federation of Garden Clubs in Convention Assembled at West Palm Beach, Florida," 14–15; "Campaign History."

32. Vance, *May Mann Jennings*, 120; Jennings, "Conservation Laws Stand to the Credit of Florida."

Chapter 3. Creating Parks

1. Tebeau, *A History of Florida*, 343; Davis, *An Everglades Providence*, 216.

2. Gifford and Edwards, letter dated July 1916; Davis, *An Everglades Providence*, 216–17; Vance, *May Mann Jennings*, 58, 80–81, 154; Hays, *Conservation and the Gospel of Efficiency*, 47.

3. Blackman, *The Florida Federation of Women's Clubs*, 34; Vance, *May Mann Jennings*, 58, 80–81.

4. Vance, *May Mann Jennings*, 81; Tebeau, *A History of Florida*, 343.

5. Davis, *An Everglades Providence*, 219; Vance, *May Mann Jennings*, 81–82; Vance, "The Park Before the Park."

6. Vance, *May Mann Jennings*, 59; Blackman, *The Women of Florida*, 1:133, 136.

7. Vance, *May Mann Jennings*, 82–83; Davis, *An Everglades Providence*, 219–20.

8. Vance, *May Mann Jennings*, 83–85; Kaufman, *National Parks and the Woman's Voice*, 34; Wells, "Florida Clubwomen See Dream Realized in Everglades Park."

9. Vance, *May Mann Jennings*, 85, 87; Nemmers, "May Mann Jennings, Clubwomen and the Preservation of Royal Palm State Park in Florida," 4; Moore-Willson, letter to Mrs. I. Vanderpool, March 19, 1916.

10. Jennings, letter to Minnie Moore-Willson, May 12, 1915, 2.

11. Vance, *May Mann Jennings*, 86.

12. Kaufman, *National Parks and the Woman's Voice*, 32–34.

13. Sherman, "Safeguarding What We Have," 3; Kaufman, *National Parks and the Woman's Voice*, 32–33.

14. Nash, *Wilderness and the American Mind*, 108; Dilsaver, "The Early Years."

15. Hays, *Beauty, Health, and Permanence*, 100–101; Rome, "'Political Hermaphrodites,'" 441–42.

16. Nash, *Wilderness and the American Mind*, 180(n); Hays, *Beauty, Health, and Permanence*, 101.

17. Vance, *May Mann Jennings*, 88–91; Davis, *An Everglades Providence*, 226; Sollitt, "Report," Woman's Club of Coconut Grove Records.

18. Nemmers, "May Mann Jennings, Clubwomen and the Preservation of Royal Palm State Park in Florida," 7; Vance, *May Mann Jennings*, 39.

19. Davis, *An Everglades Providence*, 226; Vance, *May Mann Jennings*, 39.

20. Fairchild, letter to May Mann Jennings, July 18, 1916.

21. Ibid.; Jennings, letter to David Fairchild, August 15, 1916; Vance, *May Mann Jennings*, 90–117; Jennings, letter to C. S. Graham, August 11, 1928.

22. Nelson, "'Improving' Paradise," 93, 96; Davis, *An Everglades Providence*, 364.

23. Nelson, "'Improving' Paradise," 97–98; Davis, *An Everglades Providence*, 364–65.

24. Nelson, "'Improving' Paradise," 97; Highlands Hammock State Park, "History and Culture"; Werndli, *Florida State Parks*, 29.

25. FFGC, 1934, "Florida Botanical Florida Botanical Garden and Arboretum"; Highlands Hammock State Park, "History and Culture."

26. Derr, *Some Kind of Paradise*, 175, 178–82; Meindl, "Water, Water Everywhere," 125.

27. Derr, *Some Kind of Paradise*, 64, 313.

28. Ezell, "Report of Chairman Park Committee," Florida Historical Society; Dreisbach, *Umatilla*, 97–103.

29. "Fannie Veola Badger Ezell," online memorial.

30. Tippetts, "Mrs. Tippetts Lists Florida in This Class," 12; Meyer, *Leading the Way*, 103–5, 108–9.

31. McCally, "The Everglades and the Florida Dream," 150–52; Carter, *The Florida Experience*, 108–9; Douglas, *Florida: The Long Frontier*, 281–82. For fuller detail about creation of Everglades National Park, see Davis, *An Everglades Providence*; Grunwald, *The Swamp*; Douglas, *The Everglades: River of Grass*; Blake, *Land into Water—Water into Land*.

32. Davis, *An Everglades Providence*, 334–35, 338; Douglas, "Only Tropics in U.S. to Be National Park."

33. Davis, *An Everglades Providence*, 335, 338–39; Douglas and Rothchild, *Marjory Stoneman Douglas: Voice of the River*, 194.

34. Davis, *An Everglades Providence*. 340; Douglas and Stoutamire, *The Parks and Playgrounds of Florida*, 29.

35. Davis, *An Everglades Providence*, 342, 370.

36. Ibid., 333; Meyer, *Leading the Way*, 126; Vance, *May Mann Jennings*, 131, 154.

37. Vance, *May Mann Jennings*, 131–32.

38. Davis, *An Everglades Providence*, 393–94.

Chapter 4. The City and State Beautiful

1. Meyer, *Leading the Way*, 6, 7, 11, 12, 19–28.

2. Davis, "Shades of Justice," 82–83.

3. Chambliss, "Clubwomen and Municipal Housekeeping," 2–4.

4. Rimby, "'Better Housekeeping Out of Doors,'" 13–14; Wilson, *The City Beautiful Movement*, 129–32.

5. Knight, "The Environmentalism of Edward Bok," 158–59; Brown, *Setting a Course*, 30–32.

6. Runte, *National Parks*, 85; McFarland, "The New Department Beautiful America," 15.

7. Crooks, *Jacksonville after the Fire*, 3, 15.

8. Ibid., 84–85.

9. Meyer, *Leading the Way*, 38–40; Blackman, *The Florida Federation of Women's Clubs*, 5.

10. Meyer, *Leading the Way*, 93; "Miami Gets State Suffrage Meet and Dr. Anna Shaw Both in March."

11. Ezell, "Florida Parks," 5.

12. Robison and Belleville, *Along the Wekiva River*, 77.

13. Derr, *Some Kind of Paradise*, 313–14; "Rank by Population of the 100 Largest Urban Places."

14. Werndli, *Florida State Parks*, 36; King et al., eds., *Fifty Year History of Florida Federation of Garden Clubs*, 23; FFGC, 1952, "Minutes," Executive Board, October 23, 1952, 19; FFGC, 1953, "Minutes Florida Federation of Garden Clubs Twenty-Seventh Annual Convention," 19.

15. FFGC, 1949, "Minutes of the Twenty-Third Annual Convention," April 21–22, 1949, 9; "Madira Bickel Mound State Archeological Site" (website); "Gertrude Rollins," file, Rollins College; "Rollins Family" (website); "Rollins College Gets 100-Acre Estate on Fort George Island"; Blackman, *The Women of Florida*, 2:156–57; "Chinsegut Conservation Center" (website).

16. Lewis, "Orlando's 'Beautiful' Heritage," 9; "Mrs. A. B. Whitman," file, Rollins College; Blackman, *The Women of Florida*, 2:153.

17. "Mrs. A. B. Whitman," file, Rollins College; Blackman, *The Women of Florida*, 2:66, 153; Davis-Platt, "Brooksville to Celebrate Heritage."

18. Jameson, *Remembering Neighborhoods of Jacksonville, Florida*, 83; "News Among Colored People in the City and State," 13; *Jacksonville Looks at Its Negro Community*, 55; Clark, "Negro Women Leaders of Florida," 77.

19. Clark, "Negro Women Leaders of Florida," 7, 60; "Alice Mickens Park."

20. Florida Daughters of the American Revolution, "A Tree for Every D.A.R.," 71.

21. Hunter, *A Century of Service*, 192; Florida State Society of the D.A.R., *History 1933–1946*, 12; "DAR Forests—States," accessed February 15, 2012, http://www.dar.org/natsociety/content.cfm?ID=263&FO=Y&hd=n; Jones, "My Florida History"; Cridlin, "Planting Plan Blends Forestry, Genealogy."

22. Florida State Society of the D.A.R., *History 1892–1933*, 125–26, 145, 234, 288, 234, 309.

23. Derr, *Some Kind of Paradise*, 57–59.

24. "Forestry Department of the Florida State Federation of Women's Clubs," Woman's Club of Coconut Grove Records; *Florida Federation of Women's Clubs Annual*

Yearbook, 1916–1917 Reports, 94, FFGC; Hensley, *Florida Federation of Women's Clubs Annual Yearbook, 1927–1928*, 124, FFGC.

25. Garden Club of Jacksonville, "History"; FFGC, 1935, "The Florida Federation of Garden Clubs Fifth Annual Convention Minutes"; "Seminole County Big Tree Park."

26. King et al., eds., *Fifty Year History of Florida Federation of Garden Clubs*, 31; FFGC, 1952, "Minutes Twenty-Sixth Annual Convention"; Muir, *A Thousand Mile Walk to the Gulf*, 92; "Sabal Palm"; "Adoption of the Florida State Tree."

27. Wilson, *The City Beautiful Movement*, 47, 143; McFarland, "Beautiful America," 27; Knight, "The Environmentalism of Edward Bok," 154–65.

28. "Billboards Destroy Scenic Beauty," 7.

29. Lawton, "Florida Billboards," 13.

30. Ibid.

31. Brown, *Setting a Course*, 7; "Dark Years of Depression and War"; Nelson, "When Modern Tourism Was Born," 436–39.

32. FFGC, 1930, "Minutes Florida Federation of Garden Clubs Executive Board Meeting, Dec. 10, 1930"; Riggs, "President's Review," FFGC records.

33. Pryor, "Beatitudes of the Division of State Beautification," 14.

34. "Orlando Garden Club," Orange County Regional History Center; Crosby, *Fifty Years of Service*, 6, 54–55.

35. "Billboard Tax Gets Approval of Councilmen," 1–2.

36. FFGC, 1935, "Annual Convention Florida Federation of Garden Clubs" pamphlet, in *Board Reports March 21, 1929–March 20, 1935*.

37. FFGC, 1940, Resolution 4, "Florida Federation of Garden Clubs 14th Annual Convention, March 30–31, 1939," in 1940 Executive Board minutes, 10.

38. Crosby, *Fifty Years of Service*, 55.

39. Tompkins, "Annual State Convention," 10; Lurton, "Roadside Development Section," 11.

40. Vance, *May Mann Jennings*, 134–35.

41. "City Beautification Called 'Investment' at Florida Meeting," May Mann Jennings Papers.

42. Crosby, *Fifty Years of Service*, 55; "A History and Overview of the Federal Outdoor Advertising Control Program"; Floyd and Shedd, *Highway Beautification*, 1–2.

43. Pryor, "Beatitudes of the Division of State Beautification," 14.

44. Peterson, "Frederick Law Olmsted Sr. and Frederick Law Olmsted Jr.," 39, 45–49; Birch, "From Civic Worker to City Planner," 473.

45. Birch, "From Civic Worker to City Planner," 472–78.

46. Mould, "A Portrait in Black and White," 63–68.

47. Stephenson, "John Nolen," 7–13, 20–25; Eades, "City Planning in West Palm Beach," 282–83; Mohl and Mormino, "The Big Change in the Sunshine State," 428–31.

48. Seymour, "A State Plan for Florida," 197; Stephenson, "John Nolen," 45, 47; Davis, *An Everglades Providence*, 283–88.

49. Stephenson, "John Nolen," 45–46.

50. Seymour, "A State Plan for Florida," 197–99.

51. Ibid., 200–1.

52. Seymour, "Report Beautification Committee," FFGC records; FFGC, 1935, "Florida Federation of Garden Clubs in Convention Assembled at West Palm Beach, Florida," 12.

53. Trout, "We Need City Plans to Keep Property Attractive," 10.

54. Noble, ed., *The History of the Garden Club of Jacksonville*, 13; Gold, *History of Duval County Florida*, 474.

55. Noble, ed., *The History of the Garden Club of Jacksonville*, 16–17.

56. Haines, "Never Underestimate the Power of a Woman," 8.

57. Davis, *An Everglades Providence*, 426–27; Coconut Grove Committee for Slum Clearance, 2, untitled paper, Elizabeth Virrick Papers; Danahy, "Elizabeth Virrick," 250–51.

58. Davis, *An Everglades Providence*, 426–28; Coconut Grove Committee for Slum Clearance, 5–11.

59. Coconut Grove Committee for Slum Clearance, 12, 17; Danahy, "Elizabeth Virrick," 260–61; Davis, *An Everglades Providence*, 429; McGerr, *A Fierce Discontent*, 296, 310, 315–19.

60. Mohl, "Elizabeth Virrick and the 'Concrete Monsters,'" 32.

Chapter 5. The Three Marjories, Rachel, and the Rise of Ecology

1. Turcotte, "For This Is an Enchanted Land," 488–504; Rowe, *The Idea of Florida*, 108–9. For additional information about Rawlings, see Bigelow, *Frontier Eden*; Tarr, *Max and Marjorie*; and Rieger, *Clear-Cutting Eden*.

2. Rowe, *The Idea of Florida*, 108.

3. Rawlings, *Cross Creek*, 3, 7, 368

4. Ibid., 159; 233–34; 235–36; Rawlings, *Cross Creek Cookery*, 110.

5. Turcotte, "For This Is an Enchanted Land," 500–1; Rawlings, "Trees for Tomorrow," 25.

6. Turcotte, "For This Is an Enchanted Land," 501.

7. Ibid., 503; "Marjorie Kinnan Rawlings Historic State Park."

8. For a more complete story of the canal, see Noll and Tegeder, *Ditch of Dreams*. The name of the canal has varied in different publications; here it is referred to as the Cross Florida Barge Canal.

9. Marjorie Harris Carr, interview with author, October 18, 1990. For the purposes of this book, Carr refers to Marjorie Harris Carr, while any reference to her husband includes his complete name.

10. Macdonald, "'Our Lady of the Rivers,'" 30, 66–67; Rossiter, *Women Scientists in America*, xv; Lear, *Rachel Carson*, 94–97. Rossiter's book offers an important investiga-

tion of the history of women in American science. Other authors who have addressed this area include Schiebinger, *Nature's Body*, and *Has Feminism Changed Science?*; Harding, *Whose Science?*; and Merchant, *The Death of Nature*. Noll and Tegeder, *Ditch of Dreams*, 147; Macdonald, "'Our Lady of The Rivers,'" 81, 130–31. Macdonald's dissertation is the first biography of Marjorie Harris Carr and fully explores the discrimination she and others encountered in the sciences.

11. Macdonald, "'Our Lady of The Rivers,'" 66; Davis, *The Man Who Saved Sea Turtles*, 20–21, 263–64.

12. Worster, *Nature's Economy*, 192. This term also is spelled *Okologie* and *Oekologie* by historians of science; I use Worster's spelling. See also Darwin, *On the Origin of Species*, 73,102, 315, 489; de Beer, *Charles Darwin*, 93; McIntosh, "Ecology Since 1900," 353. For more on the difficult discussion of Darwin as an ecologist, see "Was Darwin an Ecologist?"; Kingsland, *The Evolution of American Ecology*, 68–69, 94.

13. McIntosh, "Ecology Since 1900," 356; Small, *From Eden to Sahara*, 1.

14. Rothra, *Florida's Pioneer Naturalist*, 4–5; Simpson, *Florida Wild Life*, 152–53, 183, 193; Davis, *An Everglades Providence*, 220–21.

15. Worster, *Nature's Economy*, 229–35, 270–71; Leopold, *A Sand County Almanac*, 137–41, 240–54.

16. Carson, *Silent Spring*, 1–3, 146–47, 189; Lear, *Rachel Carson*, 400–406, 428–29, 435–37, 455; "Rachel's Carson's Silent Spring," broadcast; Breton, *Women Pioneers for the Environment*, 73.

17. Lear, *Rachel Carson*, 435; "Rachel Carson's Silent Spring," broadcast.

18. Carson, *Silent Spring*, xv–xviii, xxvi.

19. Lear, *Rachel Carson*, 117; Gerlach and Hine, *Lifeway Leap*, 4, 234–35. For a discussion about the role of nature films in American culture see Mitman, *Reel Nature*.

20. Macdonald, "'Our Lady of the Rivers,'" 190–95, 197–204, 208–10; Anderson, *Paynes Prairie*, 134–37; Florida Defenders of the Environment, "Biography of Marjorie Harris Carr."

21. Carr, interview with author; Anthony, interview with author; Poole, "Florida: Paradise Redefined," 89–92; Irby, "A Passion for Wild Things," 177.

22. Poole, "Florida: Paradise Redefined," 95–97; Carr, "Second Keynote Address." Note: the emphasis on the word "use" is Carr's own.

23. Poole, "Florida: Paradise Redefined," 98; Dasmann, *No Further Retreat*, 147–48.

24. Carter, *The Florida Experience*, 279–81; Poole, "Florida: Paradise Redefined," 101.

25. Noll and Tegeder, *Ditch of Dreams*, 149–50, 169–70; Macdonald, "'Our Lady of the Rivers,'" 229–30.

26. Noll and Tegeder, *Ditch of Dreams*, 167–71, 174–77; Carr, interview with author; Anthony, interview with author; Partington, interview with author; Poole, "Florida: Paradise Redefined," 107–9.

27. Noll and Tegeder, *Ditch of Dreams*, 201–3; Anthony, interview with author; Poole, "Florida: Paradise Redefined," 112–13.

28. Noll and Tegeder, *Ditch of Dreams*, 201–3, 236–39; Macdonald, "'Our Lady of the Rivers,'" 26, 263; Valenti, interview with author.

29. Noll and Tegeder, *Ditch of Dreams*, 179–82.

30. Poole, "Florida: Paradise Redefined," 117–21.

31. Davis, *An Everglades Providence*, 485–86; Dasmann, *No Further Retreat*, 82–84, 93–95; Blake, *Land into Water—Water into Land*, 216–20; Carter, *The Florida Experience*, 195–208.

32. Carr, interview with author; Noll and Tegeder, *Ditch of Dreams*, 243–49.

33. Carr, interview with author; Dasmann, *No Further Retreat*, 95; Carter, *The Florida Experience*, 296–301; Blake, *Land into Water—Water into Land*, 213–18; Noll and Tegeder, *Ditch of Dreams*, 311–13.

34. MacKay, interview with author; MacKay and Edmonds, *How Florida Happened*, 76–79.

35. Carr speech, "The Fight to Save the Oklawaha"; Noll and Tegeder, *Ditch of Dreams*, 325–28.

36. Douglas, *The Everglades: River of Grass*, 5; Douglas and Rothchild, *Marjory Stoneman Douglas: Voice of the River*, 224.

37. Poole, "Marjory Stoneman Douglas," 9.

38. Douglas and Rothchild, *Marjory Stoneman Douglas: Voice of the River* 101–4, 109, 126–27, 133.

39. Ibid., 134–37.

40. Ibid., 190–91.

41. Davis, "Conservation Is Now a Dead Word," 298, 305–6; Hays, *Conservation and the Gospel of Efficiency*, 2.

42. Branch, "Writing the Swamp, 127, 131; Davis, *An Everglades Providence*, 354–59.

43. Davis, *An Everglades Providence*, 382–85, 393–94; Vance, *May Mann Jennings*, 131–32.

44. Davis, *An Everglades Providence*, 397–98.

45. Davis, *An Everglades Providence*, 472–73; Douglas and Rothchild, *Marjory Stoneman Douglas: Voice of the River*, 223–25.

46. Douglas and Rothchild, *Marjory Stoneman Douglas: Voice of the River*, 224–25.

47. Douglas, letter to Representative Robert Graham, March 28, 1970; Grunwald, *The Swamp*, 257–58; Davis, *An Everglades Providence*, 474–80, 483–84; Douglas and Rothchild, *Marjory Stoneman Douglas: Voice of the River*, 225–26.

48. Grunwald, *The Swamp*, 259, 267; Douglas and Rothchild, *Marjory Stoneman Douglas: Voice of the River*, 229–33.

49. Grunwald, *The Swamp*, 300–301; Davis, *An Everglades Providence*, 223.

50. Douglas, "Remarks by Marjory Stoneman Douglas," 8.

51. Davis, *An Everglades Providence*, 604.

52. Revello, "Environmental Awareness."; Long, interview with author.

53. MacKay, interview with author.

Chapter 6. Clearing the Air

1. Lightfoot, "Water, Air Should Be Conserved," 10–11.

2. Hays, *Beauty, Health, and Permanence*, 13–14.

3. Ibid., 22–23; Rome, *The Bulldozer in the Countryside*, 4–16, 42–43, 256; Rome, "'Give Earth a Chance,'" 534–38. Rome has much to add to Hays's description of the move from conservation to environmentalism, arguing that the story of tract home-building in America explains much about changing environmental attitudes.

4. Udall, *The Quiet Crisis*, vii, xiii, 176–77.

5. Mormino, *Land of Sunshine*, 11–13, 324–25; Dasmann, *No Further Retreat*, 55–56.

6. Dasmann, *No Further Retreat*, 12–16; Mormino, *Land of Sunshine*, 125.

7. Rowe, *The Idea of Florida*, 11–15, 28–30, 34–37; Stowe, *Palmetto Leaves*, 116–22; Lanier, *Florida: Its Scenery, Climate, and History*, 131.

8. Grinder, "The Battle for Clean Air," 83; Penna, *Nature's Bounty*, 265; Encyclopedia of Cleveland, "Environmentalism"; Blum, *Love Canal Revisited*, 125.

9. Grinder, "The Battle for Clean Air," 86, 88, 93, 101.

10. "A Woman Reformer Promotes Smoke Abatement, 1912," 422–23; Hoy, "Women and City Wastes in the Early Twentieth Century," 437; Blum, *Love Canal Revisited*, 126; Stradling, *Smokestacks and Progressives*, 59.

11. Gottlieb, *Forcing the Spring*, 77; "The Southland's War on Smog"; "Key Events in the History of Air Quality in California"; Davis, *When Smoke Ran Like Water*, 15–25; Kline, *First Along the River*, 80–81.

12. Dewey, "Is This What We Came to Florida For?," 198–99.

13. Ibid., 200.; "Irritant in Air Ruins Jacksonville Nylons."

14. McCluney, "The Solution to Pollution," 47.

15. Dewey, "Is This What We Came to Florida For?," 200–5; "Senate Hearings On Air Pollution Set for Tampa"; Carpenter, "What a Swell Party It'll Be."

16. Dewey, "Is This What We Came to Florida For?," 205–6; "Air Pollution Meet to Aid Polk Studies"; "State Orders Cities, Industries to End Pollution."

17. Hall, "Pollution," 38–50.

18. Dewey, "Is This What We Came to Florida For?," 208–12; Funk, "Pollution Problem Hanging over Sunshine State's Future"; Lightfoot, "Water, Air Should Be Conserved," 10–11.

19. Dewey, "Is This What We Came to Florida For?," 208–12; Funk, "Pollution Problem Hanging over Sunshine State's Future," 41.

20. "A Fabulous Convention," 7; "Herald-Tribune, Sarasota Couple, Win Awards."

21. Dewey, "Is This What We Came to Florida For?," 207; Groner, "Air Pollution Act 'Foggy'"; "Incinerator Verdict Due Today."

22. Knell, "Environmental Protection and Pollution Control."

23. Wisehart, "The Responsibility."

24. McCluney, "Air Pollution Problems in South Florida," 54–56; Greene, "How the Automobile Multiplies the Problems of Dade County," 69.

25. Dewey, "Is This What We Came to Florida For?," 213–14; Davis, *An Everglades Providence*, 441; Carter, *The Florida Experience*, 157.

26. Davis, *An Everglades Providence*, 441–43; Redford, "Groups Working to Save South Florida," 106; Carter, *The Florida Experience*, 158.

27. Davis, *An Everglades Providence*, 442–43.

28. Evans, *Born for Liberty*, 264–65, 273–75; Evans, *Personal Politics*, 7–10, 18; Napikoski, "Glass Ceiling for Women"; Smith and Bachu, "Women's Labor Force Attachment Patterns and Maternity Leave."

29. Friedan, *The Feminine Mystique*, 9–10, 15–20, 317.

30. "National Organization for Women's 1966 Statement of Purpose."

31. Davis, *An Everglades Providence*, 441–44; Carter, *The Florida Experience*, 158–60; Dewey, "Is This What We Came to Florida For?," 215.

32. Redford, "Small Rebellion in Miami," 96–101.

33. Davis, *An Everglades Providence*, 443–47; Carter, *The Florida Experience*, 159–62.

34. Dewey, "Is This What We Came to Florida For?," 215–16.

Chapter 7. Restoring Waters

1. Redford, *Billion-Dollar Sandbar*, 258–59; Barnett, *Mirage*, 24–25.

2. Wylie, "Florida: Polluted Paradise."

3. Ibid.; Dasmann, *No Further Retreat*, 164; Davis, *An Everglades Providence*, 442; Blake, *Land into Water—Water into Land*, 293.

4. "Sewage Is Major Florida Problem," 11; Blake, *Land into Water—Water into Land*, 293–95; Barnett, *Mirage*, 24–25; "Half of Florida Has Sewage Plants."

5. Blake, *Land into Water—Water into Land*, 295; Baljet, "Water Pollution Problems in Dade County," 51–52; Muir, *Miami, U.S.A.*, 67.

6. Hays, *Beauty, Health and Permanence*, 76–80; Cronon, *Nature's Metropolis*, 248–50; "Combined Sewer Separation in Minneapolis"; Modica, "The History of the Newark Sewage System"; "Environmental History Timeline."

7. Gottlieb, *Forcing the Spring*, 78; Hays, *Beauty, Health and Permanence*, 52, 76–78; Kline, *First Along the River*, 79.

8. Hays, *Beauty, Health, and Permanence*, 78–79; "NPG Facts & Figures."

9. Dasmann, *No Further Retreat*, 55; "Sewage Dumping 'Suicide'"; FFGC, 1955, "Synopsis of Minutes Twenty-Ninth Annual Convention," 1–2.

10. Scott, *Natural Allies*, 173–75; League of Women Voters, "History"; "League of Women Voters."

11. Rome, "'Give Earth a Chance,'" 535; Parashar, *Public Administration in the Developed World*, 308; Nott, "Sanitation Heads League's List of Top Improvements."

12. *Looking Back 50 Years*, 8, 10, 15–16; Brown, *Recollections*, 29; "Manatee Scores Anti-Pollution Victory," 3; all in League of Women Voters Collection.

13. Ryan, "Overflow Crowd Hears Miseries of Tampa Bay"; "Statement of the Florida Air and Water Pollution Control Department," legislative testimony.

14. Basse and Van Sant, "She Fought for Environment"; "Chapter 12—Ten Communities: Profiles in Environmental Progress"; Ellis, "Grizzle Fights to Keep Sewage Standards"; "Keep Up the Fight"; "House of Polluters"; Basse, "Pioneering Politician Mary Grizzle Dies."

15. Vickers, "Ruth Bryan Owen," 37–38.

16. Carter, *The Florida Experience*, 162–67; Davis, *An Everglades Providence*, 449–53; "Woman Sues to Halt Turkey Point Canal"; "About Turkey Point."

17. Davis, *An Everglades Providence*, 447–48, 456–58; Wainwright, speech acknowledging Thomas Barbour Medal.

18. Davis, *An Everglades Providence*, 466–69.

19. Ibid., 467–70; McSherry, interview with author; Browder, interview with author.

20. Funk, "Florida Mounts Heavy Attack on Pollution"; Wright, "Florida Conservationists Unite for '70s"; Carter, *The Florida Experience*, 53–55.

21. "Remarks of Reubin O'D. Askew Governor of Florida to the Izaak Walton League of America"; "Remarks of Reubin O'D. Askew Governor of Florida at the Air and Water Conference"; "Address to the Florida Legislature"; Carter, *The Florida Experience*, 55, 130–33.

22. Blake, *Land into Water—Water into Land*, 227–30.

23. "Former Board Member Archive."

24. Pignone, interview with author.

25. Ibid.; "For the Orange County Commission District 4: Fran Pignone"; Thomas, "Expressway Authority Can't Co-opt Fran Pignone."

26. Harden, interview with author.

27. Ibid.; Robison and Belleville, *Along the Wekiva River*, 113.

28. Thomas, "Litterbug," 58; Crosby, *Fifty Years of Service*, 56; Hays, *Beauty, Health, and Permanence*, 80–81; "KAB: A Beautiful History"; Rome, "'Give Earth a Chance,'" 537; "Lady Bird Johnson—The Beautification Campaign."

29. Jennings, "State Beautification," 12; "DOT Joins Garden Clubs in Fight over Litter"; Williams, "Pensacola the Beautiful?" 5; Askew, Speech to Keep Florida Beautiful Luncheon, 3, 8, 11.

30. "Plan Session Inaugurates Project ManaSota-88"; Rains, interview with author.

31. Rains, interview with author; Rains, ManaSota-88 Letter, 1–2; "A Tenacious Crusader"; "Gloria Rains' Legacy."

32. Rains, interview with author; Rains, ManaSota-88 Letter, 1–2; "A Tenacious Crusader"; "Gloria Rains' Legacy" Pitzer, "Gloria Rains Irreplaceable."

Chapter 8. Endangered Species and Lands

1. Vallee, interview with author.

2. Ibid.; Kline, *First Along the River*, 94.

3. Vallee, interview.

4. Ibid.; Pittman, *Manatee Insanity*, 95–98.

5. Vallee, "I Would Hate to See This Whole Thing Turn into a Circus"; Vallee, "Saving Manatee Important to Florida"; Vallee, interview.

6. "Florida Quick Facts"; "Threatened & Endangered"; "Florida's Endangered and Threatened Species."

7. Davis, *The Man Who Saved Sea Turtles*, 173–74, 260, 265–66; Catron, "A Fight for the Seas"; Fontenay, "Judge: Volusia Doing OK for Turtles"; "Turtles Win at Eleventh Circuit," accessed December 28, 2011, http://masglp.olemiss.edu/Water%20Log/WL18/turtles.htm.

8. Catron, "A Fight for the Seas."

9. Rossiter, *Women Scientists in America*, 161–62.

10. Forstall, "Florida: Population of Counties by Decennial Census"; Mormino, *Land of Sunshine*, 301–2, 326, 354.

11. Murphy and Leeper, Draft Narrative, 3–4, 13, 35, 45–50, 60–65, 72, 76, 95–96; Simone, "Racing, Region, and the Environment," 27–30, 68–69.

12. "Canaveral"; "The Doris Leeper Spruce Creek Preserve"; Moore, "Doris Leeper Was a 'Force for the Arts'"; "Park Units with Highest Number of Endangered Species—2010"; Henderson, e-mail to author; "History of Canaveral National Seashore."

13. Barile, interview with author.

14. Ibid.

15. Ibid.; Thomas, "The Sunshine Patriot."

16. Barile, interview; Thomas, "The Sunshine Patriot;" Wilson, "Nation's Oldest Wildlife Refuge Is Endangered."

17. Nugent, *Women Conserving the Florida Keys*, 1–11, 126–31.

18. Barley, interview.

19. Barley, interview; Green, "Mary Barley Crusades behind the Scenes for the Everglades."

20. Spivey, interview with author; Spivey, Facebook message.

21. Spivey, Facebook message.

22. Spivey, interview; Davis, *An Everglades Providence*, 529; Schultz, "Recognizing Helen Spivey," E849.

23. Davis, *An Everglades Providence*, 502–5; "Yellow Dye Trails Path of Sewage."

24. Rome, *The Genius of Earth Day*, 110.

25. Merchant, *The Columbia Guide to American Environmental History*, 180–81; Kline, *First Along the River*, 92–99.

26. Crosby, *Fifty Years of Service*, 40.

27. Revello, "Environmental Awareness"; Carter, *The Florida Experience*, 178.

28. Zaloudek, "Group Targets Pesticides in Parks"; House-Mason, "Praise for Supporters of Pesticide Posting Bill."

29. Siry, *Marshes of the Ocean Shore*, 158–64.

30. Ibid., 164–67.

31. Ibid., 167–70; Redford, "Vanishing Tidelands," 76.

32. Boardman, "Garden Clubs Are Leaders in Natural Area Preservation," 6–7.

33. Mormino, *Land of Sunshine*, 341–42; Stephenson, "A 'Monstrous Desecration,'" 326–32. Other estuarine controversies included Rookery Bay and Marco Island on the state's southwest coast. For more on these projects, see Blake, *Land into Water—Water into Land*, and Carter, *The Florida Experience*.

34. Stephenson, "A 'Monstrous Desecration,'" 331–40, 337.

35. Ibid., 337; Mitchell, "Pinellas Okays Ratner (Furen) Fill," B-1, B-24. As with many women of her day, Davis used her married name of Mrs. Robert Davis for her membership records and most newspaper interviews. Her first name was determined with the help of Mary Frances Lawrie, president of the Garden Club of St. Petersburg, August 22, 2011, and confirmed through "Garden Club to Hear County Agent."

36. Stephenson, "A 'Monstrous Desecration,'" 337; Davis, *An Everglades Providence*, 418.

37. "'Lady Hermit' Appeals for Funds to Save Lower Bay Lands."

38. "New Anti-Fill Group Begins Campaigning"; Lewis, "Opposition to Bay Lake Plan Builds."

39. Stephenson, "A 'Monstrous Desecration,'" 339–40, 343–44.

40. Ibid., 326; Weldon, "Civic Associations Term Fills a Threat to Boca Ciega Bay"; "Bayboro Shell Fill Approved"; Cubbison, "Delay Hinted on Offshore Oil Decision"; "Florida House District 61 Republican"; Basse, "Ex-Lawmaker, Civic Activist Sample Leaves Legacy of Nice."

41. Davis, *An Everglades Providence*, 418; Stephenson, "A 'Monstrous Desecration,'" 335–42.

42. Stephenson, "A 'Monstrous Desecration,'" 343–44.

Chapter 9. Seeking Environmental Justice

1. Hurley, *Environmental Inequalities*, xiii–xiv.

2. Steinberg, *Down to Earth*, 250–53; McGurty, "From NIMBY to Civil Rights," 303–5; Chelala, "Women Taking Charge to Save the Environment."

3. Grunwald, *The Swamp*, 30–31, 53; Mahon and Weisman, "Florida's Seminole and Miccosukee Peoples," 183–201.

4. Kersey, *The Stranahans of Fort Lauderdale*, 76–77, 82, 115–16, 130–33; Wright, *More Than Petticoats*, 78–79; Stranahan, untitled autobiography, 11–12, Stranahan Manuscript Collection.

5. "Friends of the Seminoles in Florida," Ft. Lauderdale Historical Society; Stranahan, untitled autobiography, 16; Jumper and West, *A Seminole Legend*, 90, 103.

6. Davis, *An Everglades Providence*, 377; Moore-Willson, *The Seminoles of Florida*, 53–55, 181.

7. Moore-Willson, *The Seminoles of Florida*, 128–30; Moore-Willson, "Snap Shots

from the Everglades of Florida," 5, 16, Florida Historical Society; Cantrell, letter to Ann Bradley, July 9, 1948; Munroe, letter to Minnie Moore-Willson, May 11, 1917.

8. Davis, *An Everglades Providence*, 377–79. For an examination of the role of government removal of native people from national parks elsewhere, see Spence, *Dispossessing the Wilderness*.

9. Covington, *The Seminoles of Florida*, 186.

10. Roux, "Sainthood confirmed for Deaconess Harriett Bedell"; Douglas, *The Everglades: River of Grass*, 372–73; Plater, "Through the Dust: Harriet Bedell"; Episcopal Café, "Speaking to the Soul: Bird Woman"; Bolin, "A Woman with a Seminole Mission"; Wright, *More Than Petticoats*, 50–53.

11. Grunwald, *The Swamp*, 257; Davis, *An Everglades Providence*, 469–70; Bigart, "Miami-Sized Jetport Threatens Everglades with Extinction," A1.

12. Grunwald, *The Swamp*, 298, 302; Klinkenberg, "A Culture Endangered," 97–100.

13. Steinberg, *Down to Earth*, 256; "Navajo Challenge Uranium Mining Permit on Tribal Lands"; Brugge et al., "Uranium Mining on Navajo Indian Land"; Merchant, *Earthcare*, 155; "Environmental Justice for the Navajo."

14. Merchant, *Earthcare*, 157–58; Kaplan, *Crazy for Democracy*, 15–18, 38–39; Breton, *Women Pioneers for the Environment*, 116–25.

15. Steinberg, *Down to Earth*, 254.

16. Kaplan, *Crazy for Democracy*, 47–61; Steinberg, *Down to Earth*, 256–58; Roberts, "The World's a Dirty Place When You Are Poor."

17. Roberts, "The World's a Dirty Place When You Are Poor"; Lerner, "Pensacola, Florida: Living Next Door to Mount Dioxin"; Williams, "Relocation from 'Mount Dioxin'"; Dunham, "Exodus from Pensacola's 'Mt. Dioxin,' 1–2, in possession of author.

18. Williams, "Relocation from 'Mount Dioxin'"; Dunham, "Exodus from Pensacola's 'Mt. Dioxin'"; Lerner, "Pensacola, Florida"; Miller, "Green at the Grassroots," 34–35; Dunham, e-mail to author.

19. Williams, "Relocation from 'Mount Dioxin'"; Dunham, "Exodus from Pensacola's 'Mt. Dioxin,'"; Lerner, "Pensacola, Florida"; Dunham, e-mail.

20. Lerner, "Pensacola, Florida"; Dunham, "Environmental Racism," 4; Dunham, e-mail to author; "The CATE Letter."

21. Stretesky and Hogan, "Environmental Justice," 284.

22. "Bullard: Green Issue Is Black and White"; Horning, "Social Network and Environmental Justice," 42.

23. Forstall, "Florida: Population of Counties by Decennial Census"; "Is Fenholloway River Too Big A Price"; Morris, *Women in the Florida Legislature*, 127, 133.

24. Horning, "Social Network and Environmental Justice," 39–41; Andrew, "Fenholloway River Evaluation Initiative," 40; Carter, *The Florida Experience*, 46.

25. Ezell, interview with author; Ezell, telephone interview with author; Horning, "Social Network and Environmental Justice," 43–45.

26. Ezell, interview.

27. Ibid.; Pfankuch, "Florida's Rotten River."

28. Ezell, interview; Horning, "Social Network and Environmental Justice," 46–50.

29. Ezell, interview; Horning, "Social Network and Environmental Justice," 50–58; Pfankuch, "Florida's Rotten River"; Hauserman, "Dioxin at Mill Too High."

30. Ezell, interview; Ezell, telephone interview.

31. Merchant, *Earthcare*, 160–61.

32. Pitts, "'Harvest of Shame' 50 Years Later"; Florida Legal Services, Inc., "Facts."

33. Riley, "Lake Apopka," 280–83.

34. Ibid., 283–85.

35. Ibid., 285–86; "Lake Apopka."

36. Roen, "It's Always about People"; Santich, "Decades Can't Slow Nuns' Fight against Poverty"; DM-Maz, "Central Floridians of Year: Apopka Nuns."

37. "History of FWAF"; Economos, interview with author.

38. Hahamovitch, *The Fruits of Their Labor*, 114–29, 138–39, 203; Sosnick, *Hired Hands*, 326; Thissen and Roka, "Non-Governmental Organizations Serving Farmworkers in Florida"; Riley, *Florida's Farmworkers in the Twenty-first Century*, 13, 52, 66.

39. Jones, "Millions Reaped What Cesar Chavez Sowed."

40. Habin and Matthew, *Lake Apopka Farmworkers Environmental Health Project*, 3–5; Riley, "Lake Apopka," 287–88.

41. "History of FWAF"; Riley, "Lake Apopka," 286–89; Riley, *Florida's Farmworkers in the Twenty-first Century*, 126–29; Balogh, "Apopka Farmworkers Say Pesticides Caused Illnesses"; Economos, interview. For more detailed information about the effects of chemicals on the Lake Apopka workers as well as the health issues of farmworkers across Florida and the United States, see Habin and Matthew, *Lake Apopka Farmworkers Environmental Health Project*; Kamel et al., "Neurobehavioral Performance and Work Experience in Florida Farmworkers," 1765–72; Arcury et al., "Pesticide Safety among Farmworkers," S233–S240; Gordon, "Poisons in the Fields," 51–77; Natural Resources Defense Council, "Trouble on the Farm."

42. Economos, interview.

43. Ibid.; Riley, *Florida's Farmworkers in the Twenty-first Century*, 130–33.

44. Economos, interview.

45. Forstall, "Florida: Population of Counties by Decennial Census."

Chapter 10. Women Leaders

1. Wagner, interview with author.

2. Morris, *Women in the Florida Legislature*, 126; Wagner, interview; Burke, "Political Rally Remains Civilized."

3. "Helen Gordon Davis"; Morris, *Women in The Florida Legislature*, 97–98, 125–26.

4. Spivey, interview.

5. Evans, *Born for Liberty*, 276; Evans, *Personal Politics*, 212–13; Newman, *White Women's Rights*, 3–6.

6. Poucher, "One Woman's Courage," 229, 232–33; Jones, "Without Compromise or Fear," 269–70, 287; Shell-Weiss, "Exceptional Women."

7. Evans, *Born for Liberty*, 276–78, 287–89.

8. Ibid., 290–91.

9. Ellis and Hawks, "Creating a Different Pattern," 73; Rome, "'Give Earth a Chance,'" 541.

10. Morris, interview with author; Morris, e-mail; White, "Activist Brought People Together to Better Sarasota."

11. Morris, interview.

12. Carriker, "Florida's Growth Management Act: An Introduction and Overview," 3–4; DeGrove, "Growth Management in Florida"; Blake, *Land into Water—Water into Land*, 198–99.

13. Wagner, interview; Wagner, e-mail; Wagner, "Citizen Involvement Vital for Growth Management"; O'Neal, "Environment Gets 4 New Watchdogs"; *Pro Earth Times, Inc.*, Muriel Wagner Papers.

14. Hurchalla, interview with author; Samples, "Maggy Hurchalla Is Depressed"; Allison, "On Janet Reno's Campaign, It's All Relative."

15. Hurchalla, interview; Smith, "Martin County vs. the World."

16. Kline, *First Along the River*, 101–3; DeGrove, "Growth Management in Florida"; Davis, *An Everglades Providence*, 542.

17. Evans, *Born for Liberty*, 309, 313, 323, 331–32; Rymph, *Republican Women*, 10.

18. Carter, *The Florida Experience*, 63–64; Stephenson, "A 'Monstrous Desecration,'" 331; Blake, *Land into Water—Water into Land*, 198; "Florida Dept. of Natural Resources."

19. Tschinkel, interview with author; McVety, interview with author.

20. McVety, interview; McVety, e-mail.

21. Tschinkel, interview.

22. McVety, e-mail.

23. Whitfield, interview with author.

24. Tschinkel, interview.

25. Ibid.; Tschinkel, resume.

26. McVety, interview.

27. McVety, interview; Pittman, *Manatee Insanity*, 104–9.

28. Wetherell, interview with author.

29. Wetherell, interview.

30. Wetherell, interview; Wetherell, e-mail; Keller, "Both Sides Now."

31. Wetherell interview; Wetherell, e-mail.

32. McVety, e-mail.

33. Browner, interview with author; "Biography of Carol M. Browner."

34. Browner, interview; Romero, "Energy Czar: Carol Browner"; Gupte and Cohen, "Carol Browner."

35. Browner, interview; Romero, "Energy Czar: Carol Browner"; Gupte and Cohen, "Carol Browner"; Browner speech, "Governor's Commission for a Sustainable Florida."

Epilogue

1. Douglas, "Remarks by Marjory Stoneman Douglas," 2, 6.

2. Ibid., 2, 8; Davis, *An Everglades Providence*, 553–54.

3. Douglas, "Remarks by Marjory Stoneman Douglas," 2.

4. Ezell, interview.

5. "Fran Mainella"; "Sylvia Earle, PhD"; "Sylvia Earle, Marine Biologist."

Bibliography

Abbreviations

FAS	Florida Audubon Society, Maitland, Florida
FFGC	Florida Federation of Garden Clubs
RCOL	Rollins College, Olin Library, Archives and Special Collections, Winter Park, Florida
SPOHP	Samuel Proctor Oral History Program, University of Florida, Gainesville, Florida
UFSL	University of Florida, Smathers Libraries, Special and Area Studies Collections, Gainesville, Florida
UMSC	University of Miami Special Collections, Otto G. Richter Library, Coral Gables, Florida
UWFSC	University of West Florida Special Collections Department, John C. Pace Library, University Archives and West Florida History Center, Pensacola, Florida

Primary Sources

"Address to the Florida Legislature." Tallahassee, February 1, 1972. Box 1, January 1971–February 1972, File: January–February 1972. UFSL.

Alessi, Marilyn, historian of the Tampa Woman's Club. E-mail to author, November 9, 2011.

Anthony, David. Interview with author, February 4, 1991. Gainesville, Fla.

Askew, Reubin O'D. Speech to Keep Florida Beautiful Luncheon, Tallahassee, Fla., July 14, 1971. Box 1, January 1971–February 1972, File: May–July 1971. UFSL.

"Audubon Society Notes." News article from unknown newspaper, March 30, 1921. FAS.

Barile, Diane. Interview with author, March 30, 2010. Melbourne, Fla. SPOHP.

Barley, Mary. Interview with author, April 7, 2011. Islamorada, Fla. SPOHP.

Board Reports March 21, 1929–March 20, 1935. Bound volume, FFGC.

Browder, Joe. Interview with author, October 9, 2009. Gainesville, Fla. SPOHP.

Brown, Arnetta. *Recollections: A History of the League of Women Voters of Florida 1939–1989.* St. Petersburg: League of Women Voters of Florida 1989. League of Women Voters Collection. UFSL.

Browner, Carol Martha. Telephone interview with author, April 5, 2011. SPOHP.

———. "Governor's Commission for a Sustainable Florida." Speech given March 22, 1996, West Palm Beach, Fla. EPA Website, http://yosemite.epa.gov/opa/admpress. nsf/12a744ff56dbff858525759000475ob6/9c399e69a5d4fc838525701a0052e3d2!Open Document.

Burke, Michael. "Political Rally Remains Civilized." *Pensacola News Journal,* August 19, 1983, C1. Muriel Wagner Papers, UWFSC.

Byrd, Dr. Hiram. Unmarked newspaper clipping, n.d. FAS.

Cantrell, Elizabeth Aultman. Letter to Ann Bradley, July 9, 1948. Box 9, File: Notes on J. M. and Minnie Moore Willson. Minnie Moore Willson Papers, UMSC.

Carr, Marjorie Harris. "The Fight to Save the Oklawaha." Speech at 12th Biennial Sierra Club Wilderness Conference, Washington, D.C., September 25, 1971. In author's possession.

———. Interview with author, October 18, 1990, Gainesville, Fla.

———. "Second Keynote Address—Third Annual Conference, The Society for Ecological Restoration." Orlando, Fla., May 20, 1991. In author's possession.

"Citation for Outstanding Contributions to Forestry." Box 23, Misc. File: Department of Conservation and Natural Resources/Florida Federation of Women's Clubs. May Mann Jennings Papers, UFSL.

"City Beautification Called 'Investment' at Florida Meeting." *Christian Science Monitor,* May 25, 1933. Box 23a, Scrapbook. May Mann Jennings Papers, UFSL.

Coconut Grove Committee for Slum Clearance. Untitled 17-page paper chronicling group history. No author listed. Box 2, file 14: Coconut Grove Citizen's Committee for Slum Clearance. Elizabeth Virrick Papers, HistoryMiami Archives and Research Center, Miami, Florida.

Douglas, Marjory Stoneman. Letter to Representative Robert Graham, March 28, 1970. Box 26, File: Everglades Planning Commission. D. Robert "Bob" Graham Papers, UFSL.

———. Papers 1890–1998, box 40—General Files, Correspondence—Friends, folder 16: Correspondence April 10, 1939–December 30, 1947. UMSC.

———. "Remarks by Marjory Stoneman Douglas on the Occasion of the Dedication of the Marjory Stoneman Douglas Building Headquarters of the Florida Department of Natural Resources, Tallahassee, May 15, 1981." Florida Defenders of the Environment, box 33, MS204, File: Awards to Marjory Stoneman Douglas 1981–1987. UFSL.

Dunham, Frances. E-mail to author, November 18, 2011.

———. "Environmental Racism: Human Sacrifice and the Ugly Rituals of the Bottom Line." *Harbinger*, n.d., in possession of author.

———. "Exodus from Pensacola's 'Mt. Dioxin,': A Sacrifice Community Fights to Win," 1–2, in possession of author.

Economos, Jeannie. Interview with author, November 29, 2011. Apopka, Fla. SPOHP.

Ezell, Joy Towles. Interview with author, September 5, 2011. Perry, Fla. SPOHP.

———. Telephone interview with author, February 23, 2012.

Ezell, Veola Badger. "Report of Chairman Park Committee." *Florida Federation of Women's Clubs 1923–1924 Yearbook*. Minerva Jennings Papers 1908–1935, MssColl #2001-01, File: Organization Records: Florida Federation of Women's Clubs. Florida Historical Society, Cocoa, Fla.

Fairchild, David. Letter to May Mann Jennings, July 18, 1916. Box 10 Correspondence, File: 1916 June–December 1917, January–May. May Mann Jennings Papers, UFSL.

"FAS Minutes." *Bird-Lore* 2, no. 6 (December 1900): 203. FAS.

"FAS Minutes." Vanderpool files, Mrs. Kingsmill Marrs.

"Florida Audubon Society." *Bird-Lore* (December 1901): 220. Maitland Historical Society, Maitland, Fla.

Florida Audubon Society Minutes 1900–1910. FAS.

Florida Federation of Garden Clubs [1930]. "Minutes Florida Federation of Garden Clubs Executive Board Meeting, Dec. 10, 1930." Daytona Beach Shores, Fla. *Board Reports March 21, 1929–March 20, 1935*. Bound volume, FFGC.

———[1932]. "Florida Federation of Garden Clubs Board Meeting. March 14, 1932." *Board Reports, March 21, 1929–March 20, 1935*. Bound volume, FFGC.

———[1934]. "Florida Botanical Garden and Arboretum: A Growing Project." Brochure, n.d., n.p., included in Report, Executive Board Meeting, January 10, 1934, General Federation of Garden Clubs. *Board Reports, March 21, 1929–March 20, 1935*. Bound volume, FFGC.

———[1935]. "The Florida Federation of Garden Clubs Fifth Annual Convention Minutes." *Board Reports, March 21, 1929–March 20, 1935*. Bound volume, FFGC.

———[1935]. "Florida Federation of Garden Clubs in Convention Assembled at West Palm Beach, Florida." March 21–22, 1935. *Board Reports March 21, 1929–March 20, 1935*. Bound volume, FFGC.

———[1935]. "Annual Convention Florida Federation of Garden Clubs" pamphlet, March 19–21, 1935. FFGC.

———[1940]. Resolution 4. "Florida Federation of Garden Clubs 14th Annual Convention, March 30–31, 1939." In "F.F.G.C. Inc. Executive Board Meeting Florida Federation of Garden Clubs, Jan. 29, 1940." Winter Park, Fla. *Minutes 1939–1945*. Bound volume, FFGC.

———[1949]. "Minutes of the Twenty-Third Annual Convention." April 21–22, 1949. St. Petersburg, Fla. *Minutes 1947–1949*, Bound volume, FFGC.

——[1952]. "Minutes Twenty-Sixth Annual Convention." April 21–23, 1952. *Minutes 1951–1953*. Bound volume, FFGC.

——[1952]. "Minutes." Executive Board, October 23, 1952. Ocala, Fla. *Minutes 1951–1953*. Bound volume, FFGC.

——[1953]. "Minutes Florida Federation of Garden Clubs Twenty-Seventh Annual Convention." April 8–10, 1953, Miami. *Minutes 1951–1953*. Bound volume, FFGC.

——[1955]. "Synopsis of Minutes Twenty-Ninth Annual Convention." *Minutes 1954–1961*. Bound volume, FFGC.

Florida Federation of Women's Clubs Annual Yearbook, 1916–1917 Reports. FFWC.

"Forestry Department of the Florida State Federation of Women's Clubs." Box 15, folder: 5 Scrapbooks: material accompanying 1909–1911. Woman's Club of Coconut Grove Records, 1891–1991, UMSC.

"Friends of the Seminoles in Florida." Box 3, folder 13: Seminole Indians: Friends of the Seminoles Correspondence, reports, etc., 1933–1953. Ft. Lauderdale Historical Society, Ft. Lauderdale, Fla.

Garrard, Dorinda. Polk County Historical and Genealogical Library, Bartow, Fla. E-mail to author, October 7, 2011.

"Gertrude Rollins." File: Wilson, Gertrude Rollins (Mrs. Millar) Biographical, box 05D: Wilson, Gertrude (Millar—husband's name) Rollins (cousin of Alonzo Rollins). 1956. RCOL.

Gifford, Mrs. John, and Mrs. Gaston H. Edwards. Letter dated July 1916 on Florida Federation of Women's Clubs letterhead from the FFWC Conservation Department. Box 10, Correspondence File: 1916: June–December, 1917: January–May. May Mann Jennings Papers, UFSL.

Harden, Patricia. Interview with author, November 11, 2010. Gainesville, Fla. SPOHP.

Henderson, Clay. Subject: "Doc." E-mail to author, December 24, 2011.

Hensley, Mrs. N. W. *Florida Federation of Women's Clubs Annual Yearbook, 1927–1928*, 124. FFGC.

Hurchalla, Margaret "Maggy" Reno. Interview with author, April 8, 2011. Miami, Fla. SPOHP.

Jennings, May Mann. Letter to C. S. Graham, president, Florida Branch, Izaak Walton League, August 11, 1928. Stranahan Manuscript Collection, box 31, folder 172: Florida Federation of Women's Clubs: Royal Palm State Park. Ft. Lauderdale Historical Society, Ft. Lauderdale, Fla.

———. Letter to David Fairchild, August 15, 1916. Box 10 Correspondence, File: 1916 August–October. May Mann Jennings Papers, UFSL.

———. Letter to Minnie Moore-Willson, May 12, 1915. Box 1, File: MMW—Correspondence 1915. Minnie Moore-Willson Papers 1888–1949, UMSC.

"Kingsmill Marrs Photographs." Massachusetts Historical Society. Accessed November 26, 2005. www.masshist.org/findingaids/doc.cfm?fa=fab033.

Long, Theodora. Interview with author, January 18, 2011. Miami, Fla. SPOHP.

Looking Back 50 Years. St. Petersburg: League of Women Voters of the St. Petersburg Area, 1989. League of Women Voters Collection, UFSL.

MacKay, Kenneth H. "Buddy" Jr. Interview with author, March 8, 2011. Ocklawaha, Fla. SPOHP.

"Manatee Scores Anti-Pollution Victory." *Florida Voter,* newsletter of League of Women Voters of Florida, January 1968. League of Women Voters Collection, UFSL.

McSherry, December Duke. Interview with author, February 25, 2011. Gainesville, Fla. SPOHP.

McVety, Pamela Prim. Subject: "Quick question—dissertation info." E-mail to author, May 2, 2012.

———. Interview with author, February 23, 2011. Tallahassee, Fla. SPOHP.

"Memorialized by Audubon Society." *Maitland News,* April 6, 1927, Maitland Historical Society, Maitland, Fla.

Moore-Willson, Minnie. "Snap Shots from the Everglades of Florida: Jungle Life of the Seminoles." Tampa Tribune Publishing Company, 1917. Florida Historical Society, Cocoa, Florida.

———. "Letter to Mrs. I. Vanderpool, Maitland, Secretary of Florida Audubon Society, March 19, 1916. Box 1, File: MMW Correspondence—1916. Minnie Moore Willson Papers, 1888–1949, UMSC.

Morris, Julie. Interview with author, October 30, 2010. Sarasota, Fla. SPOHP.

Morris, Julie. E-mail to author, November 8, 2010.

"Mrs. A. B. Whitman." File: Whitman, Maud (Neff) (Mrs. Alton Burnett Whitman). RCOL.

———. Letter to Minnie Moore-Willson, May 11, 1917. Box 1, File: Correspondence—1917. Minnie Moore Willson Papers, UMSC.

Natural Resources Defense Council. "Trouble on the Farm: Growing Up with Pesticides in Agricultural Communities." 1998.

"Orlando Garden Club." 1932–1933. Orlando Garden Clubs archives, box 1, Scrapbooks of the Club, 1928–1939. Orange County Regional History Center, Orlando.

Partington, Bill. Interview with author, October 11, 1990. Winter Park, Fla.

Pignone, Frances Sharp. Interview with author, June 14, 2011. Winter Park, Fla. SPOHP.

"Presidents of the St. Petersburg Audubon Society." FAS.

Pro Earth Times, Inc. Gulf Breeze, Fla., November 1983. Muriel Wagner Papers, UWFSC.

Program for presentation of seat and plaque. Lina L'Engle Barnett/Francis Philip Fatio collection, File 05C—Fatio Garden Seat. RCOL.

Rains, Gloria. Interview with author, December 17, 1990. Palmetto, Fla.

———. ManaSota-88 Letter. March 28, 1988, 1–2.

Reed, Nat. Interview with author, January 14, 1991. Hobe Sound, Fla.

"Remarks of Reubin O'D. Askew Governor of Florida at the Air and Water Conference." Miami, July 2, 1971, 5, 7, box 1: January 1971–February 1972, File: May–July 1971. Reubin O'Donovan Askew Speeches, UFSL.

"Remarks of Reubin O'D. Askew Governor of Florida to the Izaak Walton League of America." West Palm Beach, Fla., May 1, 1971. Box 1, January 1971–February 1972, File: May–July 1971. Reubin O'Donovan Askew Speeches, UFSL.

Riggs, Cora Scott, "President's Review." In "Florida Federation of Garden Clubs Sixth Annual Convention." March 4–5, 1931. Orlando, Fla. *Board Reports March 21, 1929– March 20, 1935.* Bound volume, FFGC.

Seymour, Jessica. "Report Beautification Committee." October 30, 1933. *Board Reports March 21, 1929–March 20, 1935.* Bound volume, FFGC.

Sherman, Mrs. John Dickinson. "Safeguarding What We Have." *Ladies' Home Journal,* September 1916, 31. Box 23A, MS 57. May Mann Jennings Papers, UFSL.

Smocovitis, Vassiliki "Betty." Telephone conversation with author, June 14, 2011. Gainesville, Fla.

Sollitt, Eleanor H. "Report." Box 1, Folder 1: Woman's Club of Coconut Grove—Reports. Woman's Club of Coconut Grove Records, 1891–1991, UMSC.

Spivey, Helen Digges. Facebook message to author, October 17, 2013.

———. Interview with author, December 8, 2010. Yankeetown, Fla. SPOHP.

"Statement of the Florida Air and Water Pollution Control Department, Tampa, Fla. Feb. 26, 1970." Box 8, File: League of Women Voters Legislative Testimony 1956– 1970. UFSL.

Stranahan, Ivy. Untitled autobiography. Box 28, folder 149: Stranahan, Ivy: autobiographies, 11–12, Stranahan Manuscript Collection 71-1. Ft. Lauderdale Historical Society, Ft. Lauderdale, Florida.

Tippetts, Katherine. "Notes on the founding and current status of St. Petersburg Audubon Society. Inc." FAS.

Tracy L'Engle Anglas Papers. UF Record Group 98, box 3: Memorabilia and Photographs, file 3: L'Engle/Fatio Families. RCOL.

Tschinkel, Victoria Jean Nierenberg. Interview with author, February 24, 2011. Tallahassee, Fla. SPOHP.

Udall, Stewart L. "The Conservation Challenge of the Sixties," lecture given April 19, 1963, Berkeley, CA. Accessed July 30, 2013. http://cnr.berkeley.edu/site/lectures/albright/1963.php.

Valenti, JoAnn Myer. Interview with author, April 1, 2011. SPOHP.

Vallee, Judith. Interview with author, April 13, 2010. Maitland, Fla. SPOHP.

Vanderpool, Whipple, and Dommerich Files. Randall and Allied Families: Sherman Newton Bronson. Maitland Historical Society, Maitland, Florida.

Wagner, Muriel Wright. "Citizen Involvement Vital for Growth Management." *Pensacola News-Journal,* December 24, 1988, 8A. Muriel Wagner Papers, UWFSC.

———. E-mail to author, June 29, 2011.

———. Interview with author, June 28, 2011. Pensacola, Fla. SPOHP.

Wainwright, Alice. Speech acknowledging Thomas Barbour Medal, n.d. Alice Cutts

Wainwright Papers, box 1, File: Brochures, Notes, Speeches, etc., 1950–1990. HistoryMiami Archives and Research Center, Miami, Florida.

Wells, Mildred White. "Florida Clubwomen See Dream Realized in Everglades Park." In *General Federation Clubwoman*, December 1947. Box 23, File: Biographical. May Mann Jennings Papers, UFSL.

Wetherell, Virginia Bass. E-mail to author, January 25, 2012.

———. Interview with author, February 23, 2011. Lamont, Fla. SPOHP.

Whitfield, Estus. Telephone conversation with author, October 29, 2013.

Secondary Sources

"About Turkey Point." Accessed October 22, 2011. http://www.fpl.com/environment/nuclear/about_turkey_point.shtml.

Adams-Williams, Lydia. "Conservation—Woman's Work." *Forestry and Irrigation*, 14 (1908): 350–51. Cited in Jarvis, Kimberly A., "How Did the General Federation of Women's Clubs Shape Women's Involvement in the Conservation Movement, 1900–1930?" In *Women and Social Movements in the United States, 1600–2000*, ed. Kathryn Kish Sklar and Thomas Dublin. Alexander Street Press. http://wass.alexanderstreet.com.

"Adoption of the Florida State Tree." Accessed September 28, 2011. http://www.netstate.com/states/symb/trees/fl_sabal_palmetto_palm.htm.

"Air Pollution Meet to Aid Polk Studies." *Lakeland Ledger,* November 23, 1958, A1.

"Alice Mickens Park." http://wpb.org/park/alice-mickens-park/#tabs.

Allison, Wes. "On Janet Reno's Campaign, It's All Relative." *St. Petersburg Times,* July 8, 2002.

Anderson, Lars. *Paynes Prairie—The Great Savanna: A History and Guide*. Sarasota, Fla.: Pineapple Press, 2001.

Andrew, Simon A. "Fenholloway River Evaluation Initiative: Collaborative Problem-Solving within the Permit System." In *Adaptive Governance and Water Conflict: New Institutions for Collaborative Planning*, ed. John T. Scholz and Bruce Stiftel, 40–51. Washington, D.C.: Resources for the Future, 2005.

Arcury, Thomas A., Sara A. Quandt, and Gregory B. Russell. "Pesticide Safety among Farmworkers: Perceived Risk and Perceived Control as Factors Reflecting Environmental Justice." Supplement, *Environmental Health Perspectives* 110, no. S2 (April 2002): S233-S240.

Baljet, Peter P. "Water Pollution Problems in Dade County." In *The Environmental Destruction of South Florida: A Handbook for Citizens*, ed. Ross McCluney, 51–53. Coral Gables: University of Miami Press, 1971.

Balogh, Christopher. "Apopka Farmworkers Say Pesticides Caused Illnesses." *Orlando Weekly,* June 2, 2001.

Barnett, Cynthia. *Mirage: Florida and the Vanishing Water of the Eastern U.S.* Ann Arbor: University of Michigan Press, 2007.

Basse, Craig. "Ex-Lawmaker, Civic Activist Sample Leaves Legacy of Nice." *St. Petersburg Times,* September 4, 2002.

———. "Pioneering Politician Mary Grizzle Dies." *St. Petersburg Times,* November 9, 2006.

Basse, Craig, and Will Van Sant. "She Fought for Environment, Women's Rights." *St. Petersburg Times,* November 10, 2006.

"Bayboro Shell Fill Approved." *Evening Independent* (St. Petersburg, Fla.), November 16, 1971.

Bigart, Homer. "Miami-Sized Jetport Threatens Everglades with Extinction." New York Times News Service, *Berkshire Eagle* (Pittsfield, Mass.), August 12, 1969, A1.

Bigelow, Gordon. *Frontier Eden: The Literary Career of Marjorie Kinnan Rawlings.* Gainesville: University of Florida Press, 1966.

"Billboards Destroy Scenic Beauty." *Florida Clubwoman* 9, no. 3 (July 1929): 7.

"Billboard Tax Gets Approval of Councilmen." *Evening Independent* (St. Petersburg, Fla.), January 7, 1935, 1–2.

Binkley, Cameron. "'No Better Heritage than Living Trees'—Women's Clubs and Early Conservation in Humboldt County." *Western Historical Quarterly* 33, no. 2 (Summer 2002): 179–203.

———. "Saving Redwoods: Clubwomen and Conservation, 1900–1925." In *California Women and Politics: From the Gold Rush to the Great Depression,* ed. Robert W. Cherny, Mary Ann Irwin, and Ann Marie Wilson. Lincoln: University of Nebraska Press, 2010.

"Biography of Carol M. Browner." U.S. Environmental Protection Agency website, accessed April 4, 2011. http://www2.epa.gov/aboutepa/biography-carol-m-browner.

Birch, Eugenie L. "From Civic Worker to City Planner: Women and Planning, 1890–1980." In *The American Planner,* ed. Donald A. Krueckeberg, 472–78. New Brunswick, N.J.: Center for Urban Policy Research, 1994.

Black, Hope L. "Mounted on a Pedestal: Bertha Honoré Palmer." MLA thesis, Florida State University, 2007. Graduate School Theses and Dissertations, http://scholarcommons.usf.edu/etd/637.

Blackman, Lucy Worthington. *The Florida Audubon Society: 1900–1935.* n.p.

———. *The Florida Federation of Women's Clubs, 1895–1939.* Jacksonville, Fla.: Jacksonville Southern Historical Publishing Associates, 1939.

———. *The Women of Florida.* 2 vols. Southern Historical Publishing Associates, 1940.

Blackman, William Fremont. *History of Orange County Florida: Narrative and Biographical.* Chuluota, Fla.: Mickler House, 1973.

Blair, Karen J. *The Clubwoman as Feminist: True Womanhood Redefined, 1868–1914.* New York: Holmes and Meier, 1980.

Blake, Nelson M. *Land into Water—Water into Land: A History of Water Management in Florida.* Tallahassee: University Press of Florida, 1980.

Blum, Elizabeth D. *Love Canal Revisited: Race, Class, and Gender in Environmental Activism.* Lawrence: University Press of Kansas, 2008.

———. "Women, Environmental Rationales, and Activism during the Progressive Era." In *"To Love the Wind and the Rain": African Americans and Environmental History,* ed. Dianne D. Glave and Mark Stoll, 79–84. Pittsburgh: University of Pittsburgh Press, 2006.

Boardman, Dr. Walter S. "Garden Clubs Are Leaders in Natural Area Preservation." *National Gardener* 33, no. 3–4 (March–April 1962): 6–7.

Bolin, Lois. "A Woman with a Seminole Mission: Deaconess Harriet Mary Bedell." *Naples Florida Weekly,* January 8, 2009. http://naples.floridaweekly.com/news/2009-01-08/undercover_ historian/008.html.

Brake, Andrew S. *Man in the Middle: The and Influence of Henry Benjamin Whipple, the First Episcopal Bishop of Minnesota.* Lanham, Md.: University Press of America, 2005.

Branch, Michael P. "Writing the Swamp: Marjory Stoneman Douglas and *The Everglades: River of Grass.*" In *Such News of the Land: U.S. Women Nature Writers,* ed. Thomas S. Edwards and Elizabeth A. De Wolfe, 125–35. Hanover, N.H.: University Press of New England, 2001.

Breton, Mary Jo. *Women Pioneers for the Environment.* Boston: Northeastern University Press, 1998.

Brinkley, Douglas. *The Wilderness Warrior: Theodore Roosevelt and the Crusade for America.* New York: Harper Collins, 2009.

"Bronze Plaque Marks Coquina Garden Seat." *Florida Times-Union* (Jacksonville, Fla.), December 8, 1935.

Brown, Dorothy M. *Setting a Course: American Women in the 1920s.* Boston: Twayne Publishers, 1987.

Brugge, Doug, Timothy Benally, and Esther Yazzie-Lewis. "Uranium Mining on Navajo Indian Land." *Cultural Survival Quarterly* 25, no. 1 (Spring 2001). http://www.culturalsurvival.org/publications/cultural-survival-quarterly/united-states/uranium-mining-navajo-indian-land.

Bubil, Harold. "A Century Ago, Bertha Palmer Changed the Region." *Sarasota Herald-Tribune,* January 17, 2010.

"Bullard: Green Issue Is Black and White." *CNN US,* July 17, 2007.

"Campaign History." http://www.smokeybear.com/vault/history_main.asp.

Campen, Richard N. *Winter Park Portrait: The Story of Winter Park and Rollins College.* Beachwood, Ohio: West Summit Press, 1987.

"Canaveral." Accessed December 22, 2011. http://www.nps.gov/cana/index.htm.

Carpenter, Leslie. "What a Swell Party It'll Be." *St. Petersburg Times,* February 23, 1964, 3D.

Carriker, Roy R. "Florida's Growth Management Act: An Introduction and Overview." Accessed January 6, 2011. http://ufdcimages.uflib.ufl.edu/IR/00/00/13/52/00001/FE64300.pdf.

Carson, Rachel. *Silent Spring*. New York: Houghton Mifflin, 1962; repr. 1994.

Carter, Luther J. *The Florida Experience: Land and Water Policy in a Growth State*. Baltimore: Johns Hopkins University Press, 1974.

"The CATE Letter." May 2008, accessed November 19, 2011. http://www.cate.ws/5-08_CATE_newsletter.pdf.

Catron, Derek. "A Fight for the Seas." *Orlando Sentinel*, January 9, 2000.

Cerulean, Susan, ed. *The Book of the Everglades*. Minneapolis: Milkweed Editions, 2002.

Chambliss, Julian C. "Club Women and Municipal Housekeeping: The Beautification Movement in Chicago and Atlanta, 1900–1920." Paper delivered at Social Science History Association Annual Meeting, St. Louis, Mo., October 2002.

"Chapter 12—Ten Communities: Profiles in Environmental Progress." Accessed October 24, 2011. http://clinton4.nara.gov/CEQ/earthday/ch12.html.

Chelala, Cesar. "Women Taking Charge to Save the Environment." *Boston Globe*, May 12, 2001.

Cherny, Robert W., Mary Ann Irwin, and Ann Marie Wilson, eds. *California Women and Politics: From the Gold Rush to the Great Depression*. Lincoln: University of Nebraska Press, 2010.

"Chinsegut Conservation Center." Accessed October 10, 2011. http://myfwc.com/chinsegut.

Clark, Lottie Montgomery. "Negro Women Leaders of Florida." MA thesis, Florida State College for Women, July 1942.

Cleveland, J. Cutler, ed. "History of Pelican Island National Wildlife Refuge." In *Encyclopedia of Earth*, U.S. Fish and Wildlife Service, http://www.eoearth.org/article/History_of_Pelican_Island_National_Wildlife_Refuge.

"Combined Sewer Separation in Minneapolis." Accessed October 24, 2011. http://www.minneapolismn.gov/publicworks/stormwater/cso/cso_history.

Covington, James W. *The Seminoles of Florida*. Gainesville: University Press of Florida, 1993.

Cowdrey, Albert E. *This Land, This South: An Environmental History*. Lexington: University Press of Kentucky, 1983.

Cridlin, Jay. "Planting Plan Blends Forestry, Genealogy." *St. Petersburg Times*, February 21, 2003.

Cronon, William. *Nature's Metropolis: Chicago and the Great West*. New York: W. W. Norton, 1991.

Crooks, James B. *Jacksonville after the Fire, 1901–1919*. Jacksonville: University of North Florida Press, 1991.

Crosby, Mrs. Robert R. *Fifty Years of Service: National Council of State Garden Clubs 1929–1979*. St. Louis, Mo.: National Council of State Garden Clubs, 1979.

Cubbison, Christopher. "Delay Hinted on Offshore Oil Decision." *St. Petersburg Times,* August 24, 1973.

Danahy, Laura Brackenridge. "Elizabeth Virrick, the Maverick of Miami Slum Clearance. In *Making Waves: Female Activists in Twentieth-Century Florida,* ed. Jack E. Davis and Kari Frederickson, 250–66. Gainesville: University Press of Florida, 2003.

"DAR Forests—States." Accessed February 15, 2012. http://www.dar.org/natsociety/content.cfm?ID=263&FO=Y&hd=n.

"Dark Years of Depression and War." Accessed February 15, 2012. http://floridahistory.org/depression.htm.

Darwin, Charles. *On the Origin of Species.* 1859; facsimile ed. Cambridge, Mass.: Harvard University Press, 1964.

Dasmann, Raymond F. *No Further Retreat: The Fight to Save Florida.* New York: Macmillan, 1971.

Davis, Devra. *When Smoke Ran Like Water: Tales of Environmental Deception and the Battle against Pollution.* New York: Basic Books, 2004.

Davis, Frederick Rowe. *The Man Who Saved Sea Turtles: Archie Carr and the Origins of Conservation Biology.* Oxford: Oxford University Press, 2007.

Davis, Jack E. *An Everglades Providence: Marjory Stoneman Douglas and the American Environmental Century.* Athens: University of Georgia Press, 2009.

———. "'Conservation Is Now a Dead Word': Marjory Stoneman Douglas and the Transformation of American Environmentalism." In *Paradise Lost? The Environmental History of Florida,* ed. Jack E. Davis and Raymond Arsenault, 297–325. Gainesville: University Press of Florida, 2005.

———. "Shades of Justice: The Lynching of Jesse James Payne and Its Aftermath." Master's thesis, University of South Florida, 1989.

Davis, Jack E., and Raymond Arsenault, eds. *Paradise Lost? The Environmental History of Florida.* Gainesville: University Press of Florida, 2005.

Davis, Jack E., and Kari Frederickson, eds. *Making Waves: Female Activists in Twentieth-Century Florida.* Gainesville: University Press of Florida, 2003.

Davis-Platt, Joy. "Brooksville to Celebrate Heritage." *St. Petersburg Times,* October 5, 2001.

de Beer, Gavin. *Charles Darwin: Evolution by Natural Selection.* Garden City, N.Y.: Doubleday, 1967.

DeGrove, John M. "Growth Management in Florida: My Perspective on What Has and Hasn't Worked and Why." Accessed January 11, 2012. http://www.1000friendsofflorida.org/reform/DCA_Secretaries.asp.

Derr, Mark. *Some Kind of Paradise: A Chronicle of Man and the Land in Florida.* New York: William Morrow, 1989.

Dewey, Scott Hamilton. "'Is This What We Came to Florida For?' Florida Women and the Fight against Air Pollution in the 1960s." In *Making Waves: Female Activists in Twentieth-Century Florida,* ed. Jack E. Davis and Kari Frederickson, 197–225. Gainesville: University Press of Florida, 2003.

Dieterich, Emily Perry. "Birds of a Feather: The Coconut Grove Audubon Society, 1915–1917." *Tequesta* 45 (1985): 3–27.

Dilsaver, Lary M., ed. "The Early Years." In *America's National Park System: The Critical Documents.* Lanham, Md.: Rowman and Littlefield, 1994. http://www.cr.nps.gov/history/online_books/anps/anps_1.htm.

DM-Maz, George. "Central Floridians of Year: Apopka Nuns." *Orlando Sentinel,* January 6, 2008.

"The Doris Leeper Spruce Creek Preserve." Accessed December 22, 2011. http://www.volusia.org/services/growth-and-resource-management/environmental-management/land-management/dlspsrucecreek.stml.

Dorsey, Kurkpatrick. *The Dawn of Conservation Diplomacy: U.S.-Canadian Wildlife Protection Treaties in the Progressive Era.* Seattle: University of Washington Press, 1998.

"DOT Joins Garden Clubs in Fight over Litter." *DeFuniak Springs Herald-Breeze,* March 16, 1972, 2.

Doughty, Robin W. *Feather Fashions and Bird Preservation: A Study in Nature Protection.* Berkeley: University of California Press, 1975.

Douglas, Marjory Stoneman. *The Everglades: River of Grass.* Sarasota, Fla.: Pineapple Press, 1947; repr. 1988.

———. *Florida: The Long Frontier.* New York: Harper and Row, 1967.

———. "Only Tropics in U.S. to Be National Park." *Miami Herald,* May 25, 1930.

Douglas, Marjory Stoneman, with John Rothchild. *Marjory Stoneman Douglas: Voice of the River.* Sarasota, Fla.: Pineapple Press, 1987.

Douglas, Marjory Stoneman, and Ralph Stoutamire. *The Parks and Playgrounds of Florida.* Bulletin no. 62. Reprint. Tallahassee: Florida Department of Agriculture, January 1942.

Downing, Ann B. "Oak Lodge 1881–1910." *Indian River Journal* X, no. 1 (Spring–Summer 2012): 12–15.

Dreisbach, Rebecca Bryan. *Umatilla.* Charleston, S.C.: Arcadia Publishing, 2010.

Dutcher, William. "Report of the Committee on Bird Protection." *Auk* 21 (January 1904): 133.

Eades, John F. "City Planning in West Palm Beach during the 1920s." *Florida Historical Quarterly* 75, no. 3 (Winter 1997): 282–83.

Earley, Lawrence S. *Looking for Longleaf: The Fall and Rise of an American Forest.* Chapel Hill: University of North Carolina Press, 2004.

Eastman, Susan. "'Bird Woman' Took Wing Ahead of Time." *St. Petersburg Times,* June 18, 1997.

Edwards, Thomas S., and Elizabeth A. De Wolfe, eds. *Such News of the Land: U.S. Women Nature Writers.* Hanover, N.H.: University Press of New England, 2001.

Egerton, Frank N., ed. *History of American Ecology.* New York: Arno Press, 1977.

Ellis, Mary Carolyn, and Joanne V. Hawks. "Creating a Different Pattern: Florida's Women Legislators, 1928–1986." *Florida Historical Quarterly* 66, no. 1 (July 1987): 73.

Ellis, Virginia. "Grizzle Fights to Keep Sewage Standards." *St. Petersburg Times,* May 27, 1980, 4B.

Encyclopedia of Cleveland. "Environmentalism." http://ech.cwru.edu/ech-cgi/article. pl?id=E5.

"Environmental History Timeline." Accessed October 24, 2011. http://www.radford. edu/wkovarik/envhist/5progressive.html.

"Environmental Justice for the Navajo: Uranium Mining in the Southwest." Accessed April 25, 2012. http://www.umich.edu/~snre492/sdancy.html.

Episcopal Café. "Speaking to the Soul: Bird Woman." Accessed January 7, 2014. http:// www.episcopalcafe.com/thesoul/2010/01/.

Evans, Sara M. *Born for Liberty: A History of Women in America.* New York: Free Press Paperbacks, 1989; repr. 1997.

———. *Personal Politics: The Roots of Women's Liberation in the Civil Rights Movement* and *the New Left.* New York: Vintage, 1980.

———. "Women's History and Political Theory: Toward a Feminist Approach to Public Life." In *Visible Women: New Essays on American Activism,* ed. Nancy A. Hewitt and Suzanne Lebsock, 120–28. Urbana: University of Illinois Press, 1993.

Ezell, Veola B. "Florida Parks." *Florida Bulletin* (Florida Federation of Women's Clubs), April 1924, 5.

"A Fabulous Convention—Jacksonville, April 29–May 2." *Florida Clubwoman* 15, no. 1 (Summer 1968): 7.

"Fannie Veola Badger Ezell." Online memorial. Accessed February 9, 2012. http://www. findagrave.com/cgi-bin/fg.cgi?page=gr&GRid=30432515.

Florida Daughters of the American Revolution. "A Tree for Every D.A.R." In *Twenty-Fourth Annual Conference,* 71. DeLand, Fla.: News Publishing Company, n.d.

"Florida Dept. of Natural Resources." Accessed January 20, 2012. http://dlis. dos.state.fl.us/barm/rediscovery/default.asp?IDCFile=/fsa/DETAILSG. IDC,SPECIFIC=1190,DATABASE= GROUP.

Florida Defenders of the Environment, "Biography of Marjorie Harris Carr." Accessed June 15, 2014. http://fladefenders.org/?page_id=99; Carr, interview with author.

"Florida House District 61 Republican." *Evening Independent* (St. Petersburg, Fla.), September 7, 1974.

Florida Legal Services, Inc. "Facts." Accessed November 22, 2011. http://www.florida legal.org/facts.htm (page discontinued).

"Florida Quick Facts." Accessed October 15, 2013. http://www.stateofflorida.com/Portal/ DesktopDefault.aspx?tabid=95.

Florida State Society of the D.A.R. *History 1892–1933 The Florida State Society of the Daughters of the American Revolution of Florida,* vol. 1. Jacksonville: Douglas, 1933.

————. *History 1933–1946 The Florida State Society of the Daughters of the American Revolution*, vol. 2. Jacksonville: H. and W. B. Drew, 1946.

"Florida's Endangered and Threatened Species." Accessed October 15, 2013. http://myfwc.com/media/1515251/threatened_endangered_species.pdf.

Floyd, Charles F., and Peter J. Shedd. *Highway Beautification: The Environmental Movement's Greatest Failure*. Boulder, Colo.: Westview Press, 1979.

Fontenay, Blake. "Judge: Volusia Doing OK for Turtles." *Orlando Sentinel*, May 9, 1996.

"Former Board Member Archive." Accessed January 6, 2012. http://www.sjrwmd.com/governingboard/archive.

"For the Orange County Commission District 4: Fran Pignone." *Orlando Sentinel*, October 15, 1990.

Forstall, Richard L. "Florida: Population of Counties by Decennial Census: 1900 to 1990." U.S. Census Bureau, accessed February 20, 2012. http://www.census.gov/population/cencounts/fl190090.txt.

"Fran Mainella." Accessed October 24, 2013. http://fmainella.com/.

Funk, Ben. "Florida Mounts Heavy Attack on Pollution." *The Day* (New London, Conn.), April 24, 1970, A1.

————. "Pollution Problem Hanging over Sunshine State's Future." *Ocala Star-Banner*, December 18, 1966, 41.

Gannon, Michael, ed. *The New History of Florida*. Gainesville: University Press of Florida, 1996.

"Garden Club to Hear County Agent." *Evening Independent* (St. Petersburg, Fla.), April 20, 1958.

Garden Club of Jacksonville. "History." Accessed June 23, 2011. http://www.gardenclubofjacksonville.org/history.htm.

Gerlach, Luther P., and Virginia H. Hine. *Lifeway Leap: The Dynamics of Change in America*. Minneapolis: University of Minnesota Press, 1973.

Glave, Dianne D., and Mark Stoll, eds. *"To Love the Wind and the Rain": African Americans and Environmental History*. Pittsburgh: University of Pittsburgh Press, 2006.

"Gloria Rains' Legacy." *Sarasota Herald-Tribune*, September 19, 2000, A10.

Gold, Pleasant Daniel. *History of Duval County Florida*. St. Augustine: Record Company, 1928.

Gordon, Robert. "Poisons in the Fields: The United Farm Workers, Pesticides, and Environmental Politics." *Pacific Historical Review* 68, no. 1 (February 1999): 51–77.

Gottlieb, Robert. *Forcing the Spring: The Transformation of the American Environmental Movement*. Washington, D.C.: Island Press, 1993.

Graham, Frank Jr. *The Audubon Ark: A History of the National Audubon Society*. New York: Alfred A. Knopf, 1990.

Green, Amy. "Mary Barley Crusades behind the Scenes for the Everglades." *Christian Science Monitor*, November 5, 2008.

Greene, Juanita. "How the Automobile Multiplies the Problems of Dade County." In

The Environmental Destruction of South Florida: A Handbook for Citizens, ed. William Ross McCluney, 69. Coral Gables: University of Miami Press, 1971.

Grinder, R. Dale. "The Battle for Clean Air: The Smoke Problem in Post-Civil War America." In *Pollution and Reform in American Cities, 1870–1930*, ed. Martin V. Melosi, 83–103. Austin: University of Texas Press, 1980.

Groner, Duncan G. "Air Pollution Act 'Foggy.'" *Evening Independent* (St. Petersburg, Fla.), September 5, 1967, 1A.

Grunwald, Michael. *The Swamp: The Everglades, Florida, and the Politics of Paradise.* New York: Simon and Schuster, 2006.

Gupte, Pranay, and Bonner R. Cohen. "Carol Browner: Master of Mission Creep." *Forbes*, October 20, 1997. http://www.forbes.com/forbes/1997/1020/6009170a.html.

Habin, Ron, and Geraldean Matthew. *Lake Apopka Farmworkers Environmental Health Project.* Apopka: Farmworker Association of Florida, May 2006.

Hahamovitch, Cindy. *The Fruits of Their Labor: Atlantic Coast Farmworkers and the Making of Migrant Poverty, 1870–1945.* Chapel Hill: University of North Carolina Press, 1997.

Haines, Judge Webber. "Never Underestimate the Power of a Woman." *Florida Clubwoman* (October 1949): 8.

"Half of Florida Has Sewage Plants." *Miami News*, October 24, 1964, A13a.

Hall, Richard. "Pollution." *Life*, February 7, 1969, 38–50. http://books.google.com/books?id=s1IEAAAAMBAJ&printsec=frontcover&source=gbs_ge_summary_r&cad=0#v=onepage&q&f=false.

Harding, Sandra. *Whose Science? Whose Knowledge? Thinking from Women's Lives.* Ithaca, N.Y.: Cornell University Press, 1991.

Hartzell, Scott Taylor. "Everything She Did Was Her Way of Being Good." *St. Petersburg Times*, March 17, 1999.

Hauserman, Julie. "Dioxin at Mill Too High." *St. Petersburg Times*, February 9, 2001.

Hays, Samuel P. *Beauty, Health, and Permanence: Environmental Politics in the United States, 1955–1985.* New York: Cambridge University Press, 1987.

———. *Conservation and the Gospel of Efficiency: The Progressive Conservation Movement 1890–1920.* Cambridge, Mass.: Harvard University Press, 1959.

"Helen Gordon Davis." Accessed January 20, 2012, http://www.fcsw.net/halloffame/WHOFbios/helen_gordon_davis.

"Herald-Tribune, Sarasota Couple, Win Awards." *Sarasota Herald-Tribune*, September 11, 1967, 13.

Hewitt, Nancy A., and Suzanne Lebsock, eds. *Visible Women: New Essays on American Activism.* Urbana: University of Illinois Press, 1993.

Highlands Hammock State Park. "History and Culture" brochure. Accessed April 29, 2011. http://www.floridastateparks.org/highlandshammock/additionalinformation.cfm.

"A History and Overview of the Federal Outdoor Advertising Control Program." U.S.

Department of Transportation, Federal Highway Administration, accessed October 3, 2011. http://www.fhwa.dot.gov/realestate/oacprog.htm#HISTORY.

"History of Canaveral National Seashore." Accessed January 5, 2012. http://nbbd.com/godo/cns/PressReleases/000120.html.

"History of FWAF." Accessed November 22, 2011. http://www.floridafarmworkers.org/index.php/about-us/our-history.

Horning, Gloria G. "Social Network and Environmental Justice: A Case Study in Perry, Florida." PhD diss., Florida State University, 2005.

House-Mason, Ann. "Praise for Supporters of Pesticide Posting Bill." *Sarasota Herald-Tribune*, July 10, 1989, 10A.

"House of Polluters." *St. Petersburg Times*, May 16, 1960, 22A.

Hoy, Suellen M. "Women and City Wastes in the Early Twentieth Century." In *Major Problems in American Environmental History*, ed. Carolyn Merchant, 437. Lexington, Mass.: D. C. Heath, 1993.

Hughes, J. Donald. *What Is Environmental History?* Cambridge, Mass.: Polity Press, 2006.

Hunter, Ann Arnold. *A Century of Service: The Story of the DAR*. Washington: National Society of the Daughters of the American Revolution, 1991.

Hurley, Andrew. *Environmental Inequalities: Class, Race, and Industrial Pollution in Gary, Indiana, 1945–1980*. Chapel Hill: University of North Carolina Press, 1995.

"Incinerator Verdict Due Today." *St. Petersburg Times*, September 24, 1970, 8B.

Irby, Lee. "A Passion for Wild Things: Marjorie Harris Carr and the Fight to Free a River." In *Making Waves: Female Activists in Twentieth-Century Florida*, ed. Jack E. Davis and Kari Frederickson, 177–96. Gainesville: University Press of Florida, 2003.

"Irritant in Air Ruins Jacksonville Nylons." *New York Times*, February 17, 1949, 27.

"Is Fenholloway River Too Big a Price?" *St. Petersburg Times*, December 20, 1966, 3B.

Jacksonville Looks at Its Negro Community: A Survey of Conditions Affecting the Negro Population in Jacksonville and Duval County, Florida. Jacksonville, Fla.: Council of Social Agencies, 1946.

Jameson, Mary F. Mungen. *Remembering Neighborhoods of Jacksonville, Florida*. St. Louis, Mo.: Mira Digital Publishing, 2010.

Jarvis, Kimberly A. "How Did the General Federation of Women's Clubs Shape Women's Involvement in the Conservation Movement, 1900–1930?" In *Women and Social Movements in the United States, 1600–2000*, ed. Kathryn Kish Sklar and Thomas Dublin. Alexander Street Press. http://wass.alexanderstreet.com.

Jeffreys, Mrs. Linwood. "Forests, Their Use and Beauty Natural Resources." *Florida Bulletin* 25, no. 12 (January 1948): 13, 24.

Jennings, May Mann. "Conservation Laws Stand to the Credit of Florida." *Christian Science Monitor*, November 13, 1925, B2.

Jennings, Mrs. W. S. "State Beautification." *Florida Clubwoman* 4, no. 12 (January–February 1956): 12.

Jones, Arthur. "Millions Reaped What Cesar Chavez Sowed." *National Catholic Reporter,* May 7, 1993.

Jones, Lucy D. "My Florida History." Accessed February 15, 2012. http://myfloridahistory. blogspot.com/2009/02/hillsborough-river-bridge-at-fort.html.

Jones, Maxine D. "'Without Compromise or Fear': Florida's African American Female Activists." In *Making Waves: Female Activists in Twentieth-Century Florida,* ed. Jack E. Davis and Kari Frederickson, 269–92. Gainesville: University Press of Florida, 2003.

Jumper, Betty Mae Tiger, and Patsy West. *A Seminole Legend: The Life of Betty Mae Tiger Jumper.* Gainesville: University Press of Florida, 2001.

"KAB: A Beautiful History." Accessed November 1, 2011. http://www.kab.org/site/ PageServer?pagename=about_history.

Kamel, Freya, Andrew S. Rowland, Lawrence P. Park, W. Kent Anger, Donna D. Baird, Beth C. Gladen, Tirso Moreno, Lillian Stallone, and Dale P. Sandler. "Neurobehavioral Performance and Work Experience in Florida Farmworkers." *Environmental Health Perspectives* 111, no. 14 (November 2003): 1765–72.

Kaplan, Temma. *Crazy for Democracy: Women in Grassroots Movements.* New York: Routledge, 1997.

Kaufman, Polly Welts. *National Parks and the Woman's Voice: A History.* Albuquerque: University of New Mexico Press, 2006.

"Keep Up the Fight." *Evening Independent* (St. Petersburg, Fla.), June 6, 1980, 16A.

Keller, Amy. "Both Sides Now—Energy Regulation in Florida." *Florida Trend,* June 1, 2010. http://www.floridatrend.com/article/3867/both-sides-now-energy-regulation-in-florida.

Kersey, Harry A. Jr. *The Stranahans of Fort Lauderdale: A Pioneer Family of New River.* Gainesville: University Press of Florida, 2003.

"Key Events in the History of Air Quality in California." Accessed October 20, 2011. http://www.arb.ca.gov/html/brochure/history.htm.

King, Isabel T., Mrs. Melville Hall, and Mrs. Truman Green, eds. *Fifty Year History of Florida Federation of Garden Clubs, Inc. 1925–1975.* Winter Park, Fla.: Board of Directors of the FFGC, 1975.

Kingsland, Sharon E. *The Evolution of American Ecology, 1890–2000.* Baltimore: Johns Hopkins University Press, 2005.

Kline, Benjamin. *First Along the River: A Brief History of the U.S. Environmental Movement.* 3rd ed. Lanham, Md.: Rowman and Littlefield, 2007.

Klinkenberg, Jeff. "A Culture Endangered." In *The Book of the Everglades,* ed. Susan Cerulean, 97–106. Minneapolis: Milkweed Editions, 2002.

Knell, Gretchen. "Environmental Protection and Pollution Control." July 5, 2013, accessed September 11, 2003. http://www.lwv.org/content/environmental-protection-and-pollution-control.

Knight, Jan. "The Environmentalism of Edward Bok: The Ladies' Home Journal, the

General Federation of Women's Clubs, and the Environment, 1901–09." *Journalism History* 29, no. 4 (Winter 2004): 154–65.

Krueckeberg, Donald A., ed. *The American Planner*. New Brunswick, N.J.: Center for Urban Policy Research, 1994. http://repository.upenn.edu/cgi/viewcontent.cgi?article=1018&context=cplan_papers.

"Lady Bird Johnson—The Beautification Campaign." Accessed November 2, 2011. http://www.pbs.org/ladybird/shattereddreams/shattereddreams_report.html.

"'Lady Hermit' Appeals for Funds to Save Lower Bay Lands." *St. Petersburg Times*, August 2, 1956.

"Lake Apopka." Accessed November 20, 2011. http://floridaswater.com/lakeapopka/.

Lanier, Sidney. *Florida: Its Scenery, Climate, and History*. Facsimile of the 1875 edition. Gainesville, University of Florida Press, 1973.

Lawton, Elizabeth B. "Florida Billboards." *Florida Clubwoman* (February 1935): 13.

League of Women Voters. "History." Accessed April 6, 2012. http://www.lwv.org/history.

"League of Women Voters." Accessed April 6, 2012. http://www.u-s-history.com/pages/h1592.html.

Lear, Linda. *Rachel Carson: Witness for Nature*. New York: Henry Holt, 1997.

Leopold, Aldo. *A Sand County Almanac with Essays on Conservation from Round River*. New York: Ballantine, 1966.

Lerner, Steve. "Pensacola, Florida: Living Next Door to Mount Dioxin and a Chemical Fertilizer Superfund Site." Collaborative on Health and the Environment, accessed April 20, 2011. http://www.healthandenvironment.org/articles/homepage/2628.

Lewis, James. "Opposition to Bay Lake Plan Builds." *St. Petersburg Times*, April 29, 1965.

Lewis, Paul. "Orlando's 'Beautiful' Heritage: The City Beautiful Movement and Its Impact on Orlando." Accessed October 3, 2011. http://www.cityoforlando.net/planning/cityplanning/PDFs/Historic,%20Preservation/Orla ndo_City_Beautiful_Article.pdf.

Lightfoot, Mrs. E. N. "Water, Air Should Be Conserved." *Florida Clubwoman* 12, no. 1 (September 1964): 10–11.

Lurton, Mrs. Jack. "Roadside Development Section." *Camellia* (Pensacola Federation of Garden Clubs), March 1953, 11.

Macdonald, Margaret F. "'Our Lady of the Rivers': Marjorie Harris Carr, Science, Gender, and Environmental Activism." PhD diss., University of Florida, 2010.

Macdonald, Peggy. *Marjorie Harris Carr: Defender of Florida's Environment*. Gainesville: University Press of Florida, 2014.

MacKay, Buddy, with Rick Edmonds. *How Florida Happened: The Political Education of Buddy MacKay*. Gainesville: University Press of Florida, 2010.

"Madira Bickel Mound State Archeological Site." Accessed June 23, 2011. http://www.floridastateparks.org/madirabickelmound/default.cfm.

Mahon, John K., and Brent R. Weisman. "Florida's Seminole and Miccosukee Peoples."

In *The New History of Florida*, ed. Michael Gannon, 183–201. Gainesville: University Press of Florida, 1996.

"Marjorie Kinnan Rawlings Historic State Park." Accessed September 18, 2013. http://www.floridastateparks.org/marjoriekinnanrawlings/.

Marrs, Mrs. Kingsmill. "Florida Audubon Society." *Bird-Lore* 3, no. 6 (December 1901): 220.

———. "State Reports—Florida." *Bird-Lore* 7, no. 6 (December 1905): 316.

———. "State Audubon Reports—Florida." *Bird-Lore* 12, no. 6 (November–December 1911): 367.

———. "State Audubon Reports—Florida," *Bird-Lore* 15, no. 6 (December 1913): 448.

Marsh, George Perkins. "Human Responsibility for the Land." In *American Environmentalism: Readings in Conservation History*, 3rd ed., ed. Roderick Frazier Nash, 41–44. New York: McGraw-Hill Publishing Company, 1990.

McCally, David. "The Everglades and the Florida Dream." In *Paradise Lost? The Environmental History of Florida*, ed. Jack E. Davis and Raymond Arsenault, 150–52. Gainesville: University Press of Florida, 2005.

McCluney, Ross. "Air Pollution Problems in South Florida." In *The Environmental Destruction of South Florida: A Handbook for Citizens*, ed. Ross McCluney, 54–63. Coral Gables: University of Miami Press, 1971.

———. "The Solution to Pollution." In *The Environmental Destruction of South Florida: A Handbook for Citizens*, ed. Ross McCluney, 47–50. Coral Gables: University of Miami Press, 1971.

McCluney, Ross, ed. *The Environmental Destruction of South Florida: A Handbook for Citizens*. Coral Gables: University of Miami Press, 1971.

McFarland, J. Horace. "Beautiful America." *Ladies' Home Journal* (1889–1907), July 1904, 27.

———. "The New Department Beautiful America." *Ladies' Home Journal* (1889–1907), January 1904, 15.

McGerr, Michael. *A Fierce Discontent: The Rise and Fall of the Progressive Movement in America, 1870–1920*. Oxford: Oxford University Press, 2003.

McGurty, Eileen Maura. "From NIMBY to Civil Rights: The Origins of the Environmental Justice Movement." *Environmental History* 2, no. 3 (July 1997): 303–5.

McIntosh, Robert P. "Ecology Since 1900." In *History of American Ecology*, ed. Frank N. Egerton, 353–72. New York: Arno Press, 1977.

McIver, Stuart B. *Death in the Everglades: The Murder of Guy Bradley, America's First Martyr to Environmentalism*. Gainesville: University Press of Florida, 2003.

Meindl, Christopher F. "Water, Water Everywhere." In *Paradise Lost? The Environmental History of Florida*, ed. Jack E. Davis and Raymond Arsenault, 113–37. Gainesville: University Press of Florida, 2005.

Melosi, Martin V., ed. *Pollution and Reform in American Cities, 1870–1930*. Austin: University of Texas Press, 1980.

Merchant, Carolyn. *American Environmental History: An Introduction*. New York: Columbia University Press, 2007.

———. *The Columbia Guide to American Environmental History*. New York: Columbia University Press, 2002.

———. *The Death of Nature: Women, Ecology and the Scientific Revolution*. New York: Harper and Row, 1980.

———. *Earthcare: Women and the Environment*. New York: Routledge, 1996.

———. "Women of the Progressive Conservation Movement: 1900–1916." *Environmental Review* 8, no. 1 (Spring 1984): 57–85.

Merchant, Carolyn, ed. *Major Problems in American Environmental History*. Lexington, Mass.: D. C. Heath, 1993.

Meyer, Jessie Hamm. *Leading the Way: A Century of Service. The Florida Federation of Women's Clubs, 1895–1995*. Lakeland, Fla.: GFWC Florida Federation of Women's Clubs, Inc., 1994.

"Miami Gets State Suffrage Meet and Dr. Anna Shaw Both in March." *Miami Daily Metropolis,* February 3, 1917, 5.

Miller, Char. *Gifford Pinchot and the Making of Modern Environmentalism*. Washington, D.C.: Island Press–Shearwater Books, 2001.

Miller, Stuart. "Green at the Grassroots: Women Form the Frontlines of Environmental Activism." *E: The Environmental Magazine* 8, no. 1 (January–February 1997): 34–35. http://search.proquest.com.ezproxy.rollins.edu:2048/docview/229045879.

Mitchell, Paul. "Pinellas Okays Ratner (Furen) Fill." *St. Petersburg Times,* April 12, 1957, B-1, B-24.

Mitman, Gregg. *Reel Nature: America's Romance with Wildlife on Film*. Cambridge, Mass.: Harvard University Press, 1999.

Modica, Glenn R. "The History of the Newark Sewage System." Accessed October 25, 2011. http://www.usgennet.org/usa/nj/state/EssexNewarkSewer.htm.

Mohl, Raymond A. "Elizabeth Virrick and the 'Concrete Monsters': Housing Reform in Postwar Miami." *Tequesta* 51 (2001): 32. http://digitalcollections.fiu.edu/tequesta/files/2001/01_1_01.pdf.

Mohl, Raymond A., and Gary R. Mormino. "The Big Change in the Sunshine State: A Social History of Modern Florida." In *The New History of Florida*, ed. Michael Gannon, 418–47. Gainesville: University Press of Florida, 1996.

Moore, Roger. "Doris Leeper Was a 'Force for the Arts.'" *Orlando Sentinel,* April 12, 2000.

Moore-Willson, Minnie. *The Seminoles of Florida*, 8th ed. Kingsport, Tenn.: Kingsport Press, 1928.

Mormino, Gary R. *Land of Sunshine, State of Dreams: A Social History of Modern Florida*. Gainesville: University Press of Florida, 2005.

Morris, Allen Covington. *Women in the Florida Legislature*. Tallahassee: Florida House of Representatives, 1995.

Mould, Kimberley Tomlinson. "A Portrait in Black and White: The Ideal Woman's Club and the Woman's Club of Winter Park." MLS thesis, Rollins College, May 2000.

"Mrs. F. L. Ezell Pleads for Protection of Virgin Timber Lands." *Florida Bulletin* (September 1923): 5. Bound volume, *Florida Clubwoman 1–9 1921–30.*

Muir, Helen. *Miami, U.S.A.* New York: Henry Holt and Company, 1953.

Muir, John. *A Thousand-Mile Walk to the Gulf.* Boston: Mariner, 1998.

Munroe, Mary Barr. "Two Plume-bearing Birds." *Tropic Magazine,* 1915, quoted in "Reclaiming the Everglades," Everglades Digital Library, http://everglades.fiu.edu/reclaim/bios/munroemb.htm.

Murphy, James, and Doris Leeper. Draft Narrative. Unpublished manuscript in possession of author, n.d.

Napikoski, Linda. "Glass Ceiling for Women." Accessed April 6, 2012. http://womens history.about.com/ od/feminism/a/glass_ceiling_women.htm.

Nash, Roderick. *Wilderness and the American Mind.* 3rd ed. New Haven, N.J.: Yale University Press, 1982.

Nash, Roderick Frazier, ed. *American Environmentalism: Readings in Conservation History.* 3rd ed. New York: McGraw-Hill, 1990.

"National Organization for Women's 1966 Statement of Purpose." Accessed April 6, 2012. http://www.now.org/history/purpos66.html.

"Nature Program Is Presented at Florida Art School Session." *St. Petersburg Times,* January 3, 1924, 10.

"Navajo Challenge Uranium Mining Permit on Tribal Lands." *Environment News Service,* April 19, 2008.

Nelson, David. "'Improving' Paradise: The Civilian Conservation Corps and Environmental Change in Florida." In *Paradise Lost? The Environmental History of Florida,* ed. Jack E. Davis and Raymond Arsenault, 92–112. Gainesville: University Press of Florida, 2005.

———. "When Modern Tourism Was Born: Florida at the World Fairs and on the World Stage in the 1930s." *Florida Historical Quarterly* 88, no. 4 (Spring 2010): 436–39.

Nemmers, John R. "May Mann Jennings, Club Women and the Preservation of Royal Palm State Park in Florida." Paper delivered at the American Society for Environmental History annual conference, Tallahassee, Fla., February 27, 2009.

"New Anti-Fill Group Begins Campaigning." *St. Petersburg Times,* January 9, 1965.

Newman, Louise Michele. *White Women's Rights: The Racial Origins of Feminism in the United States.* New York: Oxford University Press, 1999.

"News Among Colored People in the City and State." *Florida Metropolis,* July 5, 1918, 13.

Noble, Mrs. Fred., ed. *The History of the Garden Club of Jacksonville, Florida.* Jacksonville: Garden Club of Jacksonville, 1960. https://sites.google.com/a/whitewayrealty.com/whiteway-corner/Home/garden-club-history.

Noll, Steven, and David Tegeder. *Ditch of Dreams: The Cross Florida Barge Canal and the Struggle for Florida's Future.* Gainesville: University Press of Florida, 2009.

Nott, Marian. "Sanitation Heads League's List of Top Improvements." *Evening Independent* (St. Petersburg, Fla.), September 10, 1969, A17.

"NPG Facts & Figures." Accessed September 13, 2013. http://www.npg.org/library/population-data/florida.html.

Nugent, Susan M. *Women Conserving the Florida Keys.* Portsmouth, N.H.: Peter E. Randall, 2008.

"Obituary 1—No Title." *New York Times,* November 10, 1900. *New York Times 1851–2002,* file 1857–Current, 7.

O'Neal, Donna. "Environment Gets 4 New Watchdogs." *Orlando Sentinel,* September 4, 1991.

Orr, Oliver H. Jr. *Saving American Birds: T. Gilbert Pearson and the Founding of the Audubon Movement.* Gainesville: University Press of Florida, 1992.

Parashar, Parmanand. *Public Administration in the Developed World.* New Delhi: Sarup and Sons, 1997.

"Park Units with Highest Number of Endangered Species—2010." Accessed September 23, 2014. http://www.nature.nps.gov/biology/endangeredspecies/assets/docs/TopParkUnits.pdf.

"The Pelican: His Enemies Take a Swing at Him." *Tampa Daily Times,* March 4, 1918.

"The Pelican: John Jones and Audubon Society Aid." *Tampa Daily Times,* March 8, 1918.

Penna, Anthony N. *Nature's Bounty: Historical and Modern Perspectives.* New York: M. E. Sharpe, 1991. http://books.google.com/books?id=-HN8YsINe_EC&pg=PA265&lpg=PA265&dq=smoke+committee+of+Cleveland&source=bl&ots=9v4OTimLWR&sig=QFTu8B7-ESR_lianrEwrufPPJY&hl=en&ei=Wy2fTsmWBsT10gGRlJmMCQ&sa=X&oi=book_result&ct=result&resnum=6&ved=0CCwQ6AEwBQ#v=onepage&q=smoke%20committee%20of%20Cleveland&f=false.

Peterson, Jon A. "Frederick Law Olmsted Sr. and Frederick Law Olmsted Jr.: The Visionary and the Professional." In *Planning the Twentieth Century American City,* ed. Mary Corbin Sies and Christopher Silver, 37–54. Baltimore: Johns Hopkins University Press, 1996.

Pfankuch, Thomas B. "Florida's Rotten River." *Florida Times-Union* (Jacksonville), June 5, 2002.

Philippon, Daniel J. *Conserving Words: How American Nature Writers Shaped the Environmental Movement.* Athens: University of Georgia Press, 2004.

Pinchot, Gifford. "The Birth of 'Conservation.'" In *American Environmentalism: Readings in Conservation History,* 3rd ed., ed. Roderick Frazier Nash, 73–79. New York: McGraw-Hill Publishing Company, 1990.

Pittman, Craig. *Manatee Insanity: Inside the War over Florida's Most Famous Endangered Species.* Gainesville: University Press of Florida, 2010.

Pitts, Byron. "'Harvest of Shame' 50 Years Later." *CBS Evening News,* November 24, 2010.

Pitzer, Bruce. "Gloria Rains Irreplaceable." *Sarasota Herald-Tribune,* September 19, 2000, A10.

"Plan Session Inaugurates Project ManaSota-88." *St. Petersburg Times,* June 9, 1966, B4.

Plater, Ormonde. "Through the Dust: Harriet Bedell." Accessed November 15, 2011. http://oplater.blogspot.com/2008/01/harriet-bedell.html.

Ponting, Clive. *A Green History of the World: The Environment and the Collapse of Great Civilizations.* New York: Penguin, 1991.

Poole, Leslie Kemp. "Florida: Paradise Redefined: The Rise of Environmentalism in a State of Growth." MLS thesis, Rollins College, May 1, 1991.

———. "The Florida Story Begins with Audubon Wardens." *Florida Naturalist* 73, no. 2 (Summer 2000): 6–9.

———. "Katherine Bell Tippetts: A Female Voice for Conservation during Florida's Boom." *Tampa Bay History* 22 (2008): 55–75.

———. "Marjory Stoneman Douglas: Woman of the Century," *Florida Naturalist* 71, no. 2 (Summer 1998): 9.

Poole, Leslie Kemp, and the Maitland Historical Society. *Maitland.* Charleston, S.C.: Arcadia Publishing, 2009.

Poucher, Judith G. "One Woman's Courage: Ruth Perry and the Johns Committee." In *Making Waves: Female Activists in Twentieth-Century Florida,* ed. Jack E. Davis and Kari Frederickson, 229–49. Gainesville: University Press of Florida, 2003.

Price, Jennifer. "Hats Off to Audubon." *Audubon,* November–December 2004. http://magazine.audubon.org/features0412/hats.htm.

Pryor, Mrs. Jack H. "Beatitudes of the Division of State Beautification." *Florida Bulletin* (March–April 1925): 14.

"Rachel Carson's Silent Spring." Aired June 26, 2007, WGBH-Boston, American Experience. DVD.

"Rank by Population of the 100 Largest Urban Places, Listed Alphabetically by State: 1790–1990." Accessed February 13, 2012. http://www.census.gov/population/www/documentation/twps0027/tab01.txt.

Rawlings, Marjorie Kinnan. "Trees for Tomorrow," *Collier's* 117, May 8, 1943, 25. http://www.unz.org/Pub/Colliers-1943may08?View=PDF.

———. *Cross Creek.* New York: Grosset and Dunlap, 1942.

———. *Cross Creek Cookery.* New York: Charles Scribner's Sons, 1942.

Redford, Polly. *Billion-Dollar Sandbar: A Biography of Miami Beach.* New York: E. P. Dutton, 1970.

———. "Groups Working to Save South Florida." In *The Environmental Destruction of South Florida: A Handbook for Citizens,* ed. William Ross McCluney. Coral Gables: University of Miami Press, 1971.

———. "Small Rebellion in Miami." *Harper's,* February 1964.

———. "Vanishing Tidelands." *Atlantic Monthly* 219, no. 6 (June 1967): 76.

Revello, Susan. "Environmental Awareness." Junior League of Miami website, accessed January 25, 2011. http://www.jlmiami.org/history-of-environmental-protection.

Rieger, Christopher. *Clear-Cutting Eden: Ecology and the Pastoral in Southern Literature*. Tuscaloosa: University of Alabama Press, 2009.

Riley, Nano. *Florida's Farmworkers in the Twenty-First Century*. Gainesville: University Press of Florida, 2002.

———. "Lake Apopka: From Natural Wonder to Unnatural Disaster." In *Paradise Lost? The Environmental History of Florida*, ed. Jack E. Davis and Raymond Arsenault, 280–93. Gainesville: University Press of Florida, 2005.

Rimby, Susan. "'Better Housekeeping Out of Doors': Mira Lloyd Dock, the State Federation of Pennsylvania Women, and Progressive Era Conservation." *Journal of Women's History*, 17, no. 3 (Fall 2005): 9–34.

———. *Mira Lloyd Dock and the Progressive Era Conservation Movement*. University Park: Pennsylvania State University Press, 2012.

Roberts, Diane. "The World's a Dirty Place When You Are Poor." *St. Petersburg Times*, September 9, 2007.

Robison, Jim, and Bill Belleville. *Along the Wekiva River*. Charleston, S.C.: Arcadia Publishing, 2009.

Roen, Terry O. "It's Always about People." *Florida Catholic*, n.d., accessed February 21, 2012. http://www.catholicweb.com/media_index.cfm?fuseaction=view_article&partnerid=29&article_id=533.

"Rollins Family." Timucuan Ecological and Historic Preserve website. Accessed June 22, 2011. http://www.nps.gov/timu/historyculture/kp_rollins.htm.

"Rollins College Gets 100-Acre Estate on Fort George Island. Gift from Mrs. Millar Wilson." *Florida Times-Union* (Jacksonville), December 1, 1940.

Rome, Adam. *The Bulldozer in the Countryside: Suburban Sprawl and the Rise of American Environmentalism*. Cambridge: Cambridge University Press, 2001.

———. *The Genius of Earth Day: How a 1970 Teach-In Unexpectedly Made the First Green Generation*. New York: Hill and Wang, 2013.

———. "'Give Earth a Chance': The Environmental Movement and the Sixties." *Journal of American History* 90, no. 2 (2003): 525–54.

———. "'Political Hermaphrodites': Gender and Environmental Reform in Progressive America." *Environmental History* 11, no. 3 (July 2006): 440–63. http://ezproxy. rollins.edu:2048/login?url=http://search.proquest.com/docview/216130110?accoun tid=13584.

Romero, Frances. "Energy Czar: Carol Browner." *Time*, December 15, 2008. http:// www.time.com/time/politics/article/0,8599,1866567,00.html.

Rossiter, Margaret W. *Women Scientists in America: Struggles and Strategies to 1940*. Baltimore: Johns Hopkins University Press, 1982.

———. *Women Scientists in America: Forging a New World Since 1972*. Baltimore: Johns Hopkins University Press, 2012.

Rothra, Elizabeth Ogren. *Florida's Pioneer Naturalist: The Life of Charles Torrey Simpson*. Gainesville: University Press of Florida, 1995.

Roux, Quentin. "Sainthood Confirmed for Deaconess Harriett Bedell, Missionary and Humanitarian—the 'Angel of the Swamps.'" *Naples News*, July 21, 2009.

Rowe, Anne E. *The Idea of Florida in the American Literary Imagination*. Gainesville: University Press of Florida, 1992.

Runte, Alfred. *National Parks: The American Experience*. Lincoln: University of Nebraska Press, 1979.

Ryan, James. "Overflow Crowd Hears Miseries of Tampa Bay." *St. Petersburg Times*, November 14, 1969, B4.

Rymph, Catherine E. *Republican Women: Feminism and Conservatism from Suffrage through the Rise of the New Right*. Chapel Hill: University of North Carolina Press, 2006.

"Sabal Palm." Accessed September 28, 2011. http://www.sfrc.ufl.edu/4h/Cabbage_palm/cabbpalm.htm.

Samples, Eve. "Maggy Hurchalla Is Depressed, but It Won't Last." March 12, 2011. Accessed April 6, 2011. http://www.evergladesfoundation.org/news/entry/Eve-Samples-Maggy-Hurchalla-is-depressed-but-it-wont-last.

Santich, Kate. "Decades Can't Slow Nuns' Fight against Poverty." *Chicago Tribune*, July 26, 2006.

Schiebinger, Londa. *Has Feminism Changed Science?* Cambridge, Mass.: Harvard University Press, 1999.

———. *Nature's Body: Gender in the Making of Modern Science*. Boston: Beacon Press, 1993.

Scholz, John T., and Bruce Stiftel, eds. *Adaptive Governance and Water Conflict: New Institutions for Collaborative Planning*. Washington, D.C.: Resources for the Future, 2005.

Schultz, Debbie Wasserman. "Recognizing Helen Spivey." *Congressional Record*, May 20, 2011, E849. Accessed September 26, 2014. http://www.gpo.gov/fdsys/pkg/CREC-2011-05-10/html/CREC-2011-05-10-pt1-PgE849-2.htm.

Scott, Anne Firor. *Natural Allies: Women's Associations in American History*. Urbana: University of Illinois Press, 1993.

"Seminole County Big Tree Park." Accessed October 10, 2011. http://www.seminolecountyfl.gov/parksrec/pdf/Big%20Tree%20Brochure.pdf.

"Senate Hearings on Air Pollution Set for Tampa." *St. Petersburg Times*, January 14, 1964, 2B.

"Sewage Dumping 'Suicide.'" *Evening Independent* (St. Petersburg, Fla.), March 14, 1970, A2.

"Sewage Is Major Florida Problem, Engineer Says." *St. Petersburg Times*, September 11, 1945, 11.

Seymour, Jessica (Mrs. Robert M.). "A State Plan for Florida." In *Planning Problems of*

Town, City and Region: Papers and Discussions at the Eighteenth National Conference on City Planning held at St. Petersburg and Palm Beach, FL. March 29 to April 1, 1926. Philadelphia: Wm. F. Fell, 1927. http://www.archive.org/stream/planningproblems 01natirich/planningproblems01natirich_djvu.txt.

Shell-Weiss, Melanie R. "Exceptional Women: Jewish Americans and Postwar Civil Rights in Miami." Accessed May 1, 2012. http://www.h-net.org/reviews/showrev. php?id=9032.

Sies, Mary Corbin, and Christopher Silver, eds. *Planning the Twentieth Century American City*. Baltimore: Johns Hopkins University Press, 1996.

Simone, Daniel. "Racing, Region, and the Environment: A History of American Motorsports." PhD diss., University of Florida, 2009.

Simpson, Charles Torrey. *Florida Wild Life: Observations on the Flora and Fauna of the State and the Influence of Climate and Environment on Their Development*. New York: MacMillan, 1932.

Siry, Joseph V. *Marshes of the Ocean Shore*. College Station: Texas A & M University Press, 1984.

Sklar, Kathryn Kish, and Thomas Dublin, eds. *Women and Social Movements in the United States, 1600–2000*. Alexander Street Press. http://wass.alexanderstreet.com.

Small, John Kunkel. *From Eden to Sahara: Florida's Tragedy*. Sanford, Fla.: Seminole Soil and Water Conservation District, 2004.

"Smokey Bear Woodsy Owl Poster Contest." Accessed August 8, 2013. http://www.ffgc. org/youth/smokey_bear_woodsy_owl.html.

Smith, Helen Van Roy. "Club Women Should First Be Home Makers, Declares Mrs. Jennings." *Atlanta Constitution*, March 2, 1924, accessed through ProQuest Historical Newspapers.

Smith, Kristin E., and Amara Bachu. "Women's Labor Force Attachment Patterns and Maternity Leave: A Review of the Literature." U.S. Census Bureau, accessed April 2, 2012. http://www.census.gov/population/www/documentation/ twps0032/ twps0032.html.

Smith, Nancy. "Martin County vs. the World: Here Come de Judge." *Sunshine State News*, September 23, 2013.

Sosnick, Stephen H. *Hired Hands: Seasonal Farm Workers in the United States*. Santa Barbara, Calif.: McNally and Loftin, 1978.

"The Southland's War on Smog: Fifty Years of Progress Toward Clean Air." Accessed October 20, 2011. http://www.aqmd.gov/news1/Archives/History/marchcov.html.

Spence, Mark David. *Dispossessing the Wilderness: Indian Removal and the Making of the National Parks*. Oxford: Oxford University Press, 1999.

"State Orders Cities, Industries to End Pollution." *St. Petersburg Times*, November 7, 1967, A1.

Steinberg, Ted. *Down to Earth: Nature's Role in American History*. New York: Oxford University Press, 2002.

Stephenson, R. Bruce. "A 'Monstrous Desecration': Dredge and Fill in Boca Ciega Bay." In *Paradise Lost? The Environmental History of Florida*, ed. Jack E. Davis and Raymond Arsenault, 326–32. Gainesville: University Press of Florida, 2005.

———. "John Nolen," Chapter 8: Florida: "Everything That Is Good and Bad in the Flesh," 1922–1926, unpublished manuscript, 2011.

Stowe, Harriet Beecher. *Palmetto Leaves.* 1873; facsimile ed. Gainesville: University Press of Florida, 1999.

Stradling, David. *Smokestacks and Progressives: Environmentalists, Engineers, and Air Quality in America, 1881–1951.* Baltimore: Johns Hopkins University Press, 1999.

Stretesky, Paul, and Michael J. Hogan. "Environmental Justice: An Analysis of Superfund Sites in Florida." *Social Problems* 45, no. 2 (May 1998): 268–87.

"Sylvia Earle, Marine Biologist." Accessed October 24, 2013. http://events.national geographic.com/events/speakers-bureau/speaker/sylvia-earle/.

"Sylvia Earle, PhD." Accessed October 24, 2013. http://www.achievement.org/autodoc/ page/earobio-1.

Tarr, Rodger L., ed. *Max and Marjorie: The Correspondence between Maxwell E. Perkins and Marjorie Kinnan Rawlings.* Gainesville: University Press of Florida, 1999.

Tebeau, Charlton W. *A History of Florida.* Coral Gables: University of Miami Press, 1971.

"A Tenacious Crusader." *Bradenton Herald,* September 19, 2000. ManaSota-88 files, Nokomis, Florida.

Thissen. Carlene, and Fritz Roka, "Non-Governmental Organizations Serving Farmworkers in Florida." Accessed February 22, 2012. http://edis.ifas.ufl.edu/fe836.

Thomas, Mrs. Lloyd. "Litterbug." *National Gardener* 35, no. 7–8 (July–August 1964): 58.

Thomas, Mike. "Expressway Authority Can't Co-opt Fran Pignone." *Orlando Sentinel,* June 18, 2009.

———. "The Sunshine Patriot." *Orlando Sentinel.* November 25, 1990.

"Threatened & Endangered: Protected Plants for All Scientific Names." Accessed October 12, 2013. http://plants.usda.gov/java/threat?statelist=states&stateSelect=US12.

Tippetts, Katherine Bell. "Mrs. Tippetts Lists Florida in This Class." *Florida Clubwoman* 7, no. 2 (November 1927): 12.

Tompkins, Mrs. Horace. "Annual State Convention." *Camellia* (Pensacola Federation of Garden Clubs), June 1951, 10.

Trout, Grace Wilbur. "We Need City Plans to Keep Property Attractive." *Florida Clubwoman* 9, no. 5 (September 1929): 10.

Turcotte, Florence M. "For This Is an Enchanted Land: Marjorie Kinnan Rawlings and the Florida Environment." *Florida Historical Quarterly* 90, no. 4 (Spring 2012): 488–504.

"Turtles Win at Eleventh Circuit." Accessed December 28, 2011. http://masglp.olemiss. edu/Water%20Log/WL18/turtles.htm.

Udall, Stewart L. *The Quiet Crisis.* Introduction by John F. Kennedy. New York: Holt, Rinehart and Winston, 1963.

Unger, Nancy C. *Beyond Nature's Housekeepers: American Women in Environmental History.* Oxford: Oxford University Press, 2012.

University of Florida School of Forest Resources and Conservation. "The History of the School of Forest Resources and Conservation and the Austin Cary Memorial Forest." http://sfrc.ufl.edu/history.html.

Vallee, Judith Delaney. "I Would Hate to See This Whole Thing Turn into a Circus." *Orlando Sentinel,* December 16, 1990.

———. "Saving Manatee Important to Florida." *Daytona Beach News-Journal.* November 22, 1990.

Vance, Linda D. *May Mann Jennings: Florida's Genteel Activist.* Gainesville: University of Florida Press, 1985.

———. "The Park Before the Park." *Everglade Magazine,* 1976. http://www.everglades online.com/50years/before.htm.

Vanderpool, Mrs. I. "Florida Society!" *Bird-Lore* 3, no. 5 (September–October 1901): 183.

Vickers, Sally. "Ruth Bryan Owen, Florida's First Congresswoman." In *Making Waves: Female Activists in Twentieth Century Florida,* ed. Jack E. Davis and Kari Frederickson, 23–55. Gainesville: University Press of Florida, 2003.

"Was Darwin an Ecologist?" Darwin Correspondence Project, accessed June 15, 2012. http://www.darwinproject.ac.uk/was-darwin-an-ecologist.

Weatherford, Doris. *Real Women of Tampa and Hillsborough County from Prehistory to the Millennium.* Tampa, Fla.: University of Tampa Press, 2004.

Weidensaul, Scott. *Of a Feather: A Brief History of American Birding.* Orlando: Harcourt, 2007.

Weldon, Ann. "Civic Associations Term Fills a Threat to Boca Ciega Bay." *Evening Independent* (St. Petersburg, Fla.), September 8, 1966.

Werndli, Phil. *Florida State Parks . . . 75 Years.* Altamonte Springs: Florida Media, 2010.

Whipple, H. B. *Bird-Lore* 2, no. 3 (June 1900): 97.

White, Dale. "Activist Brought People Together to Better Sarasota." *Sarasota Herald-Tribune,* June 15, 2010.

Whitley, Frances E. "Forestry and Wild Life Refuges," in Document 15: Pamphlet, Applied Education Department, Conservation Divisions, General Federation of Women's Clubs (1925–1926), President's Papers (Record Group 2), Papers of Mary Sherman, General Federation of Women's Club Archives, Washington, D.C., 2, included in Jarvis, Kimberly A., "How Did the General Federation of Women's Clubs Shape Women's Involvement in the Conservation Movement, 1900–1930?" In *Women and Social Movements in the United States, 1600–2000,* ed. Kathryn Kish Sklar and Thomas Dublin. Alexander Street Press. http://wass.alexanderstreet.com.

Whitman, Mrs. Alton B. "Report of Committee on Conservation." *Florida Bulletin* 11, no. 3 (December 1922): 6–7.

Williams, Margaret. "Relocation from 'Mount Dioxin.'" Accessed April 20, 2011. http://www.ejrc.cau.edu/voicesfromthegrassroots.htm#margaret %20williams.

Williams, Mary B. "Pensacola the Beautiful?" *Camellia* (Pensacola Federation of Garden Clubs), vol. 24, no. 8 (April 1973): 5. Bound volume: *Camellia* 23–25 (1971–74), UWFSC.

Wilson, Catherine. "Nation's Oldest Wildlife Refuge Is Endangered: Golf, Polo Projects Under Way Near Pelican Island." *Los Angeles Times,* September 3, 1989.

Wilson, Edward O. *The Future of Life.* New York: Alfred A. Knopf, 2002.

Wilson, Herbert M. "Smoke Worse Than Fire." In *Nature's Bounty: Historical and Modern Perspectives,* ed. Anthony M. Penna, 264–65. New York: M. E. Sharpe, 1991. http://books.google.com/books?id=-HN8YsINe_EC&pg=PA265&lpg=PA265&dq=smoke+committee+of+Cleveland&source=bl&ots=9v4OTimLWR&sig=QFTu8B7-ESR_lianrEwrufPPJY&hl=en&ei=Wy2fTsmWBsT10gGRlJmMCQ&sa=X&oi=book_result&ct=result&resnum=6&ved=0CCwQ6AEwBQ#v=onepage&q=smoke%20committee%20of%20Cleveland&f=false.

Wilson, William H. *The City Beautiful Movement.* Baltimore: Johns Hopkins University Press, 1989.

Wisehart, Bob. "The Responsibility: League of Women Voters Suggests Who Can Clean up the Air." *Boca Raton News,* April 25, 1971, B1.

"A Woman Reformer Promotes Smoke Abatement, 1912." In *Major Problems in American Environmental History,* ed. Carolyn Merchant, 422–23. Lexington, Mass.: D. C. Heath, 1993.

"Woman Sues to Halt Turkey Point Canal." *Daytona Beach News-Journal,* November 25, 1970, A12.

Wood, Mary. *The History of the General Federation of Women's Clubs for the First Twenty-Two Years of Its Organization.* Farmingdale, N.Y.: Dabor Social Science, 1978.

Worster, Donald. *Nature's Economy: A History of Ecological Ideas.* 2nd ed. New York: Cambridge University Press, 1998.

Wright, C. E. "Florida Conservationists Unite for '70s." *New York Times,* January 11, 1970.

Wright, E. Lynne. *More Than Petticoats: Remarkable Florida Women.* Guilford, Conn.: Globe Pequot Press, 2001.

Wylie, Philip. "Florida: Polluted Paradise." *Miami Daily News,* March 20, 1949, 1A.

"Yellow Dye Trails Path of Sewage." *St. Petersburg Times,* April 23, 1970, 3B.

Zaloudek, Mark. "Group Targets Pesticides in Parks." *Sarasota Herald-Tribune,* March 11, 1997, 5B.

Index

LESLIE KEMP POOLE is assistant professor in the Environmental Studies Department at Rollins College. She is the author of Maitland.